John Cary

The Plymouth Pilgrim – Biography and Genealogy of a New England Pioneer

By Seth C. Cary

A people which takes no pride in noble achievements of remote ancestors, will never achieve anything worthy to be remembered with pride by remote descendants. – Macaulay.

Published by Pantianos Classics

ISBN-13: 978-1-78987-560-7

First published in 1911

Contents

The Story of the Cary Coat of Arms ix

The Roses' Message to Us x

The Line of Descent xi

Preface xii

Introduction xiii

Sketch of John Cary 16

Index of Carys 21

Intermarriages with Carys 38

Section 1 50
Section 2 51
Section 3 51
Section 3-A 52
Section 4 52
Section 5 52
Section 6 53
Section 7 53
Section 7-A 54
Section 7-B 54
Section 8 55
Section 9 55
Section 10 56
Section 11 57
Section 12 57
Section 13 58
Section 14 59
Section 15 60
Section 16 60
Section 17 61
Section 18 61
Section 19 61
Section 19-A 62
Section 20 63
Section 21 63
Section 22 64
Section 23 64
Section 24 64
Section 25 65
Section 25-A 66
Section 26 66
Section 27 66
Section 28 67
Section 28-A 67
Section 28-C 70
Section 29 71
Section 30 71
Section 31 71
Section 32 72
Section 33 72
Section 34 74
Section 35 74
Section 36 75
Section 37 75
Section 38 75
Section 39 76
Section 40 76
Section 41 76
Section 42 77
Section 43 77
Section 44 77
Section 45 78

Section 46............78	Section 66............98	Section 86..........117
Section 47............79	Section 67............99	Section 87..........117
Section 48............79	Section 68............99	Section 88..........117
Section 49............80	Section 69............99	Section 89..........117
Section 50............80	Section 69-A......100	Section 90..........118
Section 51............81	Section 70..........101	Section 91..........118
Section 52............81	Section 71..........102	Section 92..........119
Section 53............82	Section 71-A......102	Section 93..........119
Section 53-A........82	Section 71-B......104	Section 94..........119
Section 54............83	Section 71-C......104	Section 94-A......120
Section 55............83	Section 72..........105	Section 95..........121
Section 56............83	Section 73..........106	Section 96..........121
Section 57............84	Section 74..........106	Section 97..........122
Section 58............84	Section 75..........106	Section 97-A......122
Section 59............84	Section 76..........107	Section 98..........122
Section 60............85	Section 77..........107	Section 99..........123
Section 60-A........85	Section 78..........108	Section 99-A......123
Section 61............91	Section 79..........108	Section 100........123
Section 62............91	Section 79-A......108	Section 101........124
Section 63............92	Section 80..........111	Section 102........124
Section 63-A........92	Section 81..........112	Section 103........125
Section 63-B........93	Section 82..........112	Section 104........125
Section 63-C........95	Section 83..........113	Section 105........126
Section 63-D........96	Section 84..........114	Section 105-A..126
Section 63-E........96	Section 85..........114	Section 106........128
Section 64............97	Section 85-A......114	Section 107........128
Section 65............98	Section 85-B......115	Section 108........129

Section 109 129	Section 132 143	Section 153-A .. 158
Section 110 129	Section 133 144	Section 153-B .. 158
Section 111 130	Section 134 144	Section 154 158
Section 112 130	Section 135 144	Section 155 159
Section 113 131	Section 136 145	Section 156 159
Section 114 131	Section 137 145	Section 157 159
Section 115 132	Section 138 145	Section 157-A .. 160
Section 116 133	Section 139 146	Section 158 161
Section 117 133	Section 140 146	Section 159 161
Section 118 133	Section 141 146	Section 160 161
Section 118-A .. 134	Section 141-A .. 147	Section 161 162
Section 119 135	Section 142 147	Section 162 162
Section 120 136	Section 142-A .. 149	Section 163 163
Section 121 136	Section 142-B .. 150	Section 164 163
Section 122 137	Section 142-C .. 150	Section 165 163
Section 123 137	Section 142-D .. 151	Section 166 164
Section 124 137	Section 143 152	Section 167 164
Section 125 138	Section 144 153	Section 168 165
Section 126 138	Section 145 153	Section 169 165
Section 126-A .. 139	Section 146 154	Section 170 165
Section 127 139	Section 147 154	Section 171 166
Section 128 140	Section 148 154	Section 172 166
Section 128-A .. 141	Section 149 154	Section 173 167
Section 129 141	Section 150 155	Section 174 167
Section 129-A .. 142	Section 151 156	Section 175 170
Section 130 143	Section 152 156	Section 176 170
Section 131 143	Section 153 157	Section 177 170

Section 178 171	Section 204 184	Section 228 196
Section 179 172	Section 205 184	Section 229 197
Section 180 172	Section 206 185	Section 230 197
Section 181 172	Section 206-A .. 185	Section 231 197
Section 182 173	Section 206-B .. 186	Section 232 198
Section 183 173	Section 207 186	Section 233 198
Section 184 173	Section 208 186	Section 234 198
Section 185 174	Section 209 187	Section 235 198
Section 186 174	Section 209-A .. 187	Section 236 199
Section 187 175	Section 210 187	Section 237 199
Section 188 175	Section 211 188	Section 238 200
Section 189 175	Section 212 189	Section 239 200
Section 190 176	Section 213 189	Section 240 201
Section 191 176	Section 214 189	Section 241 201
Section 192 176	Section 215 189	Section 242 201
Section 193 176	Section 216 190	Section 243 202
Section 194 177	Section 217 190	Section 244 202
Section 195 178	Section 218 190	Section 245 202
Section 196 179	Section 219 193	Section 246 202
Section 197 179	Section 220 193	Section 247 203
Section 198 179	Section 221 194	Section 248 203
Section 199 179	Section 222 194	Section 249 203
Section 200 181	Section 223 194	Section 250 203
Section 201 181	Section 224 194	Section 251 203
Section 202 182	Section 225 195	Section 252 204
Section 202-A .. 183	Section 226 196	Section 253 205
Section 203 184	Section 227 196	Section 254 205

Section 255 205	Section 276-A .. 215	Section 297 225
Section 256 206	Section 277 215	Section 298 225
Section 257 206	Section 278 216	Section 299 226
Section 258 206	Section 279 216	Section 300 226
Section 259 207	Section 279-A .. 216	Section 301 228
Section 260 207	Section 279-B .. 217	Section 302 229
Section 261 207	Section 280 218	Section 303 229
Section 262 208	Section 281 219	Section 304 230
Section 263 208	Section 281-A .. 219	Section 305 230
Section 264 209	Section 282 220	Section 306 230
Section 265 209	Section 283 220	Section 307 230
Section 266 210	Section 284 221	Section 308 231
Section 267 210	Section 285 221	Section 309 231
Section 268 211	Section 286 221	Section 310 231
Section 269 211	Section 287 221	Section 311 231
Section 270 211	Section 288 222	Section 312 232
Section 271 212	Section 288-A .. 222	Section 313 232
Section 272 212	Section 289 222	Section 314 232
Section 272-A .. 212	Section 290 223	Section 315 233
Section 272-B .. 212	Section 291 223	Section 316 233
Section 272-C ... 213	Section 292 223	Section 317 234
Section 273 213	Section 293 224	Section 318 234
Section 274 214	Section 294 224	Section 319 234
Section 275 214	Section 295 224	
Section 276 215	Section 296 225	

Dedicated to the descendants of John Cary

The Story of the Cary Coat of Arms

As Told by the Old Chroniclers.

"In the beginning of the reign of Henry V. (1413-1422) a certain Knight-errant of Aragon, having passed through divers countries, and performed many feats of Arms, arrived here in England, where he challenged any man of his rank and quality to make a trial of his skill in arms. This challenge was accepted by Sir Robert Cary, between whom a cruel encounter, and a long and doubtful combat was waged in Smithfield, London. But at length this noble Champion vanquished the presumptuous Aragonois, for which King Henry V. restored unto him a good part of his father's lands, which for his loyalty to Richard II. he had been deprived of by Henry IV. and authorized him to bear the Arms of a Knight of Aragon, which the noble posterity continue to wear unto this day; for according to the laws of Heraldry, whoever fairly in the field conquers his adversary may justify the wearing of his Arms."— *Burke's Heraldry*.

SETH C CARY,
PUBLISHER

Another account is so quaint that it is placed before the reader:

"In the time of Henry V. cam out of Aragon a lusty gentleman into England, and challenged to do feites of armes, with any English gentleman without exception. This Sir Robert Cary hearing thereof, made suite forthwith to the Prince, that he might answer the challange, which was granted, and Smithfield was the place appointed for the same, who, at the day and time prefixed, both parties mett and did performe sundrie feates of armes, but in the end this Robert gave the foils and overthrow to the Aragon Knight, disarmed and spoiled him, which his doinge so well pleased the Prince, that he receyved him into great favor, caused him to be restored to the most part of his father's landes, and willed him also for a perpetuall memorie of his victorie, that he should henceforth give the same armes as the Aragon Knight, which is Argent, on bend sable three roses argent, for before they did beare gules, chevron entre, three swans argent."— *Herald's Visitation*, 1620.

The Roses' Message to Us

   The age of chivalry has passed away;
We cannot now on tourney-fields display
Our strength and courage; neither did we flee
From native land to find beyond the sea
Freedom and justice; these we now possess,
And need not seek them in the wilderness.
Yet even now must we fierce battles fight,
And firmly stand as champions of the right.
Valor is needed if we hope to win
Our victories over greed, and wrong and sin.
The roses white must we preserve from stain,
And other trophies by our valor gain.
Then let each one who bears the Cary name
Remember whence his shield and motto came:
Remember, too, the one who brought them o'er
The ocean's waves to this New England shore.
All that the fathers have by valor gained
Must by the sons be valiantly maintained.
Then take the shield; go forward to the fight;
Guard well the roses; may their silvery light
Shine on brave deeds performed for truth and right.

        —From Later Cary Poems, by permission.

The Line of Descent

OF THE AUTHOR OF THE BOOK.   **OF THE OWNER OF THE BOOK**

John Cary, Sec. 1.   _____

John Cary, Sec. 2.   _____

James Cary, Sec. 10.   _____

James Cary, Sec. 25-A.   _____

John Cary, Sec. 60-A.   _____

John Cary, Sec. 105-A.   _____

Seth C. Cary, Sec. 206-B.   _____

Knibloe B. Cary, Sec. 318.   _____

Preface

The plan of this book is very simple, and that is to tell the story of *John Cary the Plymouth Pilgrim,* and his descendants. This can not be done wisely and disregard the monumental work of the Hon. Samuel Fenton Cary, who published the "Cary Memorials" in 1874. He laid the foundations, and they need not be relaid. All that can be done is to add to the superstructure, making here and there a correction, and adding such new material as further research has developed.

The last word has not yet been said in regard to the early years of John Cary. The time does not yet seem ripe to say more than has already been said; but to put together the best that can be done for the multitude that are coming after. The most recent thing published is Prof. Henry Grosvenor Cary's "The Cary Family in England."

It is rare to find a man who gathered to himself so much of good, and then to send down through family life, cleaner morals, higher ideals, or a more pervasive personality. He was quiet yet firm; true and aggressive, persistent and successful. He was one who could afford "to labor and to wait."

It will be noted that in this book our name is invariably spelled C-a-r-y. It is also well known that some of the branches of the Family prefer and use the longer form, C-a-r-e-y. In some cases this is from choice, and in others it is what has descended to them from the recent past. The writer has no question but that the shorter form is correct. And yet when asked by those who seek to know what they should do under the circumstances, he has no hesitancy in saying this: If you are tied up in business, and entangled by legal forms and documents, such as wills, deeds, patents, etc., keep on as you are; but the younger members of the family, who are not thus hampered, can make the change, and thus bring about uniformity. The only reason why we do not print the name as each line or branch is accustomed to do, is because of the utter confusion that would result, and our proof-reading would be interminable.

At first it was thought possible that the book could be quite largely illustrated, but it was soon discovered that this would make the work altogether too bulky, and also too expensive.

Years of work have been put upon this book, and many hands have been occupied in its production. It is the best that the conditions and surroundings allow. And it is now entrusted to your hands to be studied, to be enlarged and filled out to its proper capacity and its fullest development. Many of its Sections can and should be worked up into biographies, or sketches, and out of this scores of families could enrich their own family life. The author cheerfully resigns the work to the optimism and enthusiasm of the younger Carys.

SETH C. CARY.

Dorchester Center, Boston, Massachusetts.

Introduction

This book contains the names of the descendants of John Cary, so far as they have been reported, or discovered in any other way. No claim that it includes them all is made, but a wide search has been instituted and carried on for years, and none are knowingly omitted. If others report themselves, it will be a pleasure to add their names to the already long list.

So far as known this is the only work devoted to this Family that is now in print and brought up to date.

The family is English, and they appear first in the Domesday Book, and are traced back to Adam De Kari, who was Lord of Castle Cary in 1198.

The three principal lines which came to America are descended from John, who came to Plymouth about 1634; James, who came to Charlestown in 1639, and Miles, who came to Virginia in 1640. There are numerous other individuals or families who have come to this land of opportunity at various times, but there seems as yet no complete list of them.

In England the Family is represented in almost all grades of the nobility, all orders in the Church, and among the people. Their tombs are found in St. Paul's, Westminster, and various other Cathedrals and Churches. They attained distinction in Statesmanship, Poetry, Music, and Letters; in the Army and Navy; as Diplomats, Courtiers, and Representatives of the English Crown abroad. William Cary, the great Baptist missionary to India, well represents the family by his work as a Translator; while a Moravian preacher bearing our name was instrumental in the conversion of Captain Webb, an English officer, who planted Methodism in Philadelphia.

This book will be valuable to all Carys, whether their names are included or not; if not here, and they belong to the family, all the original ancestors are easily found, and thus connection can be made with the proper branch. It is equally valuable for all the lines of intermarriage, since in many cases these have been traced to considerable length, in order that the work may be most complete.

A singular fact has recently come to light: Some German-speaking Russians at Mandan, North Dakota, spell their name Kari, and pronounce it Cary.

The quaint statement of Oliver Wendell Holmes, that "A person with a known Grandfather is too distinguished to find it necessary to put on airs," is doubtless somewhat exaggerated; yet it has in it just enough of a great truth to make it stick, and at the same time teach a lesson that the race really needs to know. A careful indoctrination of somewhat of the Chinese respect for their ancestors would go a long way toward making the American people more self-respecting, and in this way lay a foundation for a better citizenship, with higher ideals and a far better outcome.

Occasionally the plain, blunt question comes to us in this form: Are the Carys keeping up their old-time vigor, strength, and mental and moral qualities? This is a serious question, and should not be answered without careful thought, and a wide knowledge of the Family. Having known many, and corresponded with more, the following statement seems wholly warranted as the result of a thoughtful analysis: I can see no special lack in muscular strength, no failing in general vigor, no falling off in mental quality, rather an increase in musical taste, and no decline in the consecration to God and to the uplift of the race. They are as hard-working, with as much inventive genius, literary ability, far seeing, with the other qualities which make up patriotic and useful citizenship, as well as all the home virtues, with as much persistency coupled with quiet, peaceable dispositions, as the Family has ever presented. Let it be distinctly understood, that I can point out the individuals who go to make up this array of strong, sturdy, and desirable characteristics. And this new book will be found full of illustrations of all these qualities.

As we near the completion of this book, we find people still asking about it; and if they belong to the Family, and are their names included? Many such requests have been answered, and their lines definitely connected. But in other cases the queries have come so late, and the time for securing the needed data is so short, that we shall be compelled to disappoint these good people. This we greatly regret. But we have a plan by which such friends, and a great host behind them, can have their data put into form for permanent preservation. The plan is this: Let all such records be properly edited and printed in our Bulletin, which would thus become a permanent organ for the preservation of the records of our Family.

The John Cary Monument Erected On His Homestead West Bridgewater. Mass. 1905.

NEAR THIS SPOT WAS THE HOME OF
JOHN CARY
BORN IN SOMERSETSHIRE, ENGLAND.
HE BECAME IN 1651 AN ORIGINAL PROPRIETOR.
AND HONORED SETTLER ON THIS RIVER.
WAS CLERK OF THE PLANTATION.
WHEN THE TOWN OF BRIDGEWATER WAS
INCORPORATED, IN 1656, HE WAS ELECTED
CONSTABLE, THE FIRST AND ONLY OFFICER OF
THAT YEAR.
WAS TOWN CLERK UNTIL HIS DEATH IN 1681.
TRADITION SAYS,
HE WAS THE FIRST TEACHER OF LATIN IN
PLYMOUTH COLONY.
THIS TABLET IS ERECTED BY HIS DESCENDANTS
IN MEMORY
OF THEIR HISTORIC AND NOBLE ANCESTOR.

Bronze Tablet on Monument

Sketch of John Cary

Chronological

Samuel F. Cary, in "Cary Memorials," says: "The writer has had access to a manuscript more than one hundred years old, and written by a grandson of John, which says that John Cary, when a youth, was sent by his father to France to perfect his education, and that while absent his father died. On returning to Somersetshire he differed with his brothers about the settlement of his father's estate. He compromised by receiving one hundred pounds as his portion and immediately sailed for America."

Tradition says that he was the first Latin School teacher in the Plymouth Colony, and that he taught Elder Brewster the Hebrew.

He removed to Duxbury where he had ten acres of land allotted to him. At a Court of Assistants, held October 2, 1637, "A proporcon of land is granted to John Carew, about the lands graunted to Robte Mendall, contayning X acrees." And at a Court of Assistants, January 7, 1639 _____ "are appoynted to lay forth Robte Mendloues & John Carews land" _____.

The history of Duxbury is interesting and is as follows: In 1630 and 1631 there were a few settlers in Duxbury, but they went back to Plymouth in the winter to be nearer public worship, and also because their houses were more comfortable for the cold weather. Some of them signed an agreement to this effect. In 1632, probably, the real settling began, but it was not till June 7, 1637, that the town was incorporated: "It is enacted by the Court that Ducksborrow shall become a township and unite together for their better securitie and to have the p'veledges of a towne, onley their bounds and limmits shall be sett and appoynted by the next Court."

The name probably came from Duxbury Hall, the seat of the Standish Family in England.

So many people had left Plymouth that there was an effort made to unite the two churches, and build a new town, and committees were appointed to consider the matter. Two locations were suggested: Jones River, now Kingston, and Morton's Hole, which was west of Captain's Hill. The Indian name was Mattakeeset.

Marshfield was incorporated March 2, 1640, but the bounds were not fixed till 1642.

At a Court of Assistants, October 7, 1639, "John Carew is allowed to be for himself vpon the continuence of the good report of his carriage & demean'r; & at a Court of Assistants held the fourth of Novemb'r next after, Edmond Weston is lycenced to Hue w'th John Carew, and to be p'tner w'th him in working and planting vpon the sd John Carews land, vpon their good demean'r together."

In 1640 Marshfield was set off from Duxbury, and as a compensation for this loss of territory, the following plan was made: "The inhabitants of the town of Duxbury are granted a competent portion of lands about Saughtuchquett (Satucket), towards the west, for a plantation for them, and to have it four miles every way from the place where they shall set up their center; provided, it intrench not upon Winnytuckquett, formerly granted to Plymouth. And we have nominated Capt. Miles Standish, Mr. John Alden, George Soule, Constant Southworth, John Rogers, and William Brett, to be foefees in trust for the equal dividing and laying forth the said lands to the inhabitants." It would seem that this plan was never executed, although carried out in a larger way in the Duxbury New Plantation, bought of the Indians in 1649. Those wishing to see the old Indian Deed, will find it in "The Cary Family in America," pages 5, 6.

In June, 1644, John Cary and Elizabeth Godfrey were married; she was the daughter of Francis Godfrey of Duxbury and Bridgewater. John, their first child, was born November 4, 1645, and died in 1721.

It also appears that in 1646, according to the records of Marshfield: "At the Town meeting it was agreed that Edward Winsloe (afterward Governor) should agree with F. Godfrey for making a bridge over South River and what he shall agree the town are ready to affirm."

Francis, his second son, was born January 19, 1647, and died in 1718.

October 23, 1648, he sold to James Lindell all the land, both upland and meadow, granted him by the town, and at the same time "testified and affirmed" that his father-in-law, Francis Godfrey, "did acknowledge and confess that he had sold his present right and interest of his said land lying upon Green Harbor River," to James Lindell.

March 23, 1649, Duxbury New Plantation, which was fourteen miles square, was deeded to trustees for the benefit of the people of Duxbury. John Cary was one of the fifty-six who had shares, but only a few ever settled on them.

Elizabeth was born December 20, 1649.

January 16, 1650, he sold two acres of meadow land to Steven Briant.

John Cary was Clerk of the Plantation, which was a kind of land company, and this year it began to be settled.

Francis Godfrey, of Marshfield, sold to Anthony Eames and his son, Mark Eames, one hundred acres of land and dwelling-house on North River, near Mr. Vassells, "for four-score pounds," December 10, 1650.

March 18, 1652, James was born in Braintree, Massachusetts Bay Colony. It is quite likely that on account of some stress of the times, they were living there.

Mary was born at Duxbury New Plantation. July 8, 1654.

The town records contain the following item: "It was agreed upon by the Towne the twelfe of March, 1656, that there shall be five woulfe traps made."

June 3 (O. S.), 1656, the General Court incorporated Duxbury New Plantation as Bridgewater: "ORDERED, That henceforth Duxborrow New Plantation bee allowed to bee a tounshipe of ytselfe. destinct from Duxborrow, and to bee called by the name of Bridgewater. Provided that all publicke rates bee borne by them with Duxborrow upon equally proportions."

Plymouth Colony Records, volume 3, page 99, for June 3, 1656, have the following entry:

> "The Cunstables of the seueral Townes"
> "Bridgewater John Carew."

At this time there were but ten freemen in the town.

Jonathan was born September 24, 1656.

John Cary is mentioned as having "taken the Oath of Fidelitie at Duxborrow, in the yeare 1657." He was elected Town Clerk this year, and this was most likely the oath of office; he occupied this place until his death in 1681.

"Att the Generali Court holden att Plymouth, in New England, the first of March, 1658."

"These may certify all whom it may concerne, that the fourth of March, 1658, that these men whose names are vnderwritten, by the intelligence of an Indian, came to a place a little below Namaskett, where the Indians took vp an English man out of the Riuer of Tetacutt, with a blew paire of stockings and a gray listed garter, and likewise pte of a locorum paire of briches with wyer bottons fastened about his waist; but wee found noe blemish about the man that should any way cause his death, but as wee conceiue was drowned accedentally; and finding the man thuse, wee haue buried him, and haue satisfyed the Indians for theire paines." Signed by John Carew and eleven others "from Bridgewater."

And superscribed these: "I pray you deliur this to M'r Collyer, or M'r Alden, either of them, to doe with as they shall see meet. And by them sence ordered heer to be recorded as aboue-said."

David was born January 27, 1659.

"It is Ordered and Agreed upon by the Towne, the tenth of July, 1660, freely and willingly to give to Mr. Buckner if he shall come Heyther to supply the place of A minister the sum of twenty pounds and his diet."

Hannah was born April 30, 1661.

"Att the Generali Court holden att Plymouth the fourth day of June, 1661, John Carye is admitted by the Court to haue equall entrest in the graunt made to Arthur Harris, and others, of Bridgewater, for accomodation of lands."

Joseph was born April 18, 1663.

Rev. Mr. Keith, the first pastor at Bridgewater, installed in 1663, was from Aberdeen, Scotland, and preached there fifty-six years. It is said that his sermon was preached on "Sermon Rock."

Rebecca, the tenth child of John and Elizabeth, was born March 30, 1665.

June 7, 1665, more land was granted to John Cary and others.

Francis Godfrey made his will 1666, and the property was inventoried at £117-17-5.

June 5, 1667, "a Jury was named and ordered to bee impaneled to lay out waies requisett to the township of Bridgewater." Among the twelve appointed was John Carrey, and "Captaine Bradford ordered by the Court to impanell this jury."

John Cary was also appointed with Deacon Willis "to take all the charges of the late war (King Philip's) since June last and expenses of the scouts before and since June last."

Sarah was born August 2, 1667.

June 3, 1668, land was laid out to John Cary and others.

June 7, 1668, the Jury appointed to lay out the lands reported to the Court and John Cary signed the document with the eleven others.

John Cary was on "The Grand Enquest," June 3, 1662; June 5, 1672, and June 5, 1678.

John Cary's name appears in "An Exact List of all the Names of the Freemen of the Jurisdiction of New Plymouth, transcribed by Nathaniel Morton, Secretary to the Court for the said Jurisdiction, the 29th of May, Anno Dom. 1670."

John Cary, 2nd, and Abigail Allen, daughter of Samuel Allen, were married December 7, 1670.

Mehitabel, the last child of John and Elizabeth, was born December 24, 1670.

A son (John) was born to John Cary, 2nd, November 6, 1671, and died the 29th of the same month.

John Cary was "Celect Man for Bridgewater" from 1667 to 1679 consecutively.

"It was agreed upon by the towne mett togeyther, the first of November, 1675, that there should be a fortification aboute the meeting house for the safety of the towne."

The Records of the Proprietors of Bridgewater was in John Cary's handwriting, "The First Book of Records was begun 1675 by John Cary, Sen. Clerk, who had 4pence for each lot."

"The town being mett together by order from the Governor, and warned thereto by the Constable, the 21st of August 1676, I, John Cary Cleark, being cald upon by the Inhabitants to call for a vote, who should have the money that was made of the Indians that was sold last. And the vote passed that the souldiears that took them should have the money; the contrary vote being cald, I see but three at most who held up their hands to the contrary."

His son Francis married Hannah, daughter of William Brett, in 1676.

"March 16, 1676-7, the Town granted to John Cary, Sen., 10 acres on condition that he would book all the 106 acres then laid out and the three meadow lots to each."

The fourth day of December, 1676, "Agreed with Samuel Tomkins to sweep and look to the meeting house A full year after the date hereof. And he was to have 12 s for his pains or labor."

"The towne made choice of John Ames Seynior and John Cary Junior, for this year, to be helpful to the Constable and the Grand Jury man. About their inspection into such houses that may be thought to harbour Any English or Indians to sell or give Liquor, or sider to make them drunke."

November 1, 1680, Elizabeth Godfrey, for thirty-six years the beloved wife of John Cary, passed from the labor and hardships incident to the life of a Pilgrim of the Plymouth Colony, to the heritage of the just.

In 1680, the Cary family, which had lived in Bridgewater for nearly thirty years, like most families, began to scatter. It is quite probable that Joseph was the first to go, although John and Francis were married and Elizabeth also, before this. Joseph went to Norwich, and not long after removed to Windham, where he well sustained the family reputation.

John and David removed to Bristol, where they were original proprietors, deacons in the Church, and useful citizens in the community.

Most likely James went to Bristol a little later, as he was not married till 1682, when he married Mary Shaw, of Weymouth, and settled in Bristol, where he lived and died.

The History of Plymouth says that, "John Cary was a man of superior education, and had great influence in the Colony and as an officer in the Church."

The following is the record of his death: "John Cary Seniour inhabytant in the town of Bridgewater deceased the last day of October in the yeare of our lord 1681."

At a Court held March 7, 1682: "Letters of adminestration is graunted vnto Serjeant John Cary to adminester on the estate of John Cary, Seni'r deceased."

The family of John Cary at his death, October 31, 1681, consisted of the following children and grandchildren:

1. John, thirty-five years old, was called "Serjeant Cary" and had five living children—Seth, John, Nathaniel, Eleazer, James.
2. Francis, two children—Samuel, Ephraim.
3. Elizabeth, married Deacon William Brett.
4. James.
5. Mary.
6. Jonathan.
7. David.
8. Hannah.
9. Joseph.
10. Rebecca.
11. Sarah.
12. Mehitabel.

This makes a family of twelve children and seven grandchildren.

Index of Carys

Numbers Refer to Sections.

Aaron ... 70
Aaron ... 135
Aaron ... 138
Aaron ... 256
A. Barkley ... 288-A
Abby T ... 61
Abel ... 33
Abel ... 33
Abel ... 136
Dr. Abel ... 255
Abel De Forest ... 113
Abia H. ... 69-A
Abigail ... 2
Abigail ... 8
Abigail ... 9
Abigail ... 12
Abigail ... 16
Abigail ... 20
Ablgail ... 23
Abigail ... 26
Abigail ... 27
Abigail ... 28
Abigail ... 76
Abigail ... 91
Abigail ... 110
Abigail ... 153-A
Abigail A. ... 101
Abigail K. ... 188
Abigail P. ... 156
Abner ... 84
Abner L. ... 84
Abraham ... 79-A
Abraham J. ... 173
Abram ... 159
Abram ... 281
Abram M. ... 256
Abram Stever ... 197
Ada ... 79-A

Ada ... 142-A
Ada ... 209-A
Ada G. ... 250
Adaline ... 60-A.
Adalyn S. ... 200
Adam ... 63
Addie B. ... 60-A
Adeline E. ... 278
Agnes B. ... 300
Alanson ... 110
Dea Alanson ... 130
Alathea ... 183
Albert ... 60-A
Albert ... 106
Albert ... 110
Albert ... 195
Albert ... 207
Albert ... 311
Albert Alanson ... 130
Albert E. ... 314
Albert F. ... 310
Albert G. ... 93
Albert G. ... 190
Albert H. ... 202-A
Albert Q. ... 239
Albert St. Clair. ... 170
Albigense Waldo ...209-A
Alden ... 101
Alena A. ... 228
Alexander C. ... 279
Alex. Claxton. ... 279
Col. Alfred. ... 85-B
Alfred ... 90
Alfred ... 109
Alfred ... 165
Alfred ... 180
Alfred D. ... 216
Alfred H. ... 170
Alfred L. ... 85-B
Alfred Roswell. ... 85-B
Alfred W. ... 296
Alfred X. ... 211
Alice ... 13
Alice ... 60-A

Alice ... 79-A
Alice ... 194
Alice ... 215
Alice ... 218
Alice ... 220
Alice ... 238
Alice ... 254
Alice ... 255
Alice ... 276-A
Alice ... 279
Alice A. ... 300
Alice B. ... 261
Alice E. ... 276
Alice E. ... 279-B
Alice E. ... 312
Alice G. ... 225
Alice Lela ... 264
Alice M. ... 60-A
Alice M. ... 69-A
Alice M. ... 127
Alice M. ... 281-A
Alice M. ... 300
Alice P. ... 315
Alice S. ... 294
Alice W. ... 202-A
Allen ... 27
Allen ... 314
Almira ... 81
Almira ... 85
Almira ... 149
Almira ... 202-A
Almira A. ... 179
Alpheus ... 76
Alpheus ... 154
Alta B. ... 202-A
Alta L. ... 300
Althea ... 24
Alvah ... 254
Alvin ... 60-A
Alvin ... 84
Alvin S. ... 274
Amanda ... 57
Amelia ... 85
Amelia ... 121

Amelia ... 285
Amelia L. ... 238
Amos L. ... 79-A
Amy ... 217
Amy Ann ... 177
Amzi ... 79-A
Amzi B. ... 174
Andrew E. ... 299
Andrew Shaw ... 114
Angeline ... 166
Ann ... 9
Ann A. ... 282
Ann B. ... 307
Ann E. ... 202-A
Ann E. ... 216
Ann E. ... 263
Ann Eliza ... 69
Ann Jane ... 60-A
Anna ... 52
Anna ... 63-C
Anna ... 79-A
Anna ... 81
Anna ... 91
Anna ... 94
Anna ... 131
Anna ... 132
Anna ... 202
Anna Cooley ... 105-A
Anna De L. ... 314
Anna E. ... 79-A
Anna E. ... 139
Anna E. ... 210
Anna F. ... 101
Anna G. ... 105-A
Anna G. ... 198
Anna K. ... 226
Anna L. ... 300
Anna M. ... 202
Annabelle ... 300
Anne ... 18
Anne ... 56
Anne ... 134.
Anne G. ... 200
Anne Jane ... 60-A

Anne Louise ... 142-A
Annie ... 271
Annie C. ... 177
Annie L. ... 313
Annie S. ... 206
Cary, Benjamin ... 27
Annis ... 97-A
Anselm ... 129
Anson ... 93
Anson ... 97-A
Anson L. ... 192
Arthur ... 218
Arthur B. ... 141-A
Arthur D. ... 142-A
Arthur W. ... 142-A
Arcy ... 126
Asa ... 44
Asa ... 84
Asa ... 85
Asa ... 85-B
Asa ... 179
Asa ... 194
Asa Bacon ... 317
Asa Clinton ... 128
Ashbel ... 255
Augustus ... 61
Augustus ... 242
Augustus C. ... 206
Augustus E. ... 185
Aurelia ... 85
Aurelia ... 121
Aurelia ... 236
Aurelius A. ... 107
Rev. Austin ... 158
Austin ... 273
Austin ... 276-A
Austin P. ... 158
Avery ... 145
Avey ... 66
Azubah ... 32

Barilla ... 47
Berkley ... 136
Barnabas ... 28-A
Barzillai ... 149

Bathsheba ... 6
Beecher B. ... 215
Bela ... 46
Belle ... 300
Lt. Beneijah ... 50
Beneijah ... 195
Benjamin ... 11
Benjamin ... 18
Benjamin ... 26

Benjamin ... 39
Benjamin ... 60-A
Benjamin ... 63-C
Benjamin ... 272
Benjamin F. ... 173
Benjamin F. ... 195
Benjamin F. ... 245
Benjamin F. ... 291
Benjamin Franklin ... 226
Benjamin H. ... 312
Benjamin L. ... 137
Benjamin W. ... 231
Beriah ... 40
Bernice W. ... 300
Bertha ... 57
Bertha ... 79-A
Bessie E. ... 298
Bessie M. ... 222
Bethany ... 160
Bethia ... 6
Bethuel ... 125
Bethuel ... 245
Betsey ... 28-A
Betsey ... 53
Betsey ... 149
Betsey M. ... 107
Betty ... 41
B. Franklin ... 226
Bridget ... 10
Bushnell B. ... 85-B
Byfield ... 103
Byron ... 79-A

Caleb ... 41
Caleb ... 150

Calthea G. ... 102
Calvin ... 30
Calvin ... 83
Calvin ... 289
Calvin C. ... 278
Carl ... 60-A
Caroline ... 115
Caroline ... 186
Caroline ... 281
Caroline E. ... 144
Caroline E. ... 214
Caroline E. ... 300
Caroline R. ... 148
Caroline T. ... 306
Caroline W. ... 128
Carrie E. ... 235
Cassander ... 127
Cassandra ... 74
Catherine ... 60-A
Catherine ... 133
Catherine ... 134
Catherine ... 227
Catherine ... 251
Catherine C. ... 28-A
Catherine H. ... 252
Cecillia ... 113
Celesta ... 63-C
Celestina C. ... 228
Cephas ... 33
Cephas ... 119
Cephas ... 240
Cephas S. ... 228
Chad ... 81
Chad B. ... 169
Charity ... 63-B
Charles ... 60-A
Charles ... 63-C
Charles ... 76
Charles ... 97-A
Charles ... 118
Charles ... 141-A
Charles ... 147
Charles ... 157
Charles ... 181

Charles ... 186
Charles ... 218
Charles ... 220
Charles ... 237
Charles ... 246
Charles ... 273
Charles ... 311
Charles A. ... 144
Charles A. ... 210
Charles A. ... 254
Charles A. ... 273
Charles A. ... 296
Charles A. ... 315
Charles D. ... 128
Charles E. ... 69-A
Charles E. ... 127
Charles F. ... 169
Charles G. ... 277
Charles H. ... 114
Charles H. ... 148
Charles H. ... 153
Charles H. ... 211
Charles H. ... 220
Charles H. ... 300
Charles H. W. ... 235
Charles J. ... 214
Charles Jerome ... 109
Charles K. ... 246
Charles M. ... 255
Charles M. ... 300
Charles P. ... 139
Charles P. ... 148
Charles P. ... 190
Charles P. ... 278
Charles W. ... 69-A
Charles W. ... 257
Charles W. ... 277
Charles W. ... 299
Charles W. ... 316
Charlotte ... 28-A
Charlotte ... 97
Charlotte ... 142
Charlotte ... 159
Charlotte A. ... 152

Charlotte A. ... 276
Charlotte H. ... 69-A
Chester E. ... 100
Chloe ... 19-A
Christopher ... 94
Christopher ... 118
Christopher ... 195
Clara ... 60-A
Clara ... 67
Clara ... 79-A
Clara ... 123
Clara ... 127
Clara ... 131
Clara ... 248
Clara ... 295
Clara B. ... 226
Clara B. ... 261
Clara E. ... 130
Clara I. ... 129
Clara I. ... 243
Clara M. ... 225
Clara S. ... 228
Clarence ... 170
Clarence ... 300
Clarence C. ... 288-A
Clarinda Bliss ... 105-A
Clarissa ... 55
Clarissa ... 73
Clarissa ... 83
Clarissa D. ... 28-A
Clarissa Olive ... 60-A
Clark H. ... 310
Clark S. ... 316
Clark W. ... 310
Clement ... 161
Clement C. ... 281-A
Clementine ... 227
Clifton ... 196
Clinton B. ... 294
Collin R. ... 263
Comfort ... 63-D
Cordelia C. ... 177
Cornelia F. ... 114
Cornelia M. ... 225

Curtis C. ... 294	David ... 19	Ebenezer ... 53-A
Cynthia ... 62	David ... 21	Ebenezer ... 62
Cynthia ... 65	David ... 122	Ebenezer ... 63-C
Cynthia ... 107	David ... 142	Ebenezer ... 80
Cynthia ... 121	David ... 228	Ebenezer ... 86
Cynthia ... 123	David A. ... 228	Ebenezer ... 97-A
Cynthia ... 240	David H. ... 106	Ebenezer ... 165
Cynthia A. ... 114	David M. ... 255	Ebenezer ... 166
Cynthia H. ... 218	Deborah ... 50	Ebenezer ... 180
Cynthia M. ... 218	Deborah ... 57	Ebenezer ... 217
Cynthia T. ... 125	Delia ... 60-A	Ebenezer ... 223
Cyrus ... 68	Delia ... 95	Ebenezer ... 280
	Delia F. ... 152	Ebenezer ... 281-A
Dale E. ... 33	Delia L. ... 293	Ebenezer F. ... 281-A
Damaris ... 8	Delia M. ... 288-A	Ebenezer L. ... 291
Damaris ... 48	Delight ... 47	Eddie L. ... 291
Damaris ... 85	Deliverance ... 52	Eddie S. ... 294
Damaris ... 175	De Witt Clinton ... 113	Edgar A. ... 300
Danforth A. ... 175	Diantha ... 88	Edgar H. ... 179
Daniel ... 32	Dillsworth ... 196	Edith ... 79-A
Daniel ... 33	Dolly ... 128	Edith ... 317
Daniel ... 34	Donald B. ... 218	Edith H. ... 225
Daniel ... 40	Donald E. ... 266	Edith M. ... 238
Daniel ... 60	Donovan ... 291	Edith V. ... 141-A
Daniel ... 63-D	Dora E. ... 69-A	Edith W. ... 313
Daniel ... 65	Dorcas ... 47	Edmond ... 257
Maj. Daniel ... 66	Dorothy ... 28-A	Edward ... 19
Daniel ... 140	Dorothy ... 37	Edward ... 60-A
Daniel ... 243	Dorothy ... 218	Edward ... 207
Daniel ... 247	Dorothea ... 28-A	Edward ... 225
Daniel B. ... 60-A	Douglass ... 116	Edward ... 226
Daniel B. ... 257	Douglass V. ... 114	Edward ... 237
Daniel Clark ... 202-A	Cary, Drusilla ... 119	Edward ... 272
Daniel H. ... 60	Drusilla ... 280	Edward A. ... 271
Daniel H. ... 142-B	Dumont R. ... 182	Edward A. ... 294
Daniel H. ... 242	Dwight ... 305	Edward Colby ... 317
Daniel I. ... 60-A	Dwight ... 307	Edward D. ... 220
Daniel L. ... 161	Dwight P. ... 300	Edward F. ... 238
Daniel M. ... 33		Edward F. ... 250
Daniel M. ... 254	Earnest ... 218	Edward G. ... 261
Daniel M. ... 272	Earnest B. ... 298	Edward H. ... 79-A
Daniel W. ... 142-A	Eben M. ... 79-A	Edward L. ... 214
Darius H. ... 108	Ebenezer ... 34	Edward L. ... 288
David ... 6	Ebenezer ... 44	Edward M. ... 69-A
David ... 13	Ebenezer ... 48	

Edward M. ... 288
Edward R. ... 249
Edward S. ... 127
Edwin ... 213
Edwin A. ... 312
Edwin F. ... 276-A
Edwin H. ... 163
Edwin H. ... 118-A
Edwin H. ... 208
Edwin S. ... 291
Edwin T. ... 170
Edwin W. ... 183
Edwin W. ... 298
Effa ... 79-A
Dr. Egbert ... 113
Egbert ... 207
Egbert ... 218
Egbert J. ... 223
Eleanor ... 181
Eleanor ... 276-A
Eleanor ... 281
Eleazer ... 9
Eleazer ... 24
Eleazer ... 25
Eleazer ... 29
Eleazer ... 41
Eleazer ... 47
Eleazer ... 54
Eleazer ... 63-C
Eleazer ... 99
Eleazer ... 116
Eleazer ... 203
Electa J. ... 112
Elias ... 63-C
Elias ... 64
Elias R. ... 162
Elijah ... 184
Eliphalet ... 18
Maj. Eliphalet ... 18
Eliphalet P. ... 242
Elisha ... 56
Elisha C. ... 274
Elisha S. ... 274
Eliza ... 9

Eliza ... 60-A
Eliza ... 73
Eliza ... 110
Eliza ... 122
Eliza ... 159
Eliza ... 207
Eliza A. ... 152
Eliza J. ... 306
Eliza M. ... 210
Eliza S. ... 143
Eliza Vilas ... 85-B
Elizabeth ... 2
Elizabeth ... 3-A
Elizabeth ... 4
Elizabeth ... 6
Elizabeth ... 7
Elizabeth ... 10
Elizabeth ... 11
Elizabeth ... 13
Elizabeth ... 19-A
Elizabeth ... 23
Elizabeth ... 28-A
Elizabeth ... 28-C
Elizabeth ... 29
Elizabeth ... 34
Elizabeth ... 40
Elizabeth ... 45
Elizabeth ... 48
Elizabeth ... 53-A
Elizabeth ... 61
Elizabeth ... 63-A
Elizabeth ... 81
Elizabeth ... 97-A
Elizabeth ... 112
Elizabeth ... 115
Elizabeth ... 118-A
Elizabeth ... 141
Elizabeth ... 163
Elizabeth ... 166
Elizabeth ... 209
Elizabeth ... 222
Elizabeth ... 279
Elizabeth C. ... 145
Elizabeth D. ... 161

Elizabeth D. ... 211
Elizabeth H. ... 225
Elizabeth M. ... 226
Elizabeth M. ... 275
Elizabeth S. ...177
Ella ... 60-A
Ella ... 226
Ella D. ... 265
Ella E. ... 314
Ella J. ... 60-A
Ella W. ... 201
Ellen ... 28-A
Ellen ... 128
Ellen ... 243
Ellen A. ... 302
Ellen B. ... 264
Ellen M. ... 142-A
Ellen M. ... 166
Ellen Fisher ... 105
Ellena A. ... 235
Elliott ... 58
Elliott ... 171
Ellsworth H. ... 291
Elma ... 167
Elmer B. ... 300
Elmer E. ... 291
Elmina ... 194
Eloise ... 300
Elvira ... 123
Elwyn A. ... 315
Emeline ... 59
Emeline ... 81
Emeline ... 108
Emeline ... 190
Emeline B. ... 28-A
Emerson J. ... 264
Emery C. ... 292
Emily ... 97-A
Emily ... 131
Emily ... 132
Emily ... 186
Emily A. ... 69-A
Emily E. ... 275
Emily I. ... 200

Emily J. ... 254
Emily L. ... 302
Emily T. ... 166
Emma ... 63-C
Emma ... 261
Emma ... 290
Emma A. ... 204
Emma C. ... 278
Emma C. ... 279
Emma J. ... 169
Emma M. ... 283
Emma Louise ... 105
Emma R. ... 195
Emmelia ... 129-A
Emory ... 295
Emory L. ... 177
Ephraim ... 14
Ephraim ... 30
Ephraim ... 32
Ephraim ... 134
Ephraim ... 290
Ephraim C. ... 143
Erastus ... 176
Ernest ... 141-A
Estella ... 63-C
Estey A. ... 79-A
Esther ... 19-A
Esther ... 28-C
Esther ... 63-A
Esther ... 63-C
Esther ... 257
Esther A. ... 166
Esther B. ... 184
Esther D. ... 60
Ethel ... 202-A
Ethel L. ... 266
Ethel M. ... 167
Ethelinda ... 263
Ethelwyn ... 201
Eunice ... 25
Eunice ... 38
Eunice ... 39
Eunice ... 42
Eunice ... 66

Eunice ... 82
Eunice ... 92
Eunice ... 99-A
Eunice ... 123
Eunice ... 126
Eunice ... 143
Eugene B. ... 174
Eugene L. ... 290
Eugenia ... 300
Eugenia A. ... 262
Eugenia L. ... 141
Eve E. ... 264
Evan F. ... 225
Evaline E. ... 301
Evelyn L. ... 300
Evelyn P. ... 275
Experience ... 18
Experience ... 40
Ezekiel ... 82
Ezekiel ... 88
Ezekiel W. ... 182
Ezra ... 30
Ezra ... 64
Ezra ... 65
Ezra ... 69
Ezra ... 110
Ezra ... 122
Ezra ... 123
Ezra ... 236
Ezra D. ... 241
Ezra H. ... 163

F. P. ... 315
Fanny ... 57
Fanny ... 90
Fanny ... 175
Fanny ... 213
Fanny B. ... 114
Fanny J. ... 222
Fanny M. ... 270
Fanny M. ... 271
Fanny O. ... 264
Ferdinand E. ... 198
Ferdinand F. ... 60
Fern E. ... 79-A

Fidelia ... 141-A
Fidelia ... 182
Finley W. ... 228
Fitch A. ... 305
Flora H. ... 230
Florence ... 170
Foster H., M. D. ... 152
Frances ... 85-B
Frances ... 116
Frances ... 159
Frances ... 192
Frances ... 247
Frances A. G. ... 129
Frances E. ... 197
Frances F. ... 28-B
Frances H. ... 183
Frances J. ... 242
Francis ... 3
Francis ... 63-B
Francis ... 68
Francis ... 71
Francis ... 126
Francis ... 159
Francis ... 195
Francis ... 242
Francis ... 247
Francis A. ... 131
Francis A. Gage. ... 129
Francis C. ... 101
Francis E. ... 197
Francis H. ... 277
Frank ... 235
Frank ... 279-B
Frank B. ... 282
Frank B. ... 300
Frank E. ... 274
Frank H. ... 149
Frank L. ... 300
Frank L. ... 141-A
Frank Pierce ... 100
Frank R. ... 284
Frank S. ... 304
Frank W. ... 307
Franklin ... 95

Franklin ... 136
Fred Asa ... 85-B
Fred E. ... 267
Fred W. ... 153
Frederic W. ... 299
Frederick ... 186
Frederick A. ... 187
Frederick A. ... 300
Frederick E. ... 169
Frederick J. ... 174
Frederick W. ... 215
Frederick W. ... 299
Freelove ... 146
Freeman Grant ... 199

Geneva H. ... 79-A
George ... 12
George ... 26
George ... 60-A
George ... 63-B
George ... 69-A
George ... 79-A
George ... 120
George ... 181
George ... 209
George ... 237
George ... 251
George ... 258
George ... 265
George ... 304
George A. ... 169
George A. ... 190
George A. ...191
George A. ... 242
George B. ... 277
George B. ... 300
George C. ... 262
George C. ... 308
George Clark ... 153
George De Forest...288-A
George E. ... 257
George E. ... 279-B
George F. ... 239
George F. ... 273
George H. ... 153

George H. ... 202-A
George H. ... 215
George H. ... 304
George L. ... 135
George L. ... 141
George L. ... 218
George L. ... 305
George Lovell ... 28-A
George M. ... 262
George N. ... 309
George Peter ... 85-B
George R. ... 206
George S. ... 168
George S. ... 307
George S. ... 286
George T. ... 235
George W. ... 152
George W. ... 154
George W. ... 167
George W. ... 186
George W. ... 216
George W. ... 286
George W. ... 316
George Washington ... 120
Georgiana ... 100
Georgiana ... 297
Gertrude ... 233
Gertrude M. ... 220
Gilbert G. ... 242
Giles ... 183
Gilman ... 28-A
Glory Ann ... 141-A
Goldy ... 33
Grace ... 218
Grafton E. ... 170
Gussie ... 63-C
Gustavus ... 240

Hannah ... 1
Hannah ... 4
Hannah ... 7
Hannah ... 20
Hannah ... 23
Hannah ... 27

Hannah ... 33
Hannah ... 34
Hannah ... 39
Hannah ... 45
Hannah ... 47
Hannah ... 53
Hannah ... 63-A
Hannah ... 63-E
Hannah ... 70
Hannah ... 82
Hannah ... 93
Hannah ... 97
Hannah ... 138
Hannah B. ... 166
Hannah C. ... 220
Hannah T. ... 101
Hannah T. ... 109
Hannah Wales ... 157
Harlan ... 141-A
Harlin E. ... 291
Harmony ... 68
Harold S. ... 225
Harold W. ... 266
Harriet ... 85
Harriet ... 93
Harriet ... 95
Harriet ... 97-A
Harriet ... 99
Harriet ... 127
Harriet ... 143
Harriet ... 271
Harriet A. ... 109
Harriet E. ... 148
Harriet E. ... 185
Harriet E. ... 223
Harriet F. ... 156
Harriet ... 193
Harriet S. ... 85-B
Harriet W. ... 28-A
Harriette G. ... 127
Harrison ... 132
Harrison Gray Otis ... 249
Harry ... 63-C
Harry ... 69-A

Harry F. ... 281-A	Henry S. ... 242	Ida F. ... 60-A
Harry G. ... 229	Henry S. ... 275	Ida M. ... 229
Harry Waldo ... 79 -A	Henry Grosvenor...206-A	Ida M. ... 293
Harvey ... 60-A	Henry Nathaniel ... 85-B	Imogene ... 203
Harvey ... 237	Henry Stephen ... 79-A	Inez ... 295
Harvey G. ... 233	Henry Shorer ... 235	Ira F. ... 33
Harvey H. ... 104	Henry W. ... 144	Ira H. ... 222
Hattie R. ... 226	Henry Y. ... 301	Irena ... 90
Helen ... 62	Hepzibah ... 62	Irving B. ... 85-B
Helen ... 276-A	Herbert ... 79-A	Irwin ... 196
Helen ... 279	Herbert ... 243	Isaac ... 28-A
Helen ... 314	Herbert B. ... 299	Isaac ... 60-A
Helen ... 319	Herbert L. ... 300	Isaac ... 78
Helen A. ... 149	Herbert O. ... 300	Herbert F. ... 266
Helen A. ... 170	Hester C. ... 228	Isaac, Dr. ... 79-A
Helen E. ... 169	Hiram ... 118-A	Isaac ... 156
Helen G. ... 63-C	Hiram F. ... 152	Isaac ... 164
Helen I. ... 210	Homer ... 179	Isaac ... 172
Helen L. ... 114	Hope ... 276-A	Isaac ... 218
Helen M. ... 193	Horace ... 97-A	Isaac ... 220
Helen M. ... 200	Horace ... 253	Isaac, Dr. ... 284
Henrietta ... 281	Horace ... 300	Isaac H. ... 208
Henrietta ... 299	Horatio ... 190	Isaac J. ... 105-A
Henry, Rev. ... 19-A	Horatio G. ... 190	Isaac N. ... 160
Henry ... 39	Hosea H. ... 242	Isabel ... 123
Henry ... 124	Howard, Capt. ... 71	Horace D. ... 202-A
Henry ... 127	Howard ... 79-A	Isabel ... 166
Henry ... 141-A	Howard ... 127	Horace K. ... 300
Henry ... 160	Howard B. ... 294	Isabella ... 128
Henry ... 242	Howard L. ... 294	Isabella ... 137
Henry A. ... 282	Howard T. ... 298	Ivy ... 79-A
Henry C. ... 227	Howard W. ... 276-A	J. Eugene ... 118-A
Henry E. ... 141-A	Hoyt F. ... 267	Jabez ... 21
Henry F. ... 133	Hubbard ... 118	Tabez ... 46
Henry F. ... 204	Hudson ... 172	Jacob ... 78
Henry G. ... 28-A	Hugh ... 131	Jacob ... 79-A
Henry G. ... 229	Huldah ... 17	Jairus ... 250
Henry G. ... 233	Huldah ... 28-C	James ... 4
Henry H. ... 141	Huldah ... 32	James ... 10
Henry H. ... 306	Huldah ... 38	James ... 15
Henry L. ... 297	Huldah ... 75	James ... 25-A
Henry Lucius ... 98		James ... 46
Henry R. ... 190	Ichabod ... 34	James ... 60-A
Henry S. ... 235	Ida ... 60-A	James ... 63-C
	Ida ... 276-A	

James ... 77
James, Capt. ... 91
James ... 132
James ... 186
James ... 188
James ... 250
James ... 276
James A. ... 128
James A. ... 263
James B. ... 135
James B. ... 254
James B. ... 305
James C. ... 128
James H. ... 239
James H. ... 254
James N. ... 280
James R. ... 218
James R. ... 255
James Rogers ... 62
James S. ... 128
James S. ... 303
James Sturges ... 114
James V. ... 63-C
James W. ... 276
James W. ... 312
James Warren ... 60-A
Jane ... 60-A
Jane ... 68
Jane ... 69
Jane ... 79-A
Jane ... 115
Jane ... 117
Jane ... 118-A
Jane ... 134
Jane ... 141-A
Jane ... 189
Jane L. ... 307
Jane M. ... 192
Jane S. ... 279
Jane W. ... 138
Jane Wesley ... 231
Jarvis ... 219
Jason S. ... 119
Jedediah T. ... 311

Jefferson ... 251
Jefferson S. ... 282
Jemima ... 45
Jeremiah ... 230
Jeremiah E. ... 210
Jennette P. ... 294
Jennie ... 63-C
Jennie ... 120
Jennie ... 181
Jennie ... 232
Jennie Wheeler ... 314
Jervis ... 218
Jesse ... 18
Jesse O. ... 225
Jesse W. ... 33
Jessica L. ... 28-A
Jessie ... 201
Jessie M. ... 300
Joanna ... 23
Joanna ... 135
Joanna ... 163
Joel ... 40
Joel ... 79-A
Joel ... 141-A
John ... 1
John ... 2
John ... 8
John ... 17
John ... 22
John ... 26
John ... 28-A
John ... 33
John ... 38
John ... 47
John ... 49
John ... 58
John ... 60-A
John ... 63-A
John ... 63-B
John ... 63-D
John ... 79
John ... 88
John ... 95
John ... 105-A

John ... 118-A
John ... 124
John ... 136
John ... 139
John ... 157
John ... 160
John ... 162
John ... 163
John ... 165
John ... 180
John ... 183
John ... 186
John ... 195
John ... 218
John ... 222
John ... 264
John A. ... 254
John A. ... 276
John Abbott ... 118-A
John B. ... 190
John Bradford ... 120
John C. ... 283
John Colman ... 132
John C. W. ... 235
John E. ... 197
John Ely ... 210
John F. ... 60
John F. ... 288-A
John G. ... 105-A
John H. ... 170
John Harris ... 79-A
John L. ... 170
John L. ... 259
John L. ... 260
John L. ... 261
John M. ... 105
John M. ... 218
John M. ... 219
John M. ... 222
John N. ... 229
John N. ... 233
John R. ... 235
John R. ... 261
John S. ... 226

John Shepherd ... 124	Joseph F. ... 300	L. B., Dr. ... 113
John T. ... 280	Joseph L. ... 210	Lanetta C. ... 223
John W. ... 167	Joseph M. ... 218	Laura ... 63-B
John W. ... 226	Joseph M. ... 281	Laura ... 108
John W. ... 295	Joseph P. ... 314	Laura A. ... 179
John W. ... 300	Joseph S. ... 142-A	Laura C. ... 231
John W. ... 301	Joseph W. ... 219	Laura E. ... 274
John Walter ... 79-A	Josephine ... 227	La Verne ... 202-A
John Watson ... 85-B	Josephine ... 319	Lavinia ... 51
Johnson ... 115	Joshua ... 34	Lazarus ... 28-A
Johnson ... 118	Joshua ... 79-A	Leander ... 19-A
Jonathan ... 5	Josiah ... 12	Leander ... 79-A
Jonathan ... 18	Josiah ... 53	Leigh R. ... 225
Jonathan Dea ... 37	Josiah ... 72	Lemuel P. ... 121
Jonathan ... 42	Josiah ... 97	Lena ... 33
Jonathan ... 75	Josiah ... 144	Leon B. ... 114
Jonathan ... 90	Josiah ... 202	Leonard ... 148
Jonathan ... 146	Josiah ... 268	Leonard ... 245
Jonathan ... 151	Josiah Addison ... 269	Leonard B. ... 261
Jonathan H. ... 133	Josiah W. ... 212	Letha ... 79-A
Jonathan T. ... 309	Josiah W. ... 310	Leta L. ... 291
Joseph ... 7	Josiah W. ... 145	Levi ... 70
Joseph ... 12	Julia ... 167	Levi ... 267
Joseph ... 12	Julia ... 181	Levi S. ... 85-B
Joseph ... 20	Julia A. ... 69-A	Levi S. ... 150
Joseph ... 22	Julia A. ... 147	Lewis ... 69
Joseph ... 28-A	Julia E. ... 182	Lewis ... 137
Joseph ... 45	Julia F. ... 250	Lewis ... 138
Joseph ... 51	Julia Knox ... 156	Lewis ... 155
Joseph ... 61	Julia M. ... 228	Lewis ... 283
Joseph ... 69-A	Lewis M. ... 256	Lewis A. ... 258
Joseph ... 78	Lewis W. ... 262	Lewis B. ... 155
Joseph ... 82	Julia Madeline ... 85-B	Lewis C. ... 239
Joseph ... 92	Julian ... 203	Lewis D. ... 263
Joseph, Dr. ... 107	Julian ... 308	Lewis H. ... 259
Joseph ... 135		Lewis M. ... 256
Joseph ... 171	Kate ... 63-C	Lewis W. ... 279
Joseph ... 172	Kate ... 271	L. Gertrude ... 28-A
Joseph ... 176	Kate M. ... 257	Lillian ... 279
Joseph ... 207	Katherine ... 111	Lillian E. ... 266
Joseph ... 214	Katherine A. ... 210	Lillian M. ... 291
Joseph A. ... 209	Kathryn ... 79-A	Lilly ... 141-A
Joseph B. ... 281-A	Keziah ... 218	Libyan Dorothy ... 202-A
Joseph C. ... 209-A	Knibloe B. ... 318	Liston D. ... 79-A

Lizzie A. ... 79-A
Lizzie Almeda ... 70-A
Lizzie O. ... 262
Lizzie T. ... 230
Lois ... 42
Lois ... 123
Lois A. ... 243
Lola ... 300
Lorana F. ... 241
Lorenzo ... 198
Lorenzo J. ... 197
Loretta ... 229
Lou ... 79-A
Louis A. ... 28-A
Louis F. ... 144
Louis F. ... 174
Louisa ... 112
Louisa E. ... 212
Louisa F. ... 149
Louisa J. ... 173
Lucia ... 99
Lucia ... 207
Lucia A. ... 142-B
Lucia Emily ... 104
Lucie A. ... 131
Lucien B. ... 303
Lucilla ... 138
Lucina ... 84
Lucinda ... 48
Lucinda ... 58
Lucinda ... 84
Lucinda ... 86
Lucinda ... 165
Lucius ... 74
Lucius ... 134
Lucius ... 149
Lucius ... 218
Lucius ... 253
Lucius C. ... 85-B
Lucius F. ...218
Lucius H. ... 203
Lucius Henry ... 98
Lucius M. ... 202-A
Lucretia ... 47

Lucretia ... 182
Lucretia ... 236
Lucretia ... 257
Lucretia ... 259
Lucretia H. ... 129
Lucy ... 46
Lucy ... 53-A
Lucy ... 63-D
Lucy ... 76
Lucy ... 82
Lucy ... 83
Lucy ... 84
Lucy ... 94
Lucy ... 97-A
Lucy ... 143
Lucy ... 242
Lucy Ann ... 104
Lucy Ann ... 125
Lucy M. ... 108
Lucy P. ... 242
Luella ... 300
Lurany ... 69
Lurany E. ...139
Luther ... 30
Luther ... 65
Luther, Dr. ... 67
Luther ... 72
Luther ... 152
Luther ... 248
Luther ... 276-A
Luther H. ... 128
Luther H. ... 174
Luther King ... 128
Luther King ... 132
Luther Messimore...79-A
Lydia ... 9
Lydia ... 13
Lydia ... 14-A
Lydia ... 25
Lydia ... 36
Lydia ... 46
Lydia ... 58
Lydia ... 62
Lydia ... 63-D

Lydia ... 69-A
Lydia ... 72
Lydia ... 77
Lydia ... 97
Lydia ... 99
Lydia ... 119
Lydia ... 123
Lydia ... 141-A
Lydia ... 202
Lydia ... 203
Lydia ... 217
Lydia ... 244
Lydia A. ... 264
Lydia H. ... 143
Lydia K. ... 234
Lydia Reed ... 28-A
Lydia S. ... 173
Lyman ... 171
Lyman ... 253
Lyman ... 141-A
Lyman F. ... 140
Lyman N. ... 263

Mabel ... 220
Mabel A. ... 79-A
Mabel E. ... 114
Mabel L. ... 202-A
Mabel V. ... 300
Mabelle B. ... 127
Mahala ... 135
Malissa A. ... 168
Malvina ... 132
Malvina E. ... 199
Manly A. ... 274
Mara A. ... 169
Marcena K. ... 33
Marcellus ... 229
Marcia A. ... 142-A
Margaret ... 85-B
Margaret ... 181
Margaret ... 215
Margaret ... 276-A
Margaret ... 28-A
Margaret J. ... 139
Margaret L. ... 210

Margaret Lovell ... 28-A	Martha E. ... 148	Mary... 281
Margaret Stone ... 85-B	Martha E. ... 152	Mary A. ... 69-A
Maria ... 62	Martha J. ... 213	Mary A. ... 143
Maria ... 94	Martha J. ... 239	Mary A. ... 148
Maria ... 97-A	Martha L. ... 201	Cary, Mary A. ... 149
Maria ... 106	Martha M. ... 259	Mary A. ... 204
Maria ... 111	Martha W. ... 60-A	Mary A. ... 207
Maria ... 112	Martin ... 153	Mary A. ... 260
Maria ... 117	Martin A. ... 153	Mary A. ... 269
Maria ... 195	Martin L. ... 276-A	Mary A. ... 218
Maria ... 200	Martin V. B. ... 195	Mary A. ... 230
Maria ... 207	Mary ... 1	Mary Adelaide ... 28-A
Maria ... 217	Mary ... 3	Mary Ann ... 57
Maria ... 221	Mary ... 4	Mary Ann ... 85-B
Maria A. ... 169	Mary ... 9	Mary Ann ... 115
Maria F. ... 121	Mary ... 12	Mary Ann ... 143
Maria S. ... 220	Mary ... 13	Mary Ann ... 161
Marilla J. ... 224	Mary ... 16	Mary Ann ... 172
Marion ... 105-A	Mary ... 19	Mary Ann ... 279-A
Marion ... 181	Mary ... 19-A	Mary Ann Short ... 28-A
Marion ... 288-A	Mary ... 21	Mary Anna ... 72
Marjorie G. ... 298	Mary ... 23	Mary B. ... 193
Mark De F. ... 215	Mary ... 25	Mary B. ... 235
Mark De F. ... 288-A	Mary ... 25-A	Mary B. ... 246
Marrel H. ... 79-A	Mary ... 28-C	Mary E. ... 33
Martha ... 17	Mary ... 34	Mary E. ... 60-A
Martha ... 46	Mary ... 36	Mary E. ... 152
Martha ... 51	Mary... 41	Mary E. ... 210
Martha ... 63-C	Mary ... 45	Mary E. ... 223
Martha ... 69	Mary ... 47	Mary E. ... 244
Martha ... 71-A	Mary ... 56	Mary E. ... 259
Martha ... 78	Mary ... 60-A	Mary E. ... 278
Martha ... 79-A	Mary ... 79	Mary E. ... 281-A
Martha ... 127	Mary ... 141	Mary E. ... 305
Martha ... 135	Mary ... 141-A	Mary Ella ... 242
Martha ... 142-B	Mary ... 145	Mary F. ... 105-A
Martha ... 148	Mary ... 149	Mary F. ... 163
Martha ... 153	Mary ... 152	Mary G. ... 313
Martha ... 159	Mary ... 153-B	Mary H. ...151
Martha ... 195	Mary ... 175	Mary H. ... 242
Martha ... 254	Mary ... 180	Mary H. ... 281
Martha ... 280	Mary ... 195	Mary J. ... 202
Martha ... 281	Mary ... 199	Mary J. ... 308
Martha B. ... 145	Mary ... 217	Mary Jane ... 105-A

Mary J. ... 118
Mary L. ... 185
Mary L. ... 299
Mary M. ... 280
Mary Scott ... 116
Mary T. ... 119
Mary W. ... 156
Mary W. ... 279
Maryette ... 162
Maryette ... 242
Matilda ... 62
Matilda ... 111
Matilda ... 113
Matilda ... 162
Matilda ... 218
Mattie ... 149
Maud ... 79-A
Maud L. ... 202-A
Maud Livsey ... 170
Maurice ... 131
Maurice ... 152
May ... 141-A
May Almeda ... 118-A
Mehitabel ... 1
Mehitabel ... 3
Mehitabel ... 6
Mehitabel ... 7-B
Mehitabel ... 14
Mehitabel ... 22
Mehitabel ... 29
Mehitabel ... 31
Mehitabel ... 35
Mehitabel ... 71-C
Melancthon ... 256
Melancthon W. ... 85-B
Melbert B. ... 85-B
Melinda ... 153
Melvin ... 235
Melvin ... 293
Mercy ... 4
Mercy ... 22
Mercy ... 52
Merritt ... 218
Meta I. ... 79-A

Michael ... 43
Milan Galusha ... 205
Mildred ... 220
Mildred J. ... 299
Milo G. ... 79-A
Milton ... 63-C
Milton ... 111
Milton T. ... 234
Minerva ... 59
Minerva ... 93
Minnie ... 79-A
Minnie L. ... 266
Mollie ... 234
Molly ... 17
Molly ... 27
Molly ... 35
Molly ... 142-C
Mordecai ... 72
Morris L. ... 300
Moses ... 53-A
Moses ... 74
Moses ... 97-A
Myra F. ... 225
Myrtle A. ... 202-A

Naba ... 61
Nabby ... 128
Nancy ... 12
Nancy ... 25
Nancy ... 63-C
Nancy ... 69
Nancy ... 76
Nancy ... 97
Nancy ... 157-A
Nancy A. ... 79-A
Nancy E. ... 281
Nancy J. ... 172
Nancy W. ... 119
Nannie L. ... 79-A
Nathan ... 19
Nathan ... 28-C
Nathan ... 48
Nathan ... 63
Nathan ... 63-B
Nathan ... 63-C

Nathan ... 80
Nathan ... 118-A
Nathan C. ... 270
Nathan S. ... 149
Nathaniel ... 2
Nathaniel ... 12
Nathaniel ... 26
Nathaniel, Col. ... 28
Nathaniel ... 47
Nathaniel, Capt. ... 51
Nathaniel ... 55
Nathaniel ... 60-A
Nathaniel ... 92
Nathaniel ... 162
Nathaniel C. ... 85-B
Nathaniel S. ... 177
Nellie ... 149
Nellie G. ... 267
Nellie L. ... 206
Nellie S. ... 177
Nelson E. ... 260
Nelson Howard ... 142-A
Nettie ... 271
Norman W. ... 269
Olive ... 46
Olive ... 60-A
Olive ... 66
Olive ... 126
Olive E. ... 288-A
Olive M. ... 291
Olivet ... 57
Olivet ... 100
Oliver Aikin ... 225
Oliver H. P. ... 280
Olney C. ... 167
Oren E. ... 300
Orinda ... 290
Ormond ... 124
Orra B. ... 291
Orrin ... 197
Oscar E. ... 300
Osee. ... 79-A
Otis, Hon. ... 157
Otis, Rev. ... 279-B

Palmer C. ... 192
Pamelia ... 28-A
Pamelia ... 59
Patty ... 60-A
Patty ... 72
Pauline ... 85-B
Paul Van Ettan ... 85-B
Pearl ... 79-A
Pearl L. ... 294
Peleg ... 10
Permelia Rosamond ... 103
Persis ... 47
Peter ... 6
Peter L. ... 233
Phebe ... 8
Phebe ... 32
Phebe ... 33
Phebe ... 45
Phebe ... 60-A
Phebe ... 64
Phebe ... 78
Phebe ... 82
Phebe ... 83
Phebe ... 94-A
Phebe ... 113
Phebe ... 159
Phebe ... 181
Phebe ... 194
Phebe ... 281
Phebe A. ... 218
Phebe A. ... 268
Phebe C. ... 218
Phebe H. ... 186
Phebe J. ... 161
Phebe J. ... 300
Philip F. ... 113
Philip H. ... 145
Philomela ... 51
Phineas ... 56
Polly ... 33
Polly ... 53
Polly ... 60-A
Polly ... 72

Polly ... 74
Polly ... 81
Preston M. ... 148
Priscilla ... 6
Priscilla P. ... 242
Priscilla P. ... 151
Prosper ... 12
Prosper ... 47

Rachel ... 63-C
Rachel ... 82
Rachel J. ... 79-A
Raiman B. ... 300
Ralph ... 187
Ralph H. ... 141-A
Ralph H. ... 161
Ralph H. ... 300
Ralph S. ... 114
Ralph W. ... 301
Ransom T. ... 141-A
Rebecca ... 7-A
Rebecca ... 10
Rebecca ... 40
Rebecca ... 49
Rebecca ... 160
Rebecca ... 161
Rebecca E. ... 118-A
Rebecca F. ... 199
Rebecca V. ... 167
Recompense, Dea ... 16
Recompense ... 73
Relief ... 83
Reuben ... 40
Rex L. ... 300
Rhoda ... 28-C
Rhoda ... 71-B
Rhoda ... 106
Rhoda ... 143-D
Rhoda ... 149
Rhoda ... 272-B
Rhoda ... 280
Rhoda J. ... 228
Rhoda S. ... 116
Rhuca ... 309
Richard ... 45

Richard ... 46
Richard ... 83
Richard ... 292
Richard L. ... 174
Richard L. ... 218
Richard M. ... 173
Robert ... 194
Robert J. ... 85-B
Robert W. ... 149
Rodolpho ... 167
Roger ... 92
Rollin B. ... 145
Rosa E. ... 281
Rosanna ... 28-C
Rosanna ... 281
Roxania ... 175
Rose B. ... 128
Roswell ... 175
Rowena ... 192
Rowena ... 194
Roy D. ... 300
Ruby ... 76
Ruby W. ... 167
Rufus ... 64
Rufus ... 237
Rufus ... 238
Rufus J. ... 101
Russell S. ... 142-A
Ruth ... 61
Ruth ... 111
Ruth ... 117
Ruth ... 217
Ruth ... 220
Ruth L. ... 300
Ruth S. ... 218

Saduska ... 85
Salmon ... 241
Sallie A. ... 119
Sally ... 44
Sally ... 69
Sally ... 75
Sally ... 84
Sally ... 91
Sally S. ... 81

Salome ... 68
Samuel ... 12
Samuel ... 13
Samuel ... 40
Samuel ... 46
Samuel ... 52
Samuel ... 63-B
Samuel ... 106
Samuel ... 217
Samuel ... 242
Samuel, Col. ... 280
Samuel A. ... 271
Samuel C. ... 232
Samuel D. ... 254
Samuel E. ... 142-A
Samuel F. ... 198
Samuel F. ... 199
Samuel F. ... 201
Samuel F. ... 301
Samuel Fenton ... 201
Samuel P. ... 242
Samuel P. ... 254
Samuel R. ... 105-A
Samuel S. D. ... 280
Samuel W. ... 140
Samuel Wills ... 140
Sanford ... 189
Sara A. ... 143
Sarah ... 1
Sarah ...15
Sarah ... 16
Sarah ... 37
Sarah ... 38
Sarah ... 48
Sarah ... 63-B
Sarah ... 63-C
Sarah ... 85-A
Sarah ... 86
Sarah ... 118-A
Sarah ... 121
Sarah ... 127
Sarah ... 141-A
Sarah ... 159
Sarah ... 172

Sarah ... 181
Sarah ... 244
Sarah ... 248
Sarah A. ... 85-B
Sarah A. ... 120
Sarah A. ... 129
Sarah A. ... 143
Sarah A. ... 197
Sarah A. M. ... 280
Sarah C. ... 240
Sarah D. ... 125
Sarah E. ... 193
Sarah E. ... 266
Sarah Etta ... 170
Sarah Flagler ... 224
Sarah T. ... 33
Sarah J. ... 163
Sarah J. ... 198
Sarah J. ... 311
Sarah L. ... 296
Sarah R. ... 307
Sarah T. ... 157
Sarah W. ... 138
Sarah W. ... 191
Sarah W. ... 254
Selesta ... 63-C
Seth ... 2
Seth ... 10
Seth ... 18
Seth ... 23
Seth ... 69-A
Seth ... 141-A
Seth Cooley ... 105-A
Seth F. ... 242
Seth S. ... 242
Seward ... 181
Shepard ... 251
Sherman G. ... 254
Sherman L. ... 202-A
Sibbel ... 47
Sibian G. ... 179
Silas J. ... 161
Silas J. ... 281-A
Simeon, Col. ... 35

Simeon ... 79-A
Simeon ... 142-A
Simeon B. ... 232
Simeon Baker ... 120
Solomon Flagler ... 114
Solomon Flagler ... 224
Sophia ... 113
Sophia ... 127
Sophia ... 28-A
Sophia A. ... 102
Sophia A. ... 235
Sophia Cornelia ... 69-A
Sophia L. ... 128
Sophronia ... 33
Sophronia ... 57
Sophronia ... 182
Sophronia ... 295
Sophronia C. ... 33
Stella ... 300
Stephen ... 40
Stephen ... 82
Stephen H. ... 231
Stephen J. ... 138
Stewart ... 118-A
Sturges ... 114
Sturges F. ... 225
Susan ... 26
Susan ... 63-A
Susan ... 115
Susan ... 118-A
Susan ... 128
Susan ... 130
Susan ... 137
Susan ... 166
Susan ... 194
Susan ... 195
Susan ... 268
Susan A. ... 242
Susan B. ... 257
Susan C. ... 140
Susan E. ... 108
Susan M. ... 300
Susan M. ... 309
Susan P. ... 242

Susan T. ... 81	Thomas ... 26	Walter ... 251
Susanna ... 10	Thomas ... 44	Walter ... 279-B
Susanna ... 11	Thomas ... 60-A	Walter B. ... 215
Susanna ... 17	Thomas ... 79-A	Walter D. ... 202-A
Susanna ... 18	Thomas ... 121	Walter E. ... 225
Susanna ... 25	Thomas ... 181	Walter E. ... 315
Susanna ... 27	Thomas ... 186	Walter H. ... 142-A
Susanna ... 29	Thomas ... 236	Walter Trumbull ... 48
Susanna ... 31	Thomas ... 240	Walter W. ... 276-A
Susanna ... 32	Thomas ... 241	Warren ... 60-A
Susanna ... 38	Thomas G. ... 69-A	Warren. ... 79-A
Susanna ... 58	Thomas H. ... 147	Warren ... 194
Susanna ... 60-A	Thomas J. ... 257	Warren ... 238
Susanna ... 63-A	Thomas M. ... 239	Warren M. ... 79-A
Susanna ... 65	Thomas Storrs ... 99	Wealthy ... 176
Susanna ... 68	Thomas W. ... 278	Wesley ... 176
Susanna ... 70	Timothy ... 2	Wilford P. ... 315
Susanna ... 74	Tolman ... 65	Willard H. ... 275
Susanna ... 83	Tom Corwin ... 226	Willard P. ... 279
Susanna ... 105-A	Tracy M. ... 225	William, Dea. ... 25
Susanna ... 143	Trillena ... 79-A	William ... 59
Susanna ... 242	Truman .175	William ... 60
Susanna ... 272-A	Trumbull . 87	William ... 63-B
Susanna Cornelia ... 140	Trumbull ..181	William ... 71
Susie Amelia ... 105	Triphena. 45	William ... 89
Sylvia ... 85		William ... 96
Sylvester ... 33	Van Renssalaer ... 174	William ... 102
Sylvester ... 177	Van Renssalaer ... 178	William ... 109
Sylvester ... 252	Varus B. ... 195	William, Dr. ... 111
Sylvester E. ... 177	Veranus L. ... 274	William ... 111
Sylvester L. ... 294	Vesta ... 149	William ... 117
	Vesta S. ... 272-C	William ... 128
Talcot P. ... 174	Viola ... 79-A	William ... 136
Tamar ... 113	Viola E. ... 266	William ... 137
Tamar A. ... 229	Volima ... 121	William ... 167
Taylor ... 112	Volney ... 79-A	William ... 185
Thankful ... 17		William ... 195
Thankful ... 26	Waitstill ... 12	William ... 199
Thankful ... 40	Waitstill ... 281	William ... 218
Thankful ... 53	Waitstill M. ... 281	William ... 220
Theda ... 240	Walcot ... 308	William ... 220
Thelma D. ... 33	Waldo ... 182	William ... 221
Theodore ... 251	Walter ... 79-A	William ... 244
Theron ... 298	Walter ... 85-B	William ... 301
Thesta S. ... 205	Walter, M. D. ... 181	

William ... 315
William A. ... 204
William A. ... 227
William A. ... 270
William A. ... 313
William Addison ... 204
William Ayres ... 146
William B. ... 255
William B. ... 308
William B. ... 314
William C. ... 157
William C. ... 228
William D. ... 60
William E. ... 224
William G. ... 260
William H. ... 28-A
William H. ... 133
William H. ... 142-A
William H. ... 187
William H. ... 202-A
William H. ... 214
William H. ... 215
William H. ... 252
William H. ... 256
William H. ... 268
William H. ... 283
William H. ... 285
William H. ... 287
William H. ... 297
William H. ... 300
William Henry ... 79-A
William Henry ... 105
William Hiram ... 28-A
William K. ... 128
William L. ... 170
William L. ... 301
William L. ... 319
William P. ... 279
William P. ... 287
William R. ... 231
William R. ... 244
William S. ... 140
William S. ... 260
William S. ... 263

William Sayre ... 263
William Stanton ... 79-A
William T. ... 227
William T. ... 229
William W. ... 197
William W. ... 266
William Woodward ... 200
Willie C. ... 158
Wilson W. ... 101
Winnefred ... 204
Winnefred R. ... 28-A
Winthrop ... 90
Winthrop H. ... 302
Wolcott ... 308
Ysabel F. ... 85-B
Zachary ... 122
Zachary ... 239
Zalmon S. ... 193
Zechariah ... 31
Zechariah ... 121
Zenas ... 34
Zenas ... 69-A
Zenas ... 71
Zenas ... 142
Zeneah ... 110
Zebulon ... 36
Zebulon ... 69-A
Zebulon ... 73
Zebulon ... 141-A
Zebulon ... 143
Zebulon E. ... 143
Zerviah ... 20
Zibiah ... 66
Zibiah ... 126
Zilla ... 50
Zina ... 82
Zoe J. ... 253

Intermarriages with Carys

Numbers Refer to Sections.

Abbott, Mercy ... 63-C
Abbey, Elvina ... 170
Ackers, A. ... 254
Adams, Aaron ... 85
　David F. ... 188
　Eliashib ... 7-B
　Elijah ... 63-C
　Mary B. ... 305
Aikin, William ... 62
Alden, Daniel ... 37
　Ezra ... 32
　Hannah ... 46
　Hannah ... 77
　Hannah C. ... 153
　Samuel ... 112
　Susanna 32
　Miss or Mrs. ... 71
Aldrich, Mr. ... 291
Alger, Betsey Ann ... 303
　Fanny ... 175
Allan, Anna E. ... 276
Allen, Abigail ... 2
　Alvah ... 135
　Benjamin ... 14
　Elizabeth M. ... 218
　George M. ... 210
　H. W. ... 60-A
　Joseph ... 71-C
　Lois ... 247
　Margaret ... 2
　Maria L. ... 201
　Sally Ann ... 63-C
　Samuel ... 7-A
　Sarah ... 5
　Simeon ... 32
　Susanna B. ... 17

Alverson, Cynthia ... 177
　Sarah ... 168
Ambrose, Daniel E. ...60-A
Anabel, Edwin E. ... 202
　Mr. ... 97
Aplin, James ... 26
Arkam, Katy ... 63-D
Arnold, Damaris ... 8
　Ella ... 60-A
　Fidelia ... 182
　Joseph ... 62
Atwood, Jemima ... 70
　William ... 103
Austin, Emons S. ... 218
　Fannie ... 294
　Phebe ... 141-A
Axtell, Martha E. ... 162
　Matilda ... 162
Ayres, Eliza ... 176
　Lucy H. ... 146
　Samuel ... 25

Babbitt, Eunice H. ... 163
William S. 115
Bacon, Harriet Ella ... 298
Bagley, Mary Kendrick ... 206-A
Bailey, Alexander D. ... 238
　Ella ... 220
　William H. ... 235
Baird, Maetha ... 75
Baker, Andrew ... 88
　Elizabeth A. ... 33
　Hiram ... 33
　John ... 22
　Walter ... 49
Baldwin, Louisa M. ... 222
Ball, Maria D. ... 197
Ballard, Roxana ... 94-A
Banks, Eunice ... 142-A
Barker, Catherine ... 114
Barker, John M. ... 166
　Mary Elizabeth ... 279

Barkley, Marian B. ... 288-A
Barnard, Mary ... 104
Barnes, James ... 172
　Sarah O. ... 277
Barney, Nathan ... 63-A
Barnum, Zacheus ... 85-A
Barrell, James B. ... 128
　Joseph ... 97-A
　William ... 15
Barrett, Alpheus ... 79-A
　B. P. ... 183
Barron, Alfred ... 129
Barry, Lewis ... 122
Bartlett, Delia ... 257
Barton, Anne ... 60-A
　Harriet ... 195
　Simon ... 60-A
Bateman, Emma V. ... 249
Bates, Rachel ... 19
Baxter, Daniel ... 38
Bass, George ... 185
　Susan ... 307
　Susanna ... 31
Bassett, Susan ... 115
Beach, James B. ... 228
Beals, L. A. ... 37
　Jonathan ... 74
Beamer, Alfred ... 139
Bearse, Mary B. ... 300
Beecher, Jane Bernice ... 215
　Lucia A. ... 174
Benham, Esther J. ... 288
Bennett, A. B. ... 93
　James S. ... 205
　Polly ... 118-A
　Mrs. Rosanna C. ... 63-B
Benson, B. Callia ... 281-A
Bentley, Mary ... 62
Bibbins, Benjamin ... 55
Bigelow, Abigail ... 12
　Rachel ... 12

Sally ... 28-A
Bilinski, Alex Adolph ... 60-A
Billings, Adaline E. ... 155
Billins, Ethan ... 82
Bingham, Gideon. 9
Bishop, Hannah. 298
Bitely, Jacob ... 53-A
Blagbrough, Elizabeth ... 266
Blake, Grenfell ... 126-A
    Harrison ... 130
    Silas, Dr. ... 67
    Silas, Dr. ... 128-A
    William L. ... 131
Blaney, Arthur ... 279
Blossom, Waldo A. ... 128
Boardman, Sarah E. ... 170
Bockover, Mary ... 282
Boenebright, Priscilla ... 176
Bolster, Mrs. (General) ... 124
Bonner, Charles R. ... 125
    Isaac .125
Bools, W. S. ... 57
Booth, Levi. ... 127
Bosley, Mr. ... 78
Boston, Caroline ... 155
Bouton, Hattie L. ... 206-B
    Mrs. Sarah W. ... 206-B
Bowen, Capt. Isaac ... 133
Bowers, John ... 60-A
Bowman, Ellen ... 79-A
Boyden, Benj. F. ... 157
Boyer, David ... 79-A
Boyle, James ... 135
Brackett, Mary Elizabeth ... 210
Bradbury, Wiley ... 33

Bradford, Mrs. Anna S. ... 91
    Ellen M. ... 128
    Sallie ... 246
    W. B., Dr. ... 66
Bradford, Miss. ... 253
    William ... 123
Brainerd, Daniel ... 53
Bradley, John H. ... 202-A
    Mr. ... 193
Braman, Mr. ... 264
Brett, Anne ... 28-A
    Cynthia ... 65
    Hannah ... 3
    Mehitabel ... 66
    Rufus ... 31
    Mrs. Sarah Alden ... 16
    Susan ... 130
    William ... 3-A
Bridgeman, Vienna ... 274
Brigham, Gideon ... 9
Briggs, D. ... 131
    Isaac B. ... 106
Bridgham, Nelson ... 151
Brillault, Armance ... 294
Brinkerhoff, Isabel ... 85-B
Brisbane, Margaret E. ... 87
Brokaw, Leah ... 94
Brooks, Dr. Jona W. ... 95
    Mr. ... 121
Bromley, Lucy Ann ... 211
Brown, Charles W. ... 197
    Cornelia E. ... 300
    George ... 207
    George E. ... 266
    Joel G. ... 166
    John ... 185
    Sarah ... 44
Brownell, R. ... 109
Bruce, Betsey ... 72

Brundadge, Harry A. ... 202-A
Bryant, E. C. ... 279-A
    Hiram, Capt. ... 126
Buck, Mr. ... 264
Bumphrey, Mr. ... 97
Burlingame, Adah ... 166
    Andrew ... 81
    Rhoda ... 166
Burlingham, Adaline ... 60-A
Burnett, Cornelia ... 234
    Emeline J. ... 169
Burnham, Lucy Jennie ... 308
Bump, Jonathan ... 83
    Mr. ... 70
Burpee, A. ... 109
Burr, Mary ... 17
Burrell, Mary ... 127
Burridge, William ... 60-A
Bush, Ebenezer ... 85-A
    Kate D. ... 300
    Mary E. ... 218
Bushnell, Abigail ... 20
    Mrs. Celia D. ... 89
    Tabitha ... 184
Butin, Joanna ... 132
Butler, Anne ... 268
    Rev. Ellery C. ... 28-A
Byron, Martha ... 39

Call, Levi E. ... 266
Canada, Mary ... 19
Canfield, Marcia ... 141-A
Cannon, Rev. Dr. ... 73
    Donald S. ... 210
Carew, Hannah ... 93
    Ruth ... 61
Carnahan, David ... 200
    Isaac B. ... 194
Carns, Elmira ... 63-B
Carson, Isabel ... 69
Carter, Arilla ... 79-A
    Augustus ... 243

Carver, Experience ... 18
Cary, Adelaide E. ... 252
   Charles ... 152
   Daniel ... 17
   Edith V. L. ... 167
   John ... 94-A
   Martha ... 33
   Mary E. ... 273
   Usual ... 33
Case, James.202-A
Chambers, Sarah ... 186
Chamberlain, Martha ... 259
Champlin, Delight. 62
Chapman, Margaret Ewing ... 235
   Mrs. Rebecca D. ... 116
Chase, Clarence O. ... 170
   Lydia ... 207
   P. B. ... 134
Cheesman, Anson ... 45
Chrisman, Priscilla ... 63-A
Church, Cordelia ... 187
   Hannah ... 27
Clapp, Samuel Worcester ... 149
   Sarah ... 127
Clark, Anne Allison ... 263
   Edith M. ... 316
   Gamaliel ... 11
   G. G. ... 173
   Lucy Ann ... 69-A
   Lydia ... 97
   Marne E. ... 291
   Harry B. ... 244
   Nellie G. ... 264
   Sophronia ... 97-A
   Theressa Gore...63-B
   Thomas Gore ... 63-B
   Wallace ... 246
Clark, Walter C. ... 114

   Miss ... 97-A
   Mr. ... 138
Clements, Sarah A. ... 218
Cleveland, Burdette ... 220
   Grace M. ... 316
   Walter G. ... 271
Coggshall, William S. ... 113
Colby, Laura M. ... 317
Cole, Miss or Mrs. ... 229
Colman, Abbie ... 63-B
   Isaac ... 139
   Lizzie ... 62-A
   Lottie ... 273
Collier, Nellie ... 141-A
Collins, Clara ... 300
   Robert M. ... 211
Coloph, Mr. ... 34
Colwell, Elma ... 167
Condit, Charles L. ... 210
Conklin, Hannah ... 53
Connett, J. ... 160
Converse, Nellie N. ... 287
Cook, Bertha ... 79-A
   Daniel ... 199
   Hannah ... 111
   Israel ... 62
   Maria ... 271
Cooke, Mary ... 40
Coolidge, Catherine ... 264
Cooley, Catherine ... 105-A
Cooper, Mrs. Augusta D. ... 281-A
   James ... 33
   Mr. ... 28-C
Cope, John ... 141
Copeland, James ... 149
Corbin, Charles Lyon ... 224
Cornell, Catherine ... 281-A

   Ruth ... 79-A
Cornwall, Elizabeth ... 106
Coswell, Erastus ... 63-D
Cox, Elias ... 112
Coy, Edward L. ... 105-A
Craig, Jesse ... 33
   N. S., Dr. ... 294
Cramer, Sarah R. ... 263
Crandall, Adaline E. ... 191
Crane, Edwin Francis ... 202-A
Crary, John ... 94-A
Crawford, Annie ... 79-A
   Frances Ives ... 238
   Sarah ... 195
Crosby, Benjamin ... 21
Cross, Sarah E. ... 296
Crossman, Joseph ... 16
   Mary ... 16
Crosswait, Mary ... 120
Crozier, Frank ... 266
Cruttenden, Mary G. ... 225
Cummings, Benjamin ... 28-A
   Mr. ... 72
Cunningham, Mrs. Elizabeth ... 86
Curtis, Helen L. ... 127
   Mary ... 37
   Roland Eliot ... 85-B
Daly, Lillian ... 279
Damon, Raymond ... 275
   Roxanna ... 152
Dancy, Lucius H. ... 177
Danforth, Phebe ... 28-A
Daniels, Clara J. ... 294
Darling, Helen ... 299
   S. R. ... 145
Dart, Susan ... 105
Davenport, Amy ... 215
   Lillian ... 279-A

Lydia D. ... 264
Davis, Claretta A. ... 285
   John ... 143
   Mary Iowa ... 235
   Mr. ... 123
Day, Ezra H., Rev. ... 79
   Mabel ... 288-A
   Sarah ... 160
   William ... 105-A
Dayton, Charles O. 141-A
Dean, Amanda M. ..202-A
   Agnes ... 63-C
   Elijah ... 20
De Forest, Helen E. ... 288-A
De Groff, Mary E. ... 223
Denison, Nathan ... 9
Dennett, Emily M. ... 205
Dent, Arthur ... 276-A
De Puy, Cora M. ... 62-A
Deulinger, Mary ... 79-A
Devine, Mrs. Almira E. J. ... 105
De Vol, Charles ... 218
   David ... 111
Dey, Lewis W. ... 115
Dickenson, Ansel ... 138
   Jean ... 62-A
Dickson, Hannah ... 63-D
   Sarah A. ... 216
Dilley, Lovina ... 63-D
Dillingham, Clarissa ... 219
Dills, William C. ... 119
Dinsmore, S. H., Dr. ... 100
Doan, Mr. ... 153
Dodder, Mary E. ... 63-B
Dodge, Althea M. ... 251
   Susan ... 101
Donahue, Rachel ... 197
Donaldson, Martha Jane ... 105-A
Doolittle, Calvin ... 83

Lucy ... 174
Dougherty, Miss ... 161
Doughty, Thomas J. ... 113
Douglass, David ... 182
Dowling, Henrietta J. ... 170
Downer, Jerusha ... 51
Downing, Ann ... 63-B
   Bateman ... 63-C
   Martin ... 63-B
Doyle, Mary E.310
Drake, Lydia. 79-A
   Mary ... 135
   Orilla S. ... 280
   Sarah ... 17
   Mr. ... 69
Dresser, Mr. ... 65
Drury, Anna ... 73
Duncan, Dr. Oscar M. ... 238
   Timothy M. ... 72
Dunham, Ebenezer ... 145
   Ezra ... 142-C
   Isaac ... 153-A
Dunlap, Ruth ... 114
Dunlop, Stewart ... 63-C
Dunn, Dr. Jennie D. ... 206-B
Dunton, George V. ... 142
Durant, Freelove ... 182
Durkee, Benjamin ... 97-A
Dyer, Dr. Edward C. ... 69-A
Eames, Caroline ... 214
Earnheart, Hannah ... 79-A
   Lydia ... 79-A
Eastman, Charles W. ... 266
Eastwood, Capitola ... 202-A
Eaton, John ... 68
   Louise ... 224

Ruby Ann ... 107
   Sophia ... 85-B
Eddy, Sarah ... 218
   Mr. ... 110
Edson, Mrs. Hannah ... 18
Edwards, M. F. ... 281
Ellery, William ... 28
Elliott, Dr. John ... 280
   Mrs. Louise M. 79-A
Ellis, Eleazer ... 125
   Mr. ... 148
Emerich, Nellie ... 141-A
Emerson, Elizabeth ... 62-A
   Ellen Maria ... 279-B
   Florence ... 251
Ensign, Julia A.283
Evans, Erma.300
   Eva ... 63-B
Farnham, Freeman C. ... 127
Farquhar, Frank C. ... 279
Fenton, Rebecca ... 96
Ferguson, Arvilla.174
   Elspeth Wilson ... 85-B
   J. B. ... 280
Ferry, Mary K. ... 238
Fields, Ann ... 169
   Harriet H. ... 182
   John ... 27
   Susanna ... 74
Finney, Jeremiah ... 27
Fish, Mary A. ... 60-A
Fisher, Arthur S. ... 313
Fitch, E. D. ... 182
   Mary L. ... 54
Flagg, Henrietta J. ... 170
Flagler, Sarah ... 114
   Tamar ... 113
Fletcher, Sally ... 58
Flint, Noadiah ... 81
Flood, Harriet N. ... 239
Fobes, Betty ... 41

Folsom, Harriet E. ... 206
Follett, Jesse ... 131
Fonda, Catherine J. ... 165
    Catherine J. ... 180
Foote, Frederick H. 224
    John. 48
Ford, Harriet G. 153
    John. 45
    Susanna . 83
Forsyth, Margaret. 276-A
Foster, Benjamin. 28-A
    Eliza W. ... 152
    George H. ... 275
    Henry L. ... 152
    John ... 48
    Sophronia M. ... 250
Fowler, Henry ... 111
    Mr. ... 60
Fozzard, Emaline ... 105
Franklin, Amos A. ... 93
Frazer, Mr. ... 82
French, Estes W. ... 126
Frobisher, Benjamin C. .. .153
    Mr. 76
Frome, John ... 23
Fuller, Elizabeth ... 173
    Freelove ... 171
    Luman ... 177
    Timothy ... 47
Fulton, Gertrude ... 63-C
Gaige, Adelia M. ... 213
    Isaac ... 108
Gaines, Dr. J. S. ... 254
Gale, Nelson B. ... 143
    Mr. ... 69
Gannett, Hannah ... 34
    Mehitabel ... 36
Gardner, Elizabeth. ... 143
    Mr. ... 99
Garland, Elizabeth ... 143
    Elvinia A. ... 170
Garman, L. M. ... 79-A

Garten, Mary E. ... 300
Gaser, Sybil ... 183
Gates, Celestine ... 272
Geaney, Nellie ... 141-A
Gee, Orson ... 101
Geer, Henry B. ... 205
    Josiah ... 51
Geer, Persis ... 306
Gerard, Isabella .228
Germand, Silas. 62
Getchell, Stephen J. 152
Gibbs, Jesse ... 117
Gibson, Jennie ... 300
Giffen, H. C. ... 101
Gifford, Ellen G. ... 235
Gilham, Elizabeth ... 149
Gill, Mr. ... 82
Gilman, Carrie ... 69-A
Gilson, Abel ... 28-A
Gladding, Jonathan ... 27
    Joseph ... 6
Gleason, Elizabeth ... 101
Goble, Sarah ... 280
Godfrey, Elizabeth ... 101
Gooding, Judith ... 28-A
Goff, Mr. ... 97-A
Gozley, Mary ... 33
Goodell, Mina L. ... 316
Goodrich, Cornelia ... 201
Gordon, Catherine G. ... 258
    Mary A. ... 260
Gore, George ... 63-A
Gorham. Alfred ... 143
    Benjamin ... 6
Gould, John ... 105-A
    Lydia ... 204
Grant, Deliverance ... 52
    Ephraim ... 48
Gray, Hannah A. ... 114
    Harriet J. ... 314
    Osee ... 79-A
    Phebe ... 79-A
    Rhoda ... 79-A

    Samuel ... 79-A
Graham, Evaline ... 301
    Mary ... 105-A
    Robert ... 170
Graves, Amasa ... 45
Green, Kezia ... 28-A
    Susanna M. ... 63-A
Greenfield, Nancy ... 141-A
Greenslit, Benjamin ... 51
Gridley, Celesta ... 221
Grubb, Martha ... 63-C
Griswold, Martha R. ... 297
Gunsey, Patty ... 43
Gurney, Augusta ... 149
    Betsey ... 144

Hackett, Charles S. ... 145
Hale, Lydia ... 72
Hall, Alice L. ... 220
    Lemuel ... 76
    Lois ... 280
Halsey, Lucinda ... 141
Hammond, Hannah ... 217
    Mrs. Rose ... 300
Handscom, Mary ... 151
Hanley, Matilda ... 147
Hanna, William ... 110
Harden, Mr. ... 53
Hardin, Mary ... 38
Harding, Judson ... 28-A
    Mary I. ... 28-A
Harkness, Isabelle D. ... 300
Harlow, Flora E. ... 142-A
Harman, W. B. ... 239
Harned, Phebe ... 63-B
Harper, William H. ... 79-A
Harrington, Frances J. ... 152
Harris, Abi ... 69-A
    John Franklin ... 288-A

Mary ... 98
Maud ... 298
Rufus ... 167
Mr. ... 64
Hart, James M. ... 235
    Virginia D. ... 225
Hascall, Catherine ... 133
Haskell, Chas. S. ... 145
    Eliza ... 133
    H. ... 253
    Rev. Wm. H. ... 142-A
    William ... 148
Haskins, Mary ... 197
    Walden L. ... 220
Hasse, William ... 300
Hastough, Laura ... 79-A
Hathaway, Thankful ... 161
Hathorn, Gilbert ... 195
Haven, Annie A. ... 304
Hayes, Prof. B. F. ... 126
Hayward, Benjamin ... 16
    Harriet 68
    Maj. Nathan ... 142-D
Hazard, Rufus ... 111
Heaton, Asa ... 281
Hebard, Abigail ... 22
    Mary ... 23
Heck, Emma ... 315
Hedley, Mr. ... 38
Hemmanway, Hiram ... 85
Hendee, Hannah ... 21
Henderson, John M. ... 199
Henghlen, Frank H. ... 114
Henry, Alex C. ... 197
    Betsey ... 149
Heywood, William T. ... 218
Hibb, William ... 104
Hibbard, Charles ... 81
Hickox, Damaris ... 85

Hicks, Mr. ... 61
Hildreth, Susanna F. ... 242
Hill, Anna ... 134
    Joseph ... 218
    Martha W. ... 286
Hills, Sarah ... 302
Hinshaw, Jesse ... 281
Hodges, Nellie ... 28-A
Hoffman, Mrs. Ardele K. ... 225
    Nicholas W. ... 263
Holcomb, Harvey ... 63-C
Holmes, Andrew ... 111
Holman, Jane ... 68
    Mary ... 30
Homan, Thomas ... 40
Hooper, Lois ... 42
    William ... 18
Hoover, Daniel L. ... 33
Hopkins, Fanny ... 222
Hopper, Mr. ... 195
Horton, Alonzo ... 200
    Daniel ... 107
Horrs, Samuel ... 72
Hotchkiss, Harris ... 97-A
Hovey, Sarah B. ... 163
Howard, Apollos ... 66
    Bela ... 35
    Bethia ... 153
    Daniel S. ... 272-B
    Darius ... 75
    Ephraim ... 77
    H. H. ... 142-B
    Dr. J. ... 138
    Howard, Martha ... 142-B
    Mary ... 35
    Phebe ... 188
    Roana ... 142-A
    Solomon ... 52
Howes, Rev. J. T. ... 128
Howland, Samuel ... 2
    Tabitha ... 12

Mr. 6
Hoyez, Kate ... 63-C
Hoyt, Francis S. ... 210
Hubbard, Ellen R. ... 101
Huber, Charles B. ... 201
Huddleson, Robert ... 281
Hufstader, Rufus ... 115
Hulbert, Lillian W. ... 145
Hull, John ... 8
    Laura M. ... 291
Humes, Mr. ... 60-A
Humphries, W. S. ... 152
Hurd, Benjamin ... 12
    Jacob ... 12
    Rachel ... 12
    Reuben ... 12
    Sophia ... 102
Hurlbert, Mary ... 118
Hurlbut, Martha ... 90
    Mary ... 56
    William H. ... 115
    William T. ... 115
Husted, Andrew ... 63-C
Huston, J. P. ... 149
Hutchins, Mrs. Clara P. ... 270
    Zeruah ... 61
Hyde, Emily ... 208
    Miss ... 106

Ingalls, Matilda A. ... 249

Jackson, Keziah ... 111
Jaquis, Mr. ... 79-A
Jarvis, Sarah M. ... 224
    Mr. ... 63-A
Jencks, Perry J. ... 85
Jenkins, Gertrude ... 269
Jenney, Lucretia P. ... 236
Jennings, Hannah ... 23
    Phebe ... 161
    William N. ... 33
Jerard, Rhoda ... 119
Jessup, Eliza ... 194
Johnson, Hamilton ... 177

Josiah ... 32
S. O. ... 143
W. ... 53
Mr. ... 148
Jones, Benjamin P. ... 108
Charles L. ... 85-B
Emily T. ... 131
J. H. ... 63-C
Joanna ... 127
Mr. ... 175
Jordan, Mr. ... 160
Joy, Clara. ... 235
Judd, Mr. ... 108

Kane, Ella ... 300
Keith, Arza B. ... 279-A
Asa ... 32
Benjamin ... 71-A
Henry K. ... 272-C
Nabby ... 68
Simeon ... 35
Solomon ... 42
Susanna ... 18
Zenas ... 68
Ziba... 75
Kellogg, Bertha ... 300
Kennard, Miss or Mrs. ... 226
Kendrick, Charles D. ... 85-B
Kenea, Emile Barton ... 85-B
Kenelly, Thomas ... 195
Kent, E. ... 143
Susanna ... 11
Keyes, Mehitabel ... 100
William H. ... 260
Kidder, Ephraim ... 2
Kimball, Rosetta ... 128
Kimberly, W. ... 48
King, Abigail ... 67
Julia ... 161
Kingsbury, Walter L. ... 28-A
Kingsley, Abigail ... 91

Jonathan ... 50
Kinsley, R. ... 68
Kirby, Charlotte ... 79-A
David ... 79-A
Kirk, Rachel ... 137
Kitchener, Mary ... 33
Kline, George R. ... 195
Knapp, Harriet ... 95
Knight, Anna E. ... 300
Knox, Julius ... 60-A
Komorinsky, Phebe E. ... 312
Konkle, Comstock ... 202-A
Krater, Nellie ... 300

Lackey, A. Goodloe ... 149
Laguin, F. ... 192
Laird, Mr. ... 63-A
Lalor, Margaret ... 85-B
Lamb, Laura ... 142
Jasper ... 79-A
Lamson, Morgan ... 129
Landing, Sira ... 63-C
Lane, Miss ... 124
Langdon, Betty ... 112
Lanning, Catherine ... 142-A
Larabee, Hannah ... 101
Latham, B. F. ... 222
Lathrop, Oliver ... 99
Lear, Lucy C. ... 309
Leaser, Christian ... 118-A
Leet, Luthera M. ... 69-A
Leonard, Abigail ... 60-A
Seth ... 142-B
William W ... 84
Leveck, Edward D. ... 166
Lewis, Eliza S. ... 261
Mary M. ... 300
Liddle, George ... 60-A
Lillie, Lucinda ... 185

Littlefair, Elizabeth A. ... 114
Littlefield, James ... 153B
Livsey, Sarah ... 170
Locke, Mary ... 26
Lockwood, James H. ... 129
Mr. ... 95
Logan, Elizabeth ... 222
Loomis, Mr. ... 97
Loop, Mary ... 63-B
Lord, Capt. Elias ... 90
Loring, John ... 94
Love, Hannah M. ... 202-A
Julia ... 181
Loveland, Miss ... 63-B
Lovell, Catherine ... 28-A
Lovell, Lydia Daniels ... 28-A
Lowe, Sarah ... 170
Loveridge, Amasa ... 99-A
Lucas, Joseph ... 3
Ludlow, Dr. Wm. B. ... 199
Lyon, Joanna ... 79
Lewis ... 161
Stephen ... 163
Lyons, Joseph ... 25-A

Macan, Malvina ... 199
Mack, Phebe ... 45
Maclaren, Miriam ... 62-A
Macy, D. ... 281
Madison, Melissa ... 93
Magdeburg, Caroline ... 85-B
Magee, Mary M. ... 201
Mann, Edward W. ... 28-A
Jane ... 63
Manning, Irena ... 89
Marble, Ebenezer ... 62-A
March, Jane ... 106
Marcy, Dorcas ... 47
Mark, Lilia B. ... 215
Marks, Lucy Ann ... 120
Miss ... 60-A

Marmaduke, Lalla ... 149
Marsh, Sarah ... 79-A
Martin, George ... 271
   John ... 63-B
   John ... 127
   Lorenzo ... 202-A
Mason, William N. ... 191
Mathers, Cordelia ... 252
Matthews, Albert ... 161
   Mary ... 218
Mattison, Margaret ... 94
Maxam, Britania ... 266
   Harriet M. ... 266
   Salome ... 142
Mayo, Hannah ... 103
McBenjamin, William ... 195
McCarty, Margaret ... 94
McCauley, Mr. ... 69
McCuan, Mary. ...118-A
McDonald, Margaret ... 170
McGinnis, James ... 94
McKenzie, Charlotte ... 140
McMullin, Francis ... 276
McNabb, Isabella ... 300
McRea, Elizabeth ... 174
Mead, Rhuca ... 309
Meeks, Lorenzo D. ... 280
Meekins, Thomas ... 45
Mendenhall, Elizabeth ... 119
Mengel, Arthur ... 60-A
Mensch, Peter ... 63-C
Mercer, Lydia ... 79-A
Merchant, D. P. ... 69
Merriam, Cynthia ... 186
   Isaac ... 186
   Mr. ... 60
   Mr. ... 137
Merrill, Charles A. ... 270
   John Cushing...142-A

Merithew, Joseph ... 105-A
Merritt, Cynthia ... 218
   James C. ... 79-A
   Rachel ... 79-A
Messimore, Cynthia ... 79-A
Metcalf, Julia ... 85-B
Midberry, Harriet E. ... 295
Miller, Maria P. ... 255
   Maj. Silas ... 79
Miner, B. A. ... 57
Mitchell, Anna ... 118
   Hon. Nathan ... 18
Monks, Richard A. ... 279
Moore, James ... 79-A
   Joseph A. ... 169
Morgan, Laura ... 63-B
   Tracy R. ... 114
Morris, Susan ... 135
Morrow, F. W. ... 162
Morse, Hazen ... 76
   Miriam ... 239
   Nelson ... 189
   Parker ... 91
   Thomas ... 91
Morton, Nathan ... 41
Mott, Amanda ... 218
   William ... 82
Moulton, Hannah ... 147
   James, Jr. ... 23
   Molly ... 72
Mowry; H. ... 184
   Samuel ... 107
Muckle, John ... 33
Mullinger, John ... 119
Munro, William ... 27
Murdock, George E. ... 169
Musdirk, Sarah ... 211
Myers, Nancy ... 256

Nash, Malcom ... 115

Neffelen, Herman P. ... 156
Nelson, H. C. ... 300
Newell, Oliver ... 57
   Sarah Maria ... 225 ..186
Newhall, Miss or Mrs. ... 122
   Mr. ... 65
Newman, Miss ... 233
Newton, James M. ... 202
Noble, Mr. ... 145 .. 105-A
Nichols, Bessie ... 63-C
   Earl William ... 266
   Polly ... 195
   Mr. ... 25
Nickerson, E. Belle ... 291
Norcross, Rev. S. G. ... 130
Northrup, Phebe ... 263
Noxon, Melissa ... 220
Noyes, Lucia P. ... 101

Oakes, Rev. Isaac ... 73
   Mr. ... 36
Ohara, Lucy Ellen ... 315
Olney, Amasa ... 81
Orcutt, Jonathan ... 17
Osborn, Julia ... 292
Osborne, F. E. ... 173
Osgood, Rowena ... 192
Osterhout, Peter ... 116
Ovens, Mary D. ... 280

Packard, Edward S. ... 149
   Elbridge H. ... 157-A
   Huldah ... 71
   Sallie ... 121
Page, Isaac ... 106
Palmer, Lucy ... 53-A
   Ruth ... 317
   Seth ... 7
   Walter L. ... 28-A
   Mr. ... 299

Palmeter, Waity W. ... 275
Parish, Asa ... 51
Parish, Eunice ... 92
   Matilda ... 99
Parker, Annie L. ... 281-A
   Caroline ... 278
   Elizabeth ... 12
   Harriet ... 146
Parkhurst, Mary ... 28-A
Pass, Hannah N. ... 176
Patchin, Talcot ... 83
Pate, Harriet Elizabeth ... 314
Patterson, Sally Ann ... 63-C
Pearce, Anna ... 28
   Col. William ... 19-A
Peck, Morgan H. ... 202
   Mrs. Sarah E. ... 198
Penn, Clara E. ... 254
Pennywit, Huldah ... 79-A
Perine, Amanda ... 162
Perkins, Abigail ... 75
   Daniel ... 166
   Deborah ... 50
   Luke ... 272-A
   Ruby ... 76
   William ... 41
Perry, Clara L. ... 279-A
   Ebenezer ... 69-A
Petersen, Nellie M. ... 300
Phelps, Catherine ... 158
Phillips, Lydia ... 36
   Sallie ... 126
   Silena ... 131
Pickett, Anna ... 63-B
Pitman, Maria Augusta ... 313
Platt, D. H. ... 113
   Miriam ... 238
Plummer, Phebe S. ... 251
Pococke, Bridget ... 10
Poestley, Jessie ... 128

Pollard, Stephen ... 129-A.
Poole, Mary ... 13
Potter, Florence E. ... 246
Powell, Mary Ann ... 79-A
Pratt, Rev. Frank W. ... 28-A
   Mr. ... 120
Prescott, George W. ... 172
Preston, Adele R. ... 202-A
Price, Dorcas ... 254
Priest, Mrs. Marian White ... 156
Prouty, E. ... 70
Purdy, James ... 63-B
   John B. R. ... 313
Purvis, Cordelia ... 262

Rail, George S. ... 199
Ransom, Harriet W. ... 141-A
Raymond, Charles Monson ... 142-A
Reach, Amelia ... 141-A
Reed, Lucretia ... 128
   Dr. N. ... 134
Reid, A. W. ... 280
Reynolds, Calvin I. ... 115
   Ruth ... 12
Rhoades, Mr. ... 69
Rhodes, Elizabeth ... 190
Rice, Laura ... 179
   Susanna ... 173
   Mr. ... 60-A
Richardson, Emons ... 103
   Mrs. Jane ... 199
   Rev. J. P. ... 67
   Nancy ... 172
Riches, John ... 140
Riggs, Elizabeth ... 38
Ripley, David ... 9
   Jeremiah ... 9
Roast, Elizabeth ... 79-A
Robinson, Lucy ... 125

   Sophia ... 245
Roby, Henry ... 127
Rock, Nancy ... 281
Rodman, Peniah ... 117
Roe, Mr. ... 290
Rodgers, George E. ... 288-A
   Jane ... 40
   Jane S. ... 135
   Walter S. ... 238
Rook, Rev. Peter R. ... 117
Roogey, Caroline ... 202-A
Root, Mrs. Tabitha ... 47
   William ... 145
Roripaugh, Stephen ... 193
Ross, Florence ... 85-B
Rost, Elizabeth ... 79-A
Roundy, Anna ... 58
Rowe, Harriet ... 284
   Martha ... 174
Rudd, Mrs. Mercy ... 7
   Rebecca ... 49
Rude, Mary ... 60-A
Rumsey, Mr. ... 181
Russell, Jane ... 60-A
   William ... 99
Rutty, Mr. ... 28-C

Sabin, Jerusha ... 59
   Dr. Silas A. ... 69-A
Sadler, Francis ... 94-A
Safford, Reuben ... 182
Salmon, Carrie H. ... 263
Sampson, Ellen A. ... 127
   Thomas R. ... 127
Sanders, John A. ... 225
Sanborn, Sherburn ... 85-B
Sanford, Anna ... 85-B
   James S. ... 145
Sargent, Nicholas E. ... 59
   Sarah ... 59
Savage, Anna ... 186
Sawyer. Caroline ... 209

Huldah ... 128
Saxton. Samuel ... 25
Sayre, Edward D. ... 201
Scales, E. S. ... 218
Schenck, A. V. C. ... 144
Schneider, Bertha ... 225
Schaffer, Andrew ... 60-A
   Elizabeth ... 60-A
Scott, Hattie C. ... 256
   Letitia ... 116
   Mr. ... 82
Scovel, Silsby ... 218
Searle, Miss or Mrs. ... 63-B
Seavey, Sarah E. ... 205
Server, Emma ... 207
Sewell, Charles A. M. ... 127
Shafer, Harriet ... 63-C
Shattuck, Herbert C. ... 313
Shaw, Comfort ... 28-C
   Hannah A. ... 114
   Rev. John ... 74
   Mary ... 4
   Sarah ... 15
Shelly, Sally ... 79-A
Shepard, Cyrus L. ... 105
Sherman, Maria ... 111
Sherwood, Ellen C. ... 254
   Frank J. ... 101
Sherwood, Nora ... 62-A
Shippee, Diana ... 265
   Dordona ... 265
   Fanny Jane ... 267
Sholtz, Herman F. ... 220
Short, Mary ... 28-A
Showerman, Ella ... 300
Shumway, Emily ... 290
Sibley, Solomon ... 143
Silvester, Zechariah ... 31
Simmons, Lora G. ... 238
   Mr. ... 26

Simons, Crissie ... 63-C
Simpson, Lavina ... 150
Singer, Tessie E. B. ... 142-A
Skiff, Dea. Nathaniel ... 7
   Zervia ... 88
Skillman, Mr. ...159
Skinner, Jane A. ... 174
   Sarah M. ... 291
   Mr. ... 97
Sliker, John ... 63-C
Slocum, Frances ... 116
Southard, Lucinda... 97-A
Southwick, Thomas ... 111
Smiley, Tane ... 63-A
   Letitia ... 63-A
Smith, Ada ... 119
   Andrew C. ... 118-A
   Anson ... 112
   Austin S. ... 176
   Daniel ... 6
   Dolly ... 128
   D. G. ... 161
   Eleanor ... 200
   Elizabeth ... 81
   Emily ... 187
   John ... 62
   Jonah ... 24
   Mary ... 118-A
   Miss ... 130
   Miss or Mrs. ... 34
Snell, Martha ... 218
   Vesta ... 149
   William ... 39
Snook, Margaret A. ... 139
Snow, Capt. James ... 90
   Zilpha ... 109
Southard, Lucinda ...97-A
Southwick, Sarah ... 63-C
   Thomas ... 111
Spencer, Dora ... 248
   Mary ... 128

Spifield, Dr. James W. ... 168
Spooner, Abiah ... 145
Sprause, Elizabeth ... 281
Sprong, Mr. ... 94
Sprague, Samuel ... 151
Squires, Betsey ... 97-A
Standish, Myles ... 7-B
Stanton, Esther ... 60
Staples, Clara ... 291
   Lois ... 123
Stark, James ... 19-A
   William ... 28-C
   Mr. ... 50
Stearnes, Calvin ... 117
   J. P. ... 121
Stedman, Arthur W. ... 279
Stein, Henry ... 118-A
Stevens, George R. ... 172
   Mr. ... 142-B
Stevenson, Thomas ... 119
Stever, Margaret E. ... 197
Stewart, Hattie ... 275
Stillwell, Lida S. ... 201
Stockbridge, Maria ... 142-A
   Rhoda G. ... 129
Stockton, Martha Burr ... 281-A
Stone, Henry A. ... 85-B
   Mae Alice ... 85-B
   Simeon E. ... 28-A
   Mr. ... 69-A
Storm, Alexander ... 300
Storer, Mr. ... 92
Storrs, Zervia ... 55
Stratton, Benjamin ... 281
Streeter, Nathaniel ... 83
   Sophia ... 178
Strong, Mrs. Caroline...12
   John ... 53

Stuart, Charles Walter ... 156
Sturdevant, Charity ... 29
Sturgis, Eben H. ... 142-A
Sumner, Capt. Roger ... 66
Surber, Anna ... 79-A
Sutherland, Thomas H. ... 60-A
Swaim, Bronson ... 280
Sweet, Francis C. ... 102
    Rufus ... 62
    Ruth ... 111
Sweeting, Experience ... 17
Swift, Alexander ... 194
Sycks, J. H. ... 79-A
Sylvester, Mary ... 118

Talbot, Sarah ... 150
    Zipporah ... 7-A
Taplin, Annie ... 25-A
Taugher, Ella K. ... 319
Taylor, Mary B. ... 215
Thankful ... 26
Teague, Daniel ... 123
Teal, Louise S. ... 114
Terrill, Elsie ... 94
Thayer, Deborah ... 154
    Hannah ... 32
    Helen ... 293
Thomas, Mr. ... 36
Thompson, Allen ... 254
    Emma L. ... 279-A
    George W. ... 129
    Judge ... 33
    Leonard ... 81
    Lydia ... 64
    Phebe ... 138
    Rachel ... 82
Throop, Daniel ... 11
Throope, Lydia ... 9
Thurbur, Thomas J. ... 166
Thurston, Daniel ... 4
    David C. ... 146

    Hannah ... 22
Tillbury, Henry ... 63-A
Titus, James ... 72
    William ... 83
Tobey, Carrie E. ... 170
Tolman, Cynthia ... 65
Toole, Benjamin ... 281-A
Torrey, Erastus ... 85
    Mary Dodge ... 157
Tracy, Caroline ... 189
Trask, Lydia ... 109
Trimback, Adolph G. ... 127
Tripp, Eunice ... 202
    Mary Frances ... 266
Troland, Archibald ... 299
Trumbull, Sarah ... 48
Tucker, Eliza ... 237
Turner, Anna ... 241
    Margaret J. ... 135

Van Benschoten, Emma ... 202-A
Vanderbin, Henry ... 26
Vandermark, Katherine ... 63-A
    Miss or Mrs. ... 227
Van Valkenburg, Mr. ... 190
Van Vleck, Frederick H. ... 210
Van Slyck, Harriet M. ... 85-B
Vaughn, Tillinghast ... 85
Verplanck, John D. ... 86
Vigor, Dr. Henry ... 163

Wade, Ellen ... 174
    N. ... 38
Wait, Joel ... 45
    Mr. ... 25
Waldo, Hannah ... 14
Wales, Hannah ... 77
    Jerusha ... 24

Walker, Maj. Merriwether L. ... 317
    William ... 81
    Miss ... 240
Wallace, Robert ... 185
Walter, Annie ... 177
Walters, Sarah ... 191
    T. ... 192
Wanton, Elizabeth ... 28
Ward, Betsey P. ... 146
    Lizzie ... 79-A
    Miss or Mrs. ... 212
Wardwell, Mr. ... 6
Ware, Daniel ... 28-A
    William ... 28-A
    Mr. ... 99
Warner, Cynthia ... 202-A
Warren, Charles McLean ... 279-A
    John Q. ... 142-A
    Lillian M. ... 167
Washburn, Isaac ... 42
    Mrs. Mary ... 41
Waters, Darius ... 63-C
Waterhouse, Miss ... 240
Waterman, Temperance ... 243
Watson, Cora E. ... 177
Watson, James ... 68
    Olive ... 264
    Mr. ... 264
Wattles, Mary M. ... 276-A
Weatherhead, Ida ... 215
Webb, Eunice ... 25
Webber, Mary ... 21
Weed, Frederick D. ... 114
Weeks, Huldah ... 63-D
Weinburg, W. ... 60-A
Welch, Reuben ... 24
    Samuel ... 99
Wellman, Hannah B. ... 101
    Dr. John D. ... 59

Wendell. Herman ... 116
Weston, James ... 97-A
   Thomas ... 52
Wharren, John ... 63-C
Wheeler, Anson ... 57
   John ... 57
   Thomas ... 143
White, Charles M. ... 300
   Lizzie J. ... 264
   Mrs. Harriet B. ... 28-A
   Mary E. ... 205
Whiteside, Jennie D. ... 167
Whitesill, J. M. ... 281
Whitman, Frank ... 241
   John ... 4
   Nicholas ... 3
   Thomas Scott ... 126
Whitney, Charles B. ... 28-A
   Patty ... 108
Whittaker, Susanna ... 251
Whittington, Eliza ... 297
Wiggins, Benjamin F. ... 118

Wigton, Mr. ... 230
Wilbour, Mr. ... 19
Wild, Richard ... 71-B
Willard, Julia ... 156
Withers, Marcellus ... 119
Wilkinson, George ... 113
   Rev. George ... 85
Willey, Lavina ... 25
   Nathan ... 25
Williams, E. ... 48
   H. W. ... 138
   Louis ... 63-B
   Moses ... 63-B
Williams, Mr. ... 267
Williamson, Andrew ... 63-C
   Jane ... 119
Willoughby, William F. ... 188
Wills, Eliza ... 140
Wilson, Frances T. ... 270
Winship, Mr. ... 57
Wiswell, J. A. ... 193
Withers, Marcellus ... 119
Wolford, Amelia ... 207
Wood, Bertha ... 57

   Clement ... 38
   Holden M. ... 145
Woods, William S. ... 149
Woodruff, Eunice ... 33
   Leah ... 194
Woodworth, Henrietta P. ... 299
Woodworth, Rachel ... 299
Worden, Mr. ... 28-C
Worthing, Jacob. ... 63-D
Wright, James ... 29
   Joshua ... 9
   Rev. William ... 182
   Mr. ... 82
Wustenfeldt, Susie L. ... 85-B
Wyart, Sarah ... 172
Wyman, Mr. ... 134

York, C. ... 182
Young, Henry ... 166
   Sarah B. ... 254

Zearing, D. S. ... 185
Zeigler, Susan ... 118-A

Section 1

John Cary was born near Bristol, Somersetshire, England, about 1610; came to America about 1634, joined the Plymouth Colony, and made his home at Duxbury, where he had a farm. In 1644 he m. Elizabeth, dau. of Francis and Elizabeth Godfrey (who was a carpenter and bridge builder, and in August, 1643, we find his name on the muster roll of the Duxbury Company commanded by Capt. Myles Standish; he removed to Bridgewater where he d. in 1669; it is thought that the name Godfrey comes from the Duke of Bouillon, the Crusader).

Concerning John Cary, Moses Cary has this: "Mr. Cary was one of the Proprietors (of Bridgewater), and one of the first settlers, and was very useful among them. The town was incorporated in 1656. Mr. Cary was the first Town Clerk and continued in that office a great number of years. At first they settled near together and around where the Town House now stands in West Bridgewater. Mr. Cary's lot was about a ¼ of a mile east of the Town House and on the farm where Dr. Reed lived; and there he spent the remainder of his days, and brought up a great family of children. He had six sons and six daughters. They all lived to grow up and have families, and all took to good courses so that it was the saying of some "that there were 12 of 'em and never a Judas among them.'"

Judge Mitchell, in his description of Bridgewater, speaking of the first settlers, says: "Mr. Cary was among the most respectable of them, and his family one of the most influential in the town."

His wife d. in 1680, and he d. in 1681.

Children:
I. John, b. Duxbury, Nov. 4, 1645. Sec. 2.
II. Francis, b. Duxbury, Jan. 19, 1647-8. Sec. 3.
III. Elizabeth, b. Duxbury, Dec. 20, 1649. Sec. 3-A.
IV. James, b. Braintree, Mar. 28, 1652. Sec. 4.
V. Mary, b. Duxbury New Plantation, July 8, 1654.
VI. Jonathan, b. Bridgewater, Sept. 24, 1656. Sec. 5.
VII. David, b. Bridgewater, Jan. 27, 1658-9. Sec. 6.
VIII. Hannah, b. Bridgewater, April 30, 1661.
IX. Joseph, b. Bridgewater, April 18, 1663. Sec. 7.
X. Rebecca, b. Bridgewater, Mar. 30, 1665. Sec. 7-A.
XI. Sarah, b. Bridgewater, Aug. 2, 1667.
XII. Mehitabel, b. Bridgewater, Dec. 24, 1670. Sec. 7-B.

Note.—Attention is called to the three daughters of John Cary, viz., Mary, Hannah, and Sarah, of whom only the date of birth is given. Moses Cary in his manuscript wrote: "The daughters of John Cary: One married a Howard; one, Dea. William Brett; one, Samuel Allen; one, a Thurston; and two of them Standishes."

Section 2

John Cary, son of John, Sec. 1, b. Duxbury, Nov. 4, 1645; m Abigail, dau. of Samuel Allen and his second wife, Margaret (French) (Lamb), at Bridgewater, Dec. 7, 1670. In 1680 he removed to Bristol, where he resided till his death in 1721. The deed to his land in Bristol was granted Sept. 14, 1680, and confirmed by the General Court, Sept. 29, 1680. The first meeting of the people and the naming of the town was Sept. 1, 1681, and John Cary and his brother David were present. He became a prominent man in the town, and was elected a Deacon of the church at its organization, and held the office till his death. He was one of the first "raters" of the town, and appointed Nov. 10, 1681; in 1693 was recording officer of the County, and Clerk of the peace; in 1694 was Representative to the General Court. His wife was also of good family; her father, Samuel Allen, came from Bridgewater, Eng., to Braintree in 1630; in 1635 he took the oath of allegiance, and was Town Clerk, Selectman, Surveyor of highways, Constable, and served as Deputy three times. He and his son Samuel, who settled in Bridgewater in 1660, both fought in King Philip's War. For eight generations this family has been identified with the best political and religious life of New England.

He d. July 14, 1721, his estate amounting to 700 pounds; the will of his wife was recorded in 1729.

Children:

I. John, b. Bridgewater, Nov. 6, 1671, d. in infancy.

II. Seth, b. Bridgewater, Jan. 28, 1672-3.

III. John, b. Bridgewater, Dec. 9, 1674. Sec. 8.

IV. Nathaniel, b. Bridgewater, Nov. 24, 1676; d. without issue, Dec. 11, 1739.

V. Eleazer, b. Bridgewater, Sept. 27, 1678. Sec. 9.

VI. James, b. Bridgewater, June 10, 1680. Sec. 10.

VII. Benjamin, b. Bristol, Aug. 29, 1681. Sec. 11.

VIII. Elizabeth, b. May 23, 1683; m. Ephraim Kidder.

IX. Abigail, b. Aug. 31, 1684; m. Samuel Howland, May 6, 1708, and had ten children, and the posterity is very numerous and widely scattered; Capt. William Pearse, who d. at Bristol in Feb. 1867, at the age of 95, was a grandson of Abigail.

X. Josiah, b. May 6, 1686. Sec. 12.

XI. Timothy, b. Feb. 15, 1687-8.

Section 3

Francis Cary, son of John, Sec. 1, b. Duxbury, Jan. 19, 1647-8; m. Hannah, dau. of William Brett, an original Proprietor and prominent citizen, in 1676; lived in Bridgewater, where he d. in 1718.

Children:

I. Samuel, b. 1677. Sec. 13.

II. Ephraim, b. 1679. Sec. 14.

III. Mary, b. 1681; m. Nicholas Whitman, 1715, and had 1. Eleazer, b. 1716; removed to Abington, Mass., and d. at 90 years of age.

2. Benjamin, b. 1719.

She d. 1719. Judge Whitman, an eminent lawyer and jurist of Cincinnati, O., is of this family.

IV. Lydia, b. 1683. Sec. 14-A.

V. Mehitabel, b. 1685; m. Joseph Lucas; no issue.

Section 3-A

Elizabeth Cary, dau. of John, Sec. 1, b. Duxbury, Dec. 20, 1649; m. William Brett, and had one child, Bethia, who m. Thomas Heywood, East Bridgewater, in 1706.

Section 4

James Cary, son of John, Sec. 1, b. Braintree, Mar. 28, 1652; m. Mary Shaw, of Weymouth, Jan. 4, 1681; settled in Bristol, where he d. 1706; his wife d. 1736.

Children:

I. Mercy, b. 1686; m. Daniel Thurston, 1713.

II. Mary, b. 1689.

III. James, b. 1692. Sec. 15.

IV. Hannah, b. 1696.

V. Elizabeth, b. 1700, d. 1742; m. John Whitman, 1728, and had

1. Samuel, b. 1730.

2. Elizabeth, b. 1732.

3. John, b. 1735.

4. James, b. 1739.

Section 5

Jonathan Cary, son of John, Sec. 1. b. Bridgewater, Sept. 24, 1656; m. Sarah, dau. of Samuel Allen and Sarah Partridge, whose mother was dau. of Gov. George Partridge of Duxbury; he d. 1695.

Children:

I. Recompense, b. about 1688. Sec. 16.

II. John, b. about 1690. Sec. 17.

III. Jonathan, b. about 1692. Sec. 18.

Section 6

David Cary, son of John, Sec. 1, b. Bridgewater, Jan. 27, 1658-9; went to Bristol in 1680, and became one of the original Proprietors of the town; was a carpenter, and his dwelling house stood for a hundred years. He was a man of education, influence, and piety, and was chosen Deacon of the Church in 1683, and held the office till his death in 1718; his estate was inventoried at 811 pounds, at that time a large fortune. In his will he provided that if his son Henry shall proceed in learning so as to enter College, then his son Peter shall pay the charges of his College education. He m. Elizabeth ———.
Children:
I. Elizabeth, b. Mar. 7, 1691; m. Daniel Smith.
II. Mehitabel, b. Aug. 14, 1693; m. Mr. Wardwell.
III. Bathsheba, b. Aug. 14, 1693; m. Mr. Howland.
IV. Sarah, b. Jan. 21, 1695, d. in childhood.
V. Bethia, b. Jan. 22, 1697; m. Benjamin Gorham, and their descendant, Wm. H. Manning, Ayer, Mass., is the compiler of the Manning genealogy.
VI. David, b. Feb. 20, 1699. Sec. 19.
VII. Peter, b. Nov. 9, 1701.
VIII. Mary, b. Nov. 6, 1703, d. in childhood.
IX. Priscilla, b. May 9, 1709; m. Joseph Gladding, 1726.
X. Henry, b. June 4, 1711. Sec. 19-A.

Section 7

Joseph Cary, son of John, Sec. 1, b. April 18, 1663, Bridgewater. When a young man he went to Norwich, Ct., and became one of the original Proprietors of Windham; Feb. 9, 1694, he bought 1,000 acres of land for ten pounds nine shillings. He took position with the first men of the town in civil and ecclesiastical affairs, and was chosen repeatedly to serve in the most important offices, civil, military, and religious; was one of the original members of the First Congregational Church in Windham, and at its organization, Dec. 10, 1700, was chosen Deacon, and held the office till his death. So highly was he esteemed that he was buried by his townsmen under arms, which was a very unusual occurrence. He m. first, Hannah __, who d. 1691; m. second, Mercy, the widow of Jonathan Rudd; he d. Jan. 10, 1722, and his widow in 1741, aged 84 years.
Children:
I. Joseph, b. May 5, 1689. Sec. 20.
II. Jabez, b. July 12, 1691. Sec. 21.
III. Hannah, b. Mar. 4, 1693; m. Dea. Nathaniel Skiff, 1716; she lived at Willimantic, Ct., and d. Aug. 22, 1775; they had 1. Joseph, who d. aged 95 years.

IV. John, b. Jan. 23, 1695. Sec. 22.
V. Seth, b. July 29, 1697. Sec. 23.
VI. Elizabeth, b. April 17, 1700; m. Seth Palmer, 1720; d. 1739.

Section 7-A

Rebecca Cary, dau. of John, Sec. i, b. Bridgewater, Mar. 30, 1665; tn. Samuel Allen, 1685, and had
I. Samuel, b. 1686.
II. Ephraim, b. 1689; m. Zipporah Crane; their dau. Rebecca Allen, m. Benjamin Talbot; their dau. Zipporah Talbot, m. Joseph Trafton; their dau., Lavinia Trafton, m. John Hathaway; their dau., Frances Hathaway, m. Moses Kimball, and had Helen Frances Kimball, Brookline, Mass. The ancestor of Moses Kimball was Richard, one of the original Proprietors of Ipswich, Mass.; in this line we find the names of Boreman, Call, Dodge, Eaton, Edwards, Hazletine, Hughett, Kimball, Knight, Lord, Low, Perkins, Scott, Smith, Waite, and Ward. While on the mother's side are found Talbot, Phillips, Deacon, Trafton, Partridge, Godfrey, Tracy, Coen, whose ancestor was Everard Bogardus, the first Minister of New York, and his wife Ahneke Jans.

The brother of Zipporah Talbot was Commodore Silas Talbot, under whose supervision the old ship Constitution was built, and in which he performed such deeds of valor. As to their "Traits," it might be said that they had sound health, strength of body, soul, and mind; most had large families and lived to a good age. They were industrious and prosperous, and there was never heard anything but good of any of them.
III. Timothy, b. 1691.
IV. Joseph, b. 1693.
V. Mehitabel, b. 1695.

Section 7-B

Mehitabel Cary, dau. of John, Sec. 1, b. Bridgewater, Dec. 24, 1670; m. first, Eliashib Adams, son of Eliashib, son of Henry, of Braintree, at Bristol, Dec. 18, 1689; he was a carpenter and d. in Bristol, 1698, and his will was probated Aug. 2, 1698, the witnesses being David Cary, John Cary, and Benjamin Jones, and it mentions his wife and his children, Eliashib, William, Lydia, and Mehitabel; she m. second, in Bristol, Miles Standish, son of Josiah and Sarah (Allen) Standish, who settled in Preston, Ct., 1687; they made their home in Preston.
Children:
I. Lydia, b. Jan. 17, 1691; bapt. Dec. 22, 1695.
II. William, b. June 3, 1693; bapt. Dec. 22, 1695.
III. Mehitabel, b. Aug. 3, 1695; bapt. Dec. 22, 1695.

IV. Eliashib, b. Sept. 11, 1697; bapt. Sept. 19, 1697; he m. and had a son Eliashib, who had a son Eliashib, b. at Canterbury, Ct., June 6, 1773, who d. at Bangor, Me., Aug. 25, 1855, a most worthy and notable citizen.

Section 8

John Cary, son of John, Sec. 2, b. Bridgewater, Dec. 9, 1674; went with the family to Bristol in 1680; m. Damaris. Arnold, dau. of Oliver Arnold and Phebe Cook; he was son of Gov. Benedict Arnold and Damaris Wescott, who was son of William Arnold and Christian, dau. of Thomas Peak, of London, who arrived in New England June 24, 1635; his first home was in Hingham, but soon removed to Providence. In 1636 William Arnold, with Roger Williams, was one of the 54 Proprietors in the first settlement of Rhode Island, and was reckoned the wealthiest man in the State. His farm included a section of the most valuable part of the City of Newport, taking in the "Old Stone Mill." He traced his line back through eighteen generations to one of the kings of Wales.

Gov. Arnold's son Oliver lived at Canonicut and was a leading citizen of the town, holding important offices, among which was that of Deputy in 1682. John Cary m. Damaris Arnold, Mar. 3, 1700. Children:

I. Phebe, b. Mar. 5, 1701.

II. Abigail, b. Nov. 4, 1702.

III. John, b. Nov. 21, 1704.

IV. Damaris, b. Oct. 10, 1706; m. John Hull, a descendant of Rev. Josep Hull, founder of the "Hull Colony," April 3, 1726, and had fourteen children and a numerous posterity. A descendant is Miss Amy Eleanor E. Hull. Baltimore, Md., author of a pamphlet, "Rev. Joseph Hull and some of His Descendants," 1904; also a "Chart of the Royal Descent of the Carys."

Section 9

Eleazer Cary, son of John, Sec. 2, b. Bridgewater, Sept. 27, 1678; removed with the family to Bristol in 1680; m. Lydia, dau. of William and Mary (Chapman) Throope, (b. July 15, 1686, at Bristol), about 1703, and removed to Windham about 1718, having bought land there Jan. 16, 1717-18; this was the "eighty-six acres of land and meadow" at the end of the Cedar Swamp, purchased of Richard Abbe, Esq., for no pounds. In 1722 he was confirmed by the General Assembly as Captain of the 2nd Company of the Trainband in Windham, and thereafter he was known as Captain Cary. He was Deputy for Windham in 1723, 1725, 1726, 1731, 1734, 1736, 1741-4, 1746-9Was chosen Deacon of the First Church in 1729, and held the place till his death; the street from his home to the Church was called Christian Street, and still retains the name. He took a prominent part in public affairs, and was an active and substantial citizen. The Rev. Thomas Clapp, afterwards President of Yale, was at that time the Pastor of the Windham Church. His will was dated Mar. 6, 1752, and he d. July 28, 1754.

Children:

I. Abigail, b. Bristol, Jan. 15, 1703. d. Oct. 16, 1766; m. first, Jeremiah Ripley (b. April 15, 1696, d. 1737), Jan. 1723, and had seven children, of whom Eleazer and Lieut. Charles were prominent men; the latter d. in captivity with the British army; she m. second, John Abbe, April 23, 1751; her son, Lieut. Charles, m. John Abbe's dau. Tabitha.

II. Lydia, b. Feb. 12, 1725-6; m. David Ripley, Windham, and was mother of Rev. Hezekiah Ripley (Sprague's Annals, Vol. I, pp. 648-50), and Rev. David Ripley, and other talented sons; Gen. William Ripley of the War of 1812-14, who d. at Painesville, O., was her grandson; she d. April 9, 1784.

Alfred L. Holman, Chicago, Ill., is a descendant, and his line is: Lydia Cary m. Jeremiah Ripley; their son Gamaliel m. and had Elizabeth, who m. Mr. Adams; their dau. m. Mr. Hemenway; Sarah Elizabeth Hemenw'ay m. Mr. Holman, and had Alfred L.

III. Ann, b. Sept. 21, 1708; m. Nathan Denison April 1, 1736, who commanded a part of the forces at Wyoming. Pa., at the massacre, 1778. She reared a large family.

IV. Eliza, b. Mar. 25, 1711; m. Joshua Wright, and had a large family in Windham.

V. Eleazer, b. Sept. 19, 1713. Sec. 24.

VI. Mary, b. Mar. 23, 1715-16; m. Gideon Bingham, Windham, and reared a large and respected family. Samuel Bingham, Cashier of the Windham Bank, and probably the Hon. John A. Bingham of Ohio, are descendants.

VII. Martha, b. Mar. i, 1717-18, d. unm. Jan. 25, 1774.

VIII. Sarah, b. April 10. 1720, d. in childhood.

IX. William, b. April 4, 1722, d. in childhood.

X. Alathea, b. May 12, 1724, d. in youth.

XI. William, b. Oct. 28, 1729. Sec. 25.

Section 10

James Cary, son of John, Sec. 2, b. Bridgewater, June 10, 1680; the youngest of the family who removed to Bristol; went to Newport; m. Bridget, dau. of John Pococke, Attorney-General of Rhode Island, Dec. 5, 1705, Rev. Walter Clark, Pastor of the Second Congregational Church of Newport, officiating. He made his home here, and the Carys intermarried with the Arnold, Ellery, Redwood, and Wanton families of Newport.

Children:

I. Rebecca, b. May, 1707.

II. Seth, b. Sept. 5, 1708; possibly went to New York.

III. Peleg, b. Mar. 6, 1710.

IV. Bridget, b. Feb. 4, 1712.
V. Elizabeth, b. Sept. 14, 17—.
VI. James, b. Oct. 7, 17—.
VII. James, bapt. Sept. 29, 1728. Sec. 25-A.
VIII. Susanna, bapt. Feb. 28, 1730.

Section 11

Benjamin Cary, son of John, Sec. 2, b. Bristol, Aug. 29, 1681; he was a man of prominence, was Town Clerk, and succeeded his father as Deacon in the Church; m. Susanna, dau. of Ensign Joseph and Susanna (George) Kent of Swansea, (b. Sept. 25, 1687, d. Aug. 10, 1764); he d. Jan. 20, 1734, and the widow was bereft of husband and six children within two years. His estate was inventoried at 8,800 pounds. Mrs. Cary in her will, proven Dec. 4, 1764, gave to her two surviving sons, Benjamin and Nathaniel, all her real estate, and to her granddaughter, Susanna. 100 pounds, to her dau. Elizabeth Clark, all her "silver plate and indoor moveables, also her servant girl named Caty."
Children:
I. Benjamin, b. about 1706. Sec. 26.
II. Allen, b. July, 1708. Sec. 27.
III. Nathaniel, b. 1710, d. in infancy.
IV. Nathaniel, b. Nov. 2, 1712. Sec. 28.
V. Bethia, b. Feb. 8, 1716; d. June 7, 1736.
VI. Abigail, b. Feb. n, 1718; d. May 10, 1736.
VII. Elizabeth, b. Feb. 20, 1720; m. Gamaliel Clark, Nov. 17, 1740.
VIII. Mehitabel, b. Sept. 22, 1722; d. June 4, 1736.
IX. John, b. Sept. 22, 1725; d. in youth.
X. Lydia, b. 1727; d. in childhood.
XI. Seth, b. 1729; d. in childhood.
XII. Joseph, b. 1730; d. in childhood.
XIII. Susanna, b. 1732; m. Daniel Throop.
XIV. Mary, b. 1734; d. in childhood.

Section 12

Josiah Cary, son of John, Sec. 2, b. Bristol, May 6, 1686; m. in Bristol, Ruth Reynolds, Nov. 9, 1710; he d. June 26, 1739.
Children:
I. Jemima, b. July 25, 1711; bapt. Oct. 2, 1715.
II. Nathaniel, b. Feb. 6, 1713; bapt. Oct. 2, 1715; m. Tabitha Howland, Dec. 11, 1737, and d. childless in 1740.
III. Joseph, b. about 1715; bapt. Oct. 27, 1717; m. Abigail Bigelow (b. Feb. 10, 1723), Oct. 24, 1739; moved to Middle Haddam; they had

1. Josiah, b. July 9, 1740; d. 1791.
2. Edward, bapt. April 24, 1743; d. young.
3. Prosper, b. about 1745; m. Elizabeth Parker, Nov. 19, 1767.
4. George, b. 1747; m. Rachel Hurd, Nov. 6, 1769; went to Sag Harbor, L. I.
5. Waitstill, b. 1749; m. Editha Bigelow, Mar. 2, 1778.
6. Joseph, b. 1752; m. Rebecca Hurd, July 1, 1774.
7. Nancy, b. April 16, 1754; m. 1st, George Lucas (b. Feb. 14, 1747; d. Feb. 10, 1776), Oct. 30, 1771; m. 2d, William Blinn (b. Sept. 14, 1742; d. Aug. 1, 1822), Nov. 7, 1782; they had

(1) Clarissa, b. June 26, 1775; m. Uzziel Adams, Sept. 15, 1794
(2) Nancy, b. Oct. 4, 1783; m. Orson Smith, April 12, 1804.
(3) Hepzibah, b. Sept. 16, 1785; m. Seth Hitchcock, May 6, 1804.
(4) Patty, b. June 14, 1788; m. Thomas Havens, Sept. 9, 1813.
(5) William, b. July 14, 1790; m. Julia A. Hamblin, Dec. 26, 1819.
(6) Emily, b. July 14, 1792; Emily Blinn m. Jesse Smith, Jr., Great Barrington, Mass., Nov. 21, 1813, and went to Lyons, N. Y.; they had

1. Orson, b. Nov. 29, 1814; d. 1843, Lyons, N. Y.
2. Nancy, b. Feb. 15, 1820; d. in infancy.
3. Charles, m. Charlotte Carr.
4. Emily Elizabeth, b. Sept. 22, 1831; m. Dr. Joseph Friend Pollock (b. June 19, 1821), 1849, and had (1) Mary Emily, b. June 14, 1851; m. Seymour Walton of New Orleans, now of Chicago, Sept. 21, 1870, and had

1. Edward, b. Dec. 5, 1871, Captain 19th U. S. Infantry; m. Emma L. Nichols, June 17, 1897.
2. Emily, b. Nov. 17, 1874.
3. Frank Richmond, b. May 27, 1876.
4. Albert, b. Oct. 24, 1877; m. Caroline Sawtelle Piers, of Philadelphia, Oct. 25, 1905, and had

(1) Mary Piers, b. July 4, 1907, Boston.
5. Margaret Maria, b. 1833; m. John Blackburn, of North Carolina; d. Jan. 1, 1903.
8. James, b. 1758; d. young.
9. Abigail, b. 1759; d. young.
10. Abigail, b. 1762; m. Jacob Hurd, Jr., Oct. 3, 1782.
11. Mary, b. Aug. 2, 1764; m. Benjamin Hurd.
12. Samuel, b. 1768.
13. Jerusha.

Section 13

Samuel Cary, son of Francis, Sec. 3, b. Bridgewater, 1677; m. Mary, dau. of Isaac and Bethia Poole, South Bridge, N. Y., 1704; removed to Dutchess County, N. Y., in 1728; he d. 1759, and she in 1766.
Children:

I. Joseph, b. 1705. Sec. 28-A.
II. Lydia, b. 1706.
III. Alice, b. 1707.
IV. Elizabeth, b. 1709.
V. Samuel, b. 1711.
VI. David, b. 1713.
VII. Nathan, b. 1716. Sec. 28-C.
VIII. Eleazer, b. 1718. Sec. 29.
IX. Mary, b. 1720.

Of the four daughters no record has as yet been found; and little is definitely known of Samuel and David, except that they had large families in Albany and Dutchess Counties, N. Y.

Section 14

Ephraim Cary, son of Francis, Sec. 3, b. Bridgewater, 1679; m. Hannah Waldo (b. July 17, 1687; d. Oct. 18, 1777), Feb. 3, 1709; lived in his native town, where he d. July 18, 1765

Children:

I. Mehitabel, b. Dec. 3, 1709; m. Benjamin Allen; reared a family, and among them was

1. Mehitabel, b. 1737; m. Caleb Washburn, May 27, 1756, Bridgewater; had

(1) Lydia, b. May 16, 1757; m. James Atherton (b. Sept. 19, 1751; d. May 5, 1828), May 3, 1774; she d. April, 1847; they had

1. Elisha Atherton, b. May 7, 1786; d. April 2, 1853; m. 1st, Zibia Perkins, Oct. 10, 1810; m. 2d, Caroline (Ross) Maffitt; they had

(1) Sarah, b. Oct. 21, 1814; m. William Henry (b. Aug. 15, 1794; d. May 23, 1878), Sept. 26, 1842, and had

1. Lydia, b. June 19, 1849; m. Winfield Scott Stites, June 16, 1874, and had

(1) Thomas H. Atherton, b. April 26, 1875; m. Mary Henry, June 27, 1905, and had 1. Mary H., b. Nov. 20, 1907.

(2) Sara H., b. July 20, 1877.

(3) Harriet M., b. Nov. 2, 1879; m. Charles Foster Tillinghast, Dec. 10, 1909.

(4) Lydia A., b. Oct. 6, 1882; m. Sidney Roby Miner, June 25, 1909.

(5) Ellen Scranton, b. June 6, 1884.

(2) Eliza Ross, b. May 10, 1831; m. Charles Abbott Miner, Jan. 1853; live at Wilkes-Barre, Pa.

II. Ezra, b. 1711. Sec. 30.
III. Zechariah, b. 1713. Sec. 31.
IV. Ephraim, b. 1714. Sec. 32.
V. Daniel, b. 1716. Sec. 33.

Section 15

James Cary, son of James, Sec. 4, b. Bridgewater, 1692; m. Sarah Shaw, 1722, and d. 1762.
Children:
I. Sarah, b. 1723; m. William Barrell, 1741.
II. Joshua, b. 1726; d. unm. 1747.

Section 16

Dea. Recompense Cary, son of Jonathan, Sec. 5, b. Bridgewater, 1688, where he lived and d. in 1759; m. 1st, Mary, dau. of Joseph Crossman, 1711, who d. 1726; m. 2d, Mrs. Sarah (Alden) Brett, dau. of Isaac Alden, and widow of Seth Brett, 1727. He was an influential citizen.
Children:
I. Seth, b. 1714; d. unm. 1742.
II. Ichabod, b. 1715. Sec. 34.
III. Ebenezer, b. 1717; d. unm. 1744.
IV. Sarah, b. 1718; m. Benjamin Hayward, 1742, and had (with possibly others)
1. Joseph, who m. and had Sarah, who m. Robert Packard;
their son Robert Packard, 2d, m. and had Robert H. Packard, who m. Ellen A.-and resided at Campello, Mass.
2. Olive H., who m. Hayward Marshall, and had
(1) Perez, who m. and had Susan Elizabeth, b. Jan. 9, 1841; m. Henry Manley, C. E., Nov. 6, 1867, and had
1. Lawrence Bradford, C. E., b. Mar. 12, 1870.
2. Howard Tisdale, C. E., b. Oct. 17, 1872; Supt. Roads and Bridges, Zamboango Province, P. I.
3. Henry, b. Oct. 13, 1880; grad. Mass. Inst. Technology.
4. Alice A., m. Charles G. Manley, Boulder, Colo., and had
(1) Sumner H., grad. Mass. Inst. Tech., 1900; m. Susie R. W. Talbot, and had Robert Cary; live Kansas City, Kan.
(2) Ruth E.; grad. Smith College, 1903; teacher Pollock Stevens Inst., Birmingham, Ala.
5. Emma Josephine, m. Josiah Edward Sears, and had Wm. Marshall, grad. Mass. Agri. Col., 1905.
V. Simeon, b. 1719. Sec. 35.
VI. Zebulon, b. 1721. Sec. 36.
VII. Jonathan, b. 1723. Sec. 37.
VIII. Josiah, b. 1724; d. 1743.
IX. Mary, b. 1726; m. Joseph Crossman, Easton, Mass.
X. Abigail, b. 1729.

Section 17

John Cary, son of Jonathan, Sec. 5, b. Bridgewater, 1690; lived in his native town and owned a Grist Mill at Orr's Works; m. 1st, Experience, dau. of Henry Sweeting of Rehoboth; m. 2d, Mary Burr of Rehoboth, 1730; m. 3d, Susanna Bryam, dau. of Elisha Allen and Mehitabel, dau. of Nicholas Bryam and Elizabeth Gannett, 1731; m. 4th, Sarah Drake of Rehoboth, 1734.

Children:
I. John, b. 1719. Sec. 38.
II. Martha, b. 1721; m. Daniel Cary, 1742.
III. Henry, b. 1723. Sec. 39.
IV. Susannah, b. 1725.
V. Beriah, b. 1729. Sec. 40.
VI. Molly, b. 1732.
VII. Thankful, b. 174s; m. Jonathan Orcutt of Cohasset, 1766.
VIII. Huldah, b. 1750.

Section 18

Jonathan Cary, son of Jonathan, Sec. 5, b. 1692, and lived in South Bridgewater; m. 1st, Susanna Keith, 1717, who d. childless; m. 2d, Experience Carver, 1719; he d. 1766.

Children:
I. Seth, b. 1721.
II. Eleazer, b. 1723. Sec. 41.
III. Susanna, b. 1725; m. William Hooper, 1759; d. 1795.
IV. Anne, b. 1728; m. Hon. Nathan Mitchell, 1754, and left a numerous family.
V. Jonathan, b. 1730. Sec. 42.
VI. Maj. Eliphalet, 1732; was an officer in the Revolutionary War; in advanced life m. Hannah, widow of Josiah Edson; d. more than 90 years of age.
VII. Experience, b. 1734.
VIII. Benjamin, b. 1738.
IX. Jesse, b. 1742.

Section 19

David Cary, son of David, Sec. 6, b. Bristol, Feb. 20, 1699; m. 1st, Rachel Bates, of Dorchester, Jan. 26, 1721; m. 2d, Mary Canada, June 9, 1729.
Children:
I. David, b. Nov. 23, 1729; went to Nova Scotia.
II. Edward, b. May 7, 1732; settled in Taunton.
III. Mary, b. Aug. 9, 1733; m. Mr. Wilbour.

IV. Thomas, b. Jan. 19, 1735. Sec. 44.
V. Nathan, b. Feb. 5, T737; removed to Vermont.
VI. Michael, b. Jan. 23, 1739. Sec. 43.

Section 19-A

Rev. Henry Cary, son of David, Sec. 6, b. Bristol, June 4, 1711; entered Harvard College in 1729, received his A. B. 1733, and A. M. in 1735, and became a Baptist minister; m. about 1734, and lived in Ashford, Ct., where his children were born. Removed to Pawling, Dutchess County, N. Y., where he was the first regularly ordained minister, and was called "Good Priest Cary;" was neighbor to James Stark, Sr., at West Mountain; afterwards removed to the John Townsend farm.

About 1754 a body of Connecticut people formed an association, known as the "Susquehanna Purchase," and bought of the Six Nations all the land between the Allegheny and Susquehanna Rivers, and organized the county of Westmoreland, Ct. The first effort at settlement, in 1763, was not successful; the actual settlement was made by forty white persons in 1769. On May 10, 1773, Henry Cary bought of William Stark, Sr., a half right in the Susquehanna Purchase; as shown by deed Mar. 10, 1774, he was resident in Westmoreland, Litchfield County, New England (now Wilkes-Barre, Pa.), as shown by deed made to him by Michael Rood, of the same place. In 1775 he was Chairman of the Committee of Safety of Dutchess County, N. Y. On June 14, 1778, we find him in the county of Luzerne, Pa., as shown by power of attorney given to Henry Stark, his grandson; perhaps about this time he left the Wyoming Valley.

Dutchess County records have it that he preached there shortly before his death, in the old Log Meeting House, near the Camp Meeting woods. The Vital Statistics of Rhode Island state that he died in Vermont. There is considerable uncertainty about some of the facts as here alleged.

Children:

I. Mary, b. Aug. 23, 1735.

II. Esther, b. Oct. 8, 1737.

III. Elizabeth, b. Aug. 18, 1739; m. James Stark, 1758; he was the son of Christopher, b. May 22, 1734, Groton, Ct., and d. of small pox, July 30, 1777. He was an early settler at Pawling, N. Y., having moved there subsequent to 1755. In the spring of 1773, the family emigrated to the Wyoming Valley, locating at Wilkes-Barre; Sept. 26, 1776, he enlisted in the Second Independent Co., located at Westmoreland, and his son joined Capt. Simon Spaulding's command, June, 1778. This son was the oldest of a large family. On the day of the Massacre— July 3, 1778, the widow saved herself and children by hiding in a held of corn; and upon finding that her home was destroyed, gathered what she could and led her children all the way back on foot to her old home in Pawling, N. Y.; she arrived at her sister Chloe's, who m. Col. Pearce, a picture of utter misery and despair. Unable to rally from the fearful strain, she d. Aug. 12, 1778, having given her life for her children.

IV. Mary, b. Nov. 17, 1741.

V. Catherine, b. May 13, 1743. d. in childhood.

VI. Henry, b. Aug. 19, 1745.

VII. Chloe, b. June 6, 1746; m. Col. William Pearce, Pawling, N. Y., Mar. 2, 1766; d. Sept. 14, 1778.

VIII. John Paul, b. Aug. 6, 1750.

Section 20

Joseph Cary, son of Dea. Joseph, Sec. 7, b. Norwich, Ct., May 5, 1689; went to Windham, Ct., with his father; m. Abigail Bushnell. July 4, 1711; his father gave him a farm in "Scotland Society," a part of Windham, where he d. 1722.

Children:

I. Abigail, b. Sept. 7, 1714; m. Elijah Dean of Middletown, Ct.

II. Joseph, b. Dec. 10, 1715; d. unm.

III. Zervia, d. in Providence, R. I., 1747.

IV. Hannah, m. Amos Spaulding, 1739, and had Amelia, who m. Marvin Ingalls, and had Olive, b. Nov. 13, 1819, who m. Pulaski Carter, 1843, and had

1. Amelia M., b. 1844; m. William De Witt Kennedy, of
Scranton, Pa., and had

(1) William P., b. Oct. 30, 1869; a bank teller.

(2) Lucius Carter, b. Sept. 8, 1872; a practicing physician.

(3) Katherine M., b. Nov. 11, 1875; m. Dr. W. A. Iverman, Newport, R. I., and had

1. William Abbey.

(4) Harold S., b. Nov. 28, 1884.

2. Pulaski P., b. June 6, 1849; m. Venitia White.

3. Marvin P., b. Nov. 28, 1857; m Pamelia Murphy.

Section 21

Jabez Cary, son of Dea. Joseph, Sec. 7, b. Norwich, Ct., July 12, 1691; m. Hannah Hendee, Nov. 15, 1722; settled first in Windham, afterwards in Preston, and finally at Mansfield, where he d. 1760. Children:

I. Joseph, b. Sept. 28, 1723. Sec. 45.

II. Hannah, b. July 6, 1725; d. 1741.

III. Jabez, b. July 30, 1727. Sec. 46.

IV. Nathaniel, b. Oct. 23, 1729. Sec. 47.

V. Ebenezer, b. 1732. Sec. 48.

VI. David, b. 1734; m. Mary Webber, 1756, Mansfield, Ct.

VII. Mary, b. Nov. 17, 1739; m. Benjamin Crosby, Mansfield, Ct.

VIII. Benjamin, b. Jan. 25, 1741; d. in infancy.

Section 22

John Cary, son of Dea. Joseph, Sec. 7, b. Windham, Ct., June 23, 1695; m. Hannah Thurston, May 15, 1716, who was of Bristol, and a sister of Mehitabel Thurston, wife of Nathaniel Huntington, and mother of Gov. Samuel Huntington, one of the Signers of the Declaration of Independence. His father gave him 100 acres of land in "Scotland Society," east of Merrick Brook; he and his wife were original members of the Third Church in Windham, organized in 1735; he was a prominent and influential citizen, and his personal estate amounted to 397 pounds; he d. Jan. 11, 1776, and his widow 1780.

Children:
I. John, b. April 12, 1717. Sec. 49.
II. Beneijah, b. Mar. 7, 1719. Sec. 50.
III. Phebe, b. July 22, 1721, d. 1738.
IV. Joseph, b. Aug. 4, 1723; m. Abigail Hebard, Dec. 10, 1747.
V. Mercy, b. Oct. 27, 1725; m. John Baker; d. 1814.
VI. William, b. Dec. 12, 1727; d. in childhood.
VII. Jonathan, b. Aug. 24, 1729; d. in youth.
VIII. Nathaniel, b. Nov. 1, 1731. Sec. 51.
IX. Samuel, b. June 13, 1734. Sec. 52.

Section 23

Seth Cary, son of Dea. Joseph, Sec. 7, b. Windham, Ct., July 29, 1697; resided on his father's farm, was a member of the First Congregational Church, a quiet man and useful citizen, but not active in public affairs; m. 1st, Mary Hebard, April 17, 1722, who d. March, 1751; m. 2d, Hannah __, and d. 1777.

Children:
I. Mary, b. Oct. 20, 1723; m. James Moulton, Jr.
II. Seth, b. July 12, 1725; m. Hannah Jennings, 1758.
III. Elizabeth, b. April 25, 1727.
IV. Josiah, b. June 18, 1729. Sec. 53.
V. Joanna, b. Dec. 28, 1731; m. John Frome.
VI. Daniel, b. Feb. 22, 1733; probably d. in youth.
VII. Abigail, b. May 15, 1736.
VIII. Hannah, b. June 25, 1738.
IX. Moses, b. Dec. 15, 1740. Sec. 53-A.

Section 24

Eleazer Cary, son of Dea. Eleazer, Sec. 9, b. Bristol, Sept. 19, 1713; went with the family to Windham, Ct.; m. Jerusha, dau. of Dea. Nathaniel Wales, Jan. 29, 1736; he d. July 24, 1754, and his widow m. Capt. James Lassell.

Children:
I. Eleazer, b. Aug. 7, 1737. Sec. 54.
II. Nathaniel, b. Jan. 17, 1739. Sec. 55.
III. Susanna, b. April 22, 1742; d. 1754.
IV. Althea, b. April i5, 1744; m. Jonah Smith.
V. Phineas, b. Oct. 7, 1746. Sec. 56.
VI. Prudence, b. Mar. 26, 1749; d. in infancy.
VII. Lydia, b. Dec. 26, 1751; d. in childhood.
VIII. Jerusha, b. Jan. 14, 1755; m. Reuben Welch.

Section 25

Dea. William Cary, son of Dea. Eleazer, Sec. 9, b. Windham, Ct., Oct. 28, 1729; m. Eunice, dau. of Nathaniel Webb, Feb. 19, 1754; resided in Windham till 1772, when he removed his family to Lempster, N. H. He was an unusually large and strong man, and some remarkable stories are recorded of his great strength; it is said that he could throw barrels of cider into a cart as fast as a man could put them on end. In 1761, when a neighbor's house was on fire, he took a tub of water holding over a barrel, carried it across four post and rail fences, dashed it on the fire, and put it out. He was Deacon of the Church in Lempster, and was influential and highly esteemed. Was Captain of Co. 1, Col. Fellows' Regiment, 1776; Captain of Co. 8, same Regiment, Sept, and Oct., 1777, which reinforced the army of Gen. Gates at Saratoga at the time of the surrender of Burgoyne's army, which took place Oct. 17, 1777. He d. May 7, 1808, and his widow in 1809.

Children:
I. Susanna, b. Dec. 11, 1754; d. in infancy.
II. Eleazer, b. April 23, 1757; m. Lavinia Willey, had a daughter, and d. May 15, 1790.
III. Mary, b. Feb. 20, 1759; m. Mr. Nichols and had a large family.
IV. Olivet, b. Oct. 20, 1761. Sec. 57.
V. Elliott, b. Dec. 20, 1763. Sec. 58.
VI. Eunice, b. Jan. 4, 1767; m. Nathan Willey, Oct. 1, 1789, and had ten children.
VII. William, b. Jan. 4, 1767. Sec. 59.
VIII. James, b. Jan. 4, 1767; d. in youth.
IX. Lydia, b. Feb. 16, 1769; d. in infancy.
X. Susanna, b. April 14, 1771; m. Mr. Wait, of New York.
XI. Throop, b. 1773; d. in childhood.
XII. Lydia, b. 1775; m. Samuel Ayres, of Pennsylvania.
XIII. John F., b. 1777. Sec. 60.
XIV. Nancy, b. 1777; m. Samuel Saxton, and had two sons, both of whom d. of cholera in Cincinnati, Ohio.
XV. Susan, b. 1799; d. young.

Section 25-A

James Cary, son of James, Sec. 10, b. Newport, R. I., and bapt. Sept. 29, 1728. Was a tanner by trade; was impressed into the British naval service, but declining this enforced service, escaped to land a mile away. He m. Annie Taplin (dau. of Mansfield and Mary (Johnson) Taplin, of Charlestown, Mass., and bapt. there Feb. 7, 1724-5), at Southboro, Mass., Mar. 23, 1747; her brother, John, was a Lieut.-Col. in the French and Indian War, in which he spent about ten years, and afterwards was appointed Judge of the Court of Common Pleas by King George III. James Cary owned land in Middletown, Ct., also a "share" of 360 acres, "be the same more or fewer," in Marlboro, Vt., and a farm of a hundred acres in Halifax, then in the Province of New York, but now in Vermont, where he died.

Children:

I. Mary, m. Joseph Lyons.

II. James, m. Margaret ___; he was probably killed at the battle of Saratoga, 1777.

III. John, b. Feb. 28, 1755, Kinderhook, N. Y. Sec. 60-A.

Section 26

Benjamin Cary, son of Dea. Benjamin, Sec. 11, b. Bristol, R. I., 1706; m. Thankful Taylor, of Plymouth, 1733; purchased real estate in Providence, R. I., and resided there, the house in which he lived being known as the "Old Deacon Cary House." He d. in old age universally esteemed for his purity of character and life.

Children:

I. John, b. 1734.

II. Joseph, b. 1736. Sec. 61.

III. Thomas, b. 1741.

IV. Nathaniel, b. 1743; m. Mary Locke, of Dutchess County, N. Y., and had
1. Absalom, d. unm.

V. Ebenezer, b. 1745Sec. 62.

VI. Thankful, b. 1747; m. James Aplin, of Otsego County, N. Y.

VII. Abigail, b. 1749; m. Mr. Simons.

VIII. Susan, b. 1761; m. Henry Vanderbin, of Dutchess County, New York.

IX. George, b. 1763; went to South Carolina, m., and settled there.

Section 27

Allen Cary, son of Dea. Benjamin, Sec. n, b. Bristol, R. I., 1708; m. Hannah Church, Oct. 9, 1731; she was the dau. of Thomas 3, (Col. Benjamin 2, Richard

1) and Edith (Woodman) Church, of Little Compton, R. I., widow of Samuel Clark, b. Sept. 23, 1714, d. Nov. 30, 1782.

Children:

I. Molly, b. Dec. 3, 1732; m. Josiah Finney (b. July 1, 1728, d. July 23, 1804), the son of Capt. Jeremiah 3, (Jeremiah 2, John 1) and Elizabeth (Bristow) Finney; their dau., Molly, m. William Coggshall; their son, Josiah, m. Mary Pease Finney; their son, Henry W. Coggshall, m. Emma or Ama Brown; their dau., M. Ella, m. Benoni R. Paine, and had

1. Jennie Elizabeth.
2. Stella Florence.

They reside in New Bedford, Mass.

II. Benjamin, b. Jan. 10, 1734.

III. Abigail, b. Dec. 23, 1736; m. John Field, of Providence. R. I.

IV. Allen, b. Jan. 1, 1738; d. in infancy.

V. Susanna, b. Aug. 7, 1740; m. Jonathan Gladding, Feb. 8. 1764.

VI. Hannah, b. Sept. 26, 1742; m. William Munro, Jan. 9, 1768; she died 1834, leaving numerous descendants.

Section 28

Col. Nathaniel Cary, son of Dea. Benjamin, Sec. 11, b. Bristol, R. I., 1712; m. Elizabeth Wanton, of Newport, R. I., Aug. 4, 1740, who d. 1769; m. 2d, Ama Pearce. He was Colonel of a Rhode Island Regiment, and a distinguished soldier and officer of the Revolution; he was large and athletic, and of splendid personal appearance. His will, proven in 1784, gave his Bristol estate to his daughter Abigail, and makes bequests to his five grandchildren, and emancipates his mulatto man, Ichabod, and provides for his support. They had one child,

I. Abigail, b. Nov. 12, 1742; m. William Ellery, of Newport, Deputy Governor of the State, and one of the Signers of the Declaration of Independence. The youngest son, George Wanton Ellery, m. Mary Goddard, and had 1. Mary Goddard, b. Sept. 5, 1833; d. Nov. 22, 1901; she was prominent in patriotic work, and for six years taught in the first evening schools established in Newport.

2. Henrietta C., resides in Newport, and is patriotic and philanthropic.

Section 28-A

Joseph Cary, son of Samuel, Sec. 13, b. Bridgewater, 17055 m Anne, dau. of Elihu Brett, 1732.

Children:

I. Barnabas, b. 1733; he was a blacksmith; served in Col. Nichols' Regiment of New Hampshire troops for nearly four months at West Point, in 1780; m.

Mary, dau. of Rev. Matthew Short, the first settled minister of Attleboro, Mass., 1759; went to Rindge, N. H., 1768, and settled in the east part of the town, where he d. 1795; their children, b. in Attleboro, Mass., were

1. Elizabeth, b. 1755, bapt. June 14, 1761; m. Lieut. Benjamin Foster, Town Clerk.

2. Sarah, b. 1757; m. Joseph Adams, d. Feb. 4, 1834.

3. Barnabas; m. Phebe, dau. of Capt. Samuel Danforth (b. 1767, Williamstown, Mass., d. Sept. 8, 1843, Medway, Mass.); he d. Feb. 4, 1834, Medway; they had

(1) Pamelia, b. Aug. 2, 1788; m. Daniel Ware (b. Aug. 21, 1789, d. Mar. 18, 1857), May 26, 1814; she d. Jan. 10, 1868, No. Wrentham, Mass.

(2) Betsey, b. Aug. 22, 1790; m. William Ware.

(3) John. b. Nov. 22, 1793; d. Jan. n, 1885, Parishville, New York.

(4) Lydia Reed. b. Mar. 11, 1796; m. Benjamin Cummings (b. Nov. 16, 1795, d. Mar. 21, 1863); she d. June 22, 1856, Medway, Mass.

(5) Charlotte, b. Aug. 16, 1798, Milltown, N. Y.; d. in infancy at Attleboro, Mass.

(6) Barnabas, b. Aug. 10, 1800, Pawtucket, R. I.; m. Kezia Green, and d. Sept., 1850, on the way to California.

(7) Clarissa Danforth, b. Mar. 6, 1803, Attleboro; m. Judson Harding (b. Jan. 11, 1800, Medfield, Mass., d. Nov. 5, 1847, Wrentham, Mass.), May 10, 1823, and d. May 29, 1872, Norfolk, Mass.

(8) William Hiram, b. Mar. 25, 1805, Attleboro, Mass.; d. June 21, 1888, Medway, Mass.; m. 1st, Lydia Daniels Lovell, dan. of Michael and Caty (Daniels) Lovell, Dec. 8, 1828; m. 2d, Harriet (Barber) White, and had

1. George Lovell, b. May 10, 1830; m. Mary Isabella Harding (b. Dec. 27, 1834), Mar. 12, 1854, and had

(1) Margaret Lovell, b. July 13, 1867; m. Rev. Frank Wright Pratt, 1892, and had three children. They reside at Calgary, Alberta, Canada.

Mr. Cary grad, at Harvard, 1852; was Professor of Greek and Latin at Antioch College, 1856-62; Professor of New Testament Literature, Meadville, Pa., 1862-1902; President Meadville Theological School, 1890-1902; since then, till his lamented death in June, 1910, Professor Emeritus; he d. while on a visit to his only child at Calgary, Can., a man highly respected.

He expected to enter the ministry, but began teaching and was never ordained, though he did at times preach. He published an Introduction to the Greek of the New Testament, and a Commentary on the Synoptic Gospels.

2. William Hiram, b. Aug. 22, 1835; m. Maria B. White, 1856, and had

(1) Emeline Barber, b. Feb. 15, 1857; m. Edward W. Mann, of Norfolk, Mass., and had two children.

(2) Harriet White, b. May 23, 1859; m Walter L. Palmer, of Medway, Feb. 24, 1893.

(3) Catherine Clark, b. 1869; m. Harry Kingsbury, of Wellesley Hills, Mass., Oct. 21, 1896, and have three children.

(4) Louis Alexander, b. Sept. 30, 1875; m. Nelly Hodges, of Medway, and have Dorothea.

3. Catherine Agnes, b. Oct. 17, 1840; d. in infancy.

4. Francis Eugene, b. Dec. 11, 1842; d. in infancy.

5. Mary Adelaide, b. Oct. 23, 1846; m. Rev. Ellery Channing Butler, Pastor "Stone Temple," Quincy, Mass.; their son Max d. 1898.

6. Henry Grattan, b. April 16, 1850; m. Nora Wood, and had

(1) Jessica Lovell, b. May 15, 1874; m. Edward K. Rundle, and have

1. Cary.

(2) L. Gertrude; m. Mr. Wilson.

(3) Winnifred H., b. Sept. 4, 1887.

(4) Dorothy C., b. Sept. 4, 1892.

(9) Samuel Danforth, b. June 30, 1807; d. in infancy.

(10) Charlotte Ann, b. May 28, 1810; d. in infancy.

(11) Mary Ann Short, b. Jan. 9, 1813, Rindge, N. H.; m. Charles B. Whitney.

4. Margaret, b. 1761; m. Abel Gilson, 1789.

5. Lazarus, b. 1765; m. Rachel ___.

6. John, b. Sept. 18, 1768, Attleboro; m. 1st, Judith, dau. of Henry and Sarah Godding (b. July 18, 1780, d. Dec. 5, 1820, Reading, Vermont), June 5, 1794; m. 2d, Sally Bigelow (b. May 30, 1789, d. Nov. 4, 1874, Cavendish, Vt.); they had

(1) John, b. May 14, 1797; d. 1812.

(2) Judith, b. May 21, 1801; d. in childhood.

(3) Isaac, b. June 10, 1803; d. in infancy.

(4) Isaac, b. April 19, 1806; d. 1854.

(5) Gilman, b. Dec. 1, 1808, New Ipswich, N. H.; m. Catherine, dau. of Michael and Caty (Daniels) Lovell, Jan. 1, 1839, and had

1. A son, b. Dec. 16, 1841; d. in infancy.

2. Josephine Maria, b. July 8, 1845; d. in infancy.

3. Edmund, b. Oct. 2, 1848; d. 1871.

4. Ellen, b. Nov. 2, 1851; m. 1st, E. M. Woodward, April 26, 1872, and had two children, who d. in infancy; he d. July 3, 1892; m. 2d, Simeon E. Stone, who d. Nov. 23, 1907; her home is in Medfield, Mass.

5. Mary, b. May 23, 1853; d. in 1883.

6. Arthur, b. April 23, 1858; d. in infancy.

(6) Alvin, b. Aug. 26, 1811; d. in infancy.

(7) John, b. July 8, 1813; d. Mar. 31, 1903; m. Mary Parkhurst (b. Sept. 27, 1818, Wethersfield, Vt., d. June 21, 1882, Cavendish, Vt.), Feb. 26, 1840; he d. Mar. 31, 1903, at Soldiers' Home, Bennington, Vt.; they had

1. William Wallace, b. Jan. 22, 1841, Poultney, Vt.; m. Hattie Spafford, 1866, and had

(1) Bertha A., b. 1866; live at Proctor, Vt.

(2) Maud, b. 1869; d. 1884.

2. Sarah Minerva, b. May 21, 1850, Cavendish, Vt.; m. Albert C. Kendall (b. June 2, 1844, d. April 21, 1897), 1870, and had

(1) Eugene A., b. April 9, 1871; m. Jessie A. L. Gilliland, Nov. 15, 1893.

(2) Fred H., b. Oct. 21, 1879; m. Ella Plunkett, Auburn, Me., April 9, 1904, and have one child.

(8) Judith, b. May 21, 1818; d. Oct. 26, 1838, Cavendish, Vermont.

7. Mary, b. 1767.

8. Theodore A., b. 1770, Goshen, Vt.; m. and had a son, Lazarus.

Section 28-C

Nathan Cary, son of Samuel, Sec. 13, b. Bridgewater, 1716; removed to Pawling, Dutchess County, N. Y., in 1728; m. Mary ___; d. in Pawling, 1800-1.
Children:

I. Elizabeth; m. Comfort Shaw.

II. Nathan.

III. Mary, b. at Pawling, N. Y.; m. William Stark 4, Christopher 3, William 2, Aaron 1, (b. 1745, Groton, Ct.); she d. Goshen, N. Y., 1795; they had

1. Nathan, b. Dec. 25, 1763; m. 1st, Dorcas Dickson, or Dixon, and had Paul Stark, who m. and had Lucretta Pauline Stark, who m. Charles Oakes Boynton, of Rockingham, Vt., and Sycamore, Ill., and had

(1) Charles Douglass, of St. Louis, Mo.; m. Cora May Farrar.

(2) Mary; m. Frederick B. Townsend, and had

1. Charles Boynton.

2. Elinor.

(3) Elmer Edward; m. Rose E. Lang-horn, and had

1. Frederick L.

2. Elmer E.

3. Mary E.

2. William, b. Feb. 13, 1765; d. Jan., 1833; m. 1st, Elizabeth Halstead; m. 2d, Mrs. Rachel Hewett.

3. Lucy, b. Dec. 30, 1768; d. Dec. 10, 1848; m. William Fancher about 1789.

4. Mary, b. Oct. 13, 1772; d. Feb. 12, 1859; m. Elijah Clark, Feb. 2, 1794.

5. Nancy, b. Mar. 12, 1774; d. Nov. 27, 1863; m. Ambrose Dickson, June 25, 1795.

6. John, b. Dec. 5, 1776; d. July 18, 1841; m. 1st, Temperance Pratt; m. 2d, Mary Camp.

7. James, b. July 2, 1779; d. June 30, 1859; m IS L Rebecca Rosencrans, Jan. 30, 1803; m. 2d, Elizabeth Wilcox, Oct. 26, 1819.

8. Oliver, b. Aug. 8, 1783; d. July 17, 1862; m. Elizabeth Dickson, April 21, 1808.

9. Elizabeth, b. Jan. 6, 1786; d. Jan. 10, 1883; m. Lewis Dixon, May 15, 1807.

10. Samuel, b. Feb. 16, 1788; d. Feb. 21, 1879; m. Mary Jones. William Stark's name is inscribed on the Wyoming Monument as one among the Rev-

olutionary citizen soldiery who fought in the memorable battle and Massacre, on July 3, 1778, and where his brother Aaron was killed.

IV. Rhoda; m. Mr. Worden.,

V. Huldah; m. Mr. Rutty.

VI. Rosanna, b. Mar. 1, 1755; d. Sept. 17, 1823; m. 1st, Mr. Bennett; m. 2d, Samuel Cary, son of Eleazer. Sec. 63-B.

VII. Esther; m. Mr. Cooper.

Section 29

Eleazer Cary, son of Samuel, Sec. 13, b. Bridgewater, 1718; removed with his father to Bond's Bridge, Dutchess County, N. Y., about 1728; m. Charity Sturdevant, and here all his children were born. He went with the first Forty Connecticut Pioneers to the Wyoming Valley in Feb., 1769, moving his family three years later, and settled in what was then known as Putnam Township, Westmoreland County, Ct. This was afterwards known as Carytown, now Cary Avenue, Wilkes-Barre, Pa.

Children:

I. Nathan, b. 1755. Sec. 63.

II. John, b. May 7, 1756. Sec. 63-A.

III. Samuel, b. Aug. 12, 1759. Sec. 63-B.

IV. Benjamin, b. 1763. Sec. 63-C.

V. Mehitabel, b. 1765; m. James Wright, Luzerne Co., Pa., and had numerous descendants.

VI. Comfort, b. 1766. Sec. 63-D.

Section 30

Ezra Cary, son of Ephraim, Sec. 14, b. Bridgewater, 1710; m. Mary, dau. of John Holman, 1734; removed to New Jersey, and afterwards to Western Pennsylvania, where he d. 1778.

Children:

I. Ezra, b. 1735. Sec. 64.

II. Luther, b. 1737.

III. Calvin, b. 1739.

IV. Ephraim, b. 1741; d. unm. at New Orleans.

Section 31

Zecheriah Cary, son of Ephraim, Sec. 14, b. Bridgewater, 1713; m. Susanna, dau. of Capt. Jonathan Bass, 1742, and settled in North Bridgewater, now the City of Brockton, where he d. Sept. 5, 1778. He with 24 others formed the First Church in North Bridgewater.

Children:
I. Ezra, b. 1749. Sec. 65.
II. Mehitabel, b. 1752; m. Zechariah Silvester, and removed to Raymond, Me.
III. Susanna, b. 1755; m. Rufus Brett, 1775, and removed to Paris, Me.
IV. Daniel, b. June 11, 1758. Sec. 66.
V. Luther, b. 1761. Sec. 67.

Section 32

Ephraim Cary, son of Ephraim, Sec. 14, b. Bridgewater, 1714; m. Susanna, dau. of Ebenezer Alden, and settled in Bridgewater, where he d. 1791; his widow d. 1803.
Children:
I. Anna, b. 1739; d. unm. 1804.
II. Azubah, b. 1741; m. Josiah Johnson (b. 1735, d. 1812), and d. 1816.
III. Phebe, b. 1742; m. Ezra Alden, and had eleven children; their son, Ethan Alden, grad, at Middlebury College, Vt., and was an Episcopal minister in Washington, D. C.
IV. Ephraim, b. 1748. Sec. 68.
V. Susanna, b. 1750; m. Asa Keith.
VI. Huldah, b. 1752; m. Simeon Allen.
VII. Daniel, b. 1754; m. Hannah Thayer.

Section 33

Daniel Cary, son of Ephraim, Sec. 14, b. Bridgewater, 1716; m. Martha, dau. of John Cary, 1742; had one son b. in Bridgewater, and removed to New Jersey; bought a large farm extending from Black River eastward, running up the mountain slope on Suckasunna Plains, Morris County, N. J., where he d. at an advanced age.
Children:
I. Lewis, b. 1742. Sec. 69.
II. Abel, b. 1744; removed to Washington Tp., Greene County, Pa., and bought a tract of land where he lived, and d. Dec., 1815; m. Elizabeth ___, and had
1. Daniel, b. Aug. 13, 1779; m., and had
(1) Abel, who m. and had four children.
(2) Sylvester, who was twice m. and had Elymas.
(3) Daniel Madison, who m. and had six children.
2. John.
3. Phebe.

4. Abel, b. Sept. 24, 1783; d. Aug. 16, 1820; he lived and d. on the old homestead; m. Eunice Woodruff (b. Mar. 4, 1787, d. May 8, 1833), and had

(1) Sophronia, b. 1815; m. Jesse Craig, and had

1. Daniel.
2. Abel.
3. Cephas.
4. Eunice.
5. Elizabeth.
6. Sarah.
7. Ellen.
8. Hannah.
9. Thomas.
10. Mary.
11. Margaret.
12. Jesse.
13. Sophronia.

(2) Lena, b. 1815; m. John Muckle.

(3) Cephas, b. Aug. 6, 1812; d. Dec. 8, 1896; m. Mary, dau. of Marcena and Mary Kitchener (b. Oct. 8, 1820, d. Sept. 10, 1897), Jan. 11, 1844, and had

1. Sarah Jane, b. Feb. 11, 1849; Nov. 22, 1876; m. Hiram Baker, March, 1870, and had

(1) Lewis C.; d. in infancy.

(2) Dale P.; d. in infancy.

(3) Mary Louisa, b. Feb. 8, 1873; m. William N. Jennings, and had

1. William H.
2. Sarah Elizabeth.
3. Ralph H.

2. Maty Elizabeth, b. Dec. 26, 1852, Indiana, Pa.

3. Sophronia Craig, b. April 7, 1854; d. Oct. 5, 1897; m. Daniel L. Hoover, and had

(1) Bertha May, who m. Frank Johnson, and had

1. Ruth.
2. Frederick.

(2) Leonora, who m. James A. Dunn, and had 1. Dorothy.

(3) Jane Pearl, who m. Byron B. Daily, and had 1. John Lewis.

(4) Frank.

This family lives in Waynesburg, Pa.

4. Marcena Kitchener, b. Sept. 14, 1857; m. Elizabeth A. Baker, live in Morgan Tp., Pa., and had

(1) Dale Emerson.

(2) Isa Florence, who m. Wiley Bradbury, and had

1. Melvin.
2. Leeta May.

(3) Goldy.

5. Jesse William, b. Feb. 1, 1861, West Bethlehem Tp., Pa.; grad. Allegheney College, taught two years, joined Pittsburg Conference, 1888, and has been in active service since; now at Indiana, Pa.; m. Anna May, dau. of Rev. John G. and Hannah Day Gogley, April 19, 1888, and had (1) Thelma Day, b. Mar. 18, 1899.

III. Hannah, b. April 26, 1747; m. Judge Thompson, an eminent jurist in New Jersey.

IV. Polly, b. 1749; m. Usual Cary, Catskill, N. Y.

V. Phebe, b. 1751; m. James Cooper.

Section 34

Ichabod Cary, son of Dea. Recompense, Sec. 16, b. Bridgewater, 1715; m. Hannah, dau. of Joseph Gannett, 1741; removed to Putney, Vermont.

Children:

I. Seth, b. 1747. Sec. 69-A.

II. Ichabod, b. 1749; m. Miss or Mrs. Smith, and had four sons and a daughter in Colrain, Mass.

III. Aaron, b. April 6, 1751. Sec. 70.

IV. Joshua, b. 1753.

V. Zenas, b. 1755.

VI. Hannah, b. 1758; m. Mr. Coloph of Burgoyne's army.

VII. Mary, b. 1761.

VIII. Daniel, b. 1762.

IX. Ebenezer, b. 1765.

Section 35

Col. Simeon Cary, son of Dea. Recompense, Sec. 16, b. 1719, Bridgewater; was a Captain in the French and Indian War, and a Colonel in the Revolution, and was a man of distinction and influence; m. Mary, dau. of Daniel Howard, 1754, and d. in 1802.

Children:

I. Molly, b. 1755; m. Simeon Keith, 1775, and had Austin Keith, who m. Betsey Copeland, and had Charles Austin Keith, who m. Hannah Copeland, and had

1. Mary Cary Keith, Principal of the School at Campello, Mass.

2. James Copeland Keith, Campello, Mass.

3. Jonathan Bradford Keith, d. Sept. 1, 1875.

II. Mehitabel, b. 1757; m. Bela Howard, 1782.

III. Howard, b. 1760. Sec. 71.

IV. Martha, b. 1765. Sec. 71-A.

V. Rhoda, b. 1772. Sec. 71-B.

Section 36

Zebulon Cary, son of Dea. Recompense, Sec. 16, b. Bridgewater, 1721; m. Mehitabel, dau. of Matthew Gannett, 1747, who d. 1748; m. 2d, Lydia Phillips, 1749; he d. at Ware, Mass., 1759.

Children:
I. Mehitabel, b. 1751. Sec. 71-C.
II. Lydia, b. 1753; m. Mr. Thomas and removed to Ware, Mass.
III. Josiah, b. 1754. Sec. 72.
IV. Zebulon, b. 1755; lost at sea.
V. Recompense, b. Jan. 25, 1757. Sec. 73.
VI. Mary, b. 1758; m. Mr. Oakes, Hawley, Mass.

Section 37

Dea. Jonathan Cary, son of Dea. Recompense, Sec. 16, b. Bridgewater, 1723; m. Mary, dau. of Capt. Joseph Curtis, Stoughton, Mass., 1747. He was remarkable for his probity and exalted Christian character; was a member of the Congregational Church for 70 years, during 60 of which he was Deacon; he d. Feb. 2, 1813, at the age of 90, and his widow at 95.

Children:
I. Moses, b. Nov. 20, 1748. Sec. 74.
II. Mary, b. 1750; d. 1768.
III. Dorothy, b. Dec. 17, 1752.
IV. Jonathan, b. Feb. 14, 1757. Sec. 75.
V. Huldah, b. 1759; d. in childhood.
VI. Alpheus, b. April 21, 1761. Sec. 76.
VII. Huldah, b. Aug. 4, 1763; d. 1775.
VIII. Sarah, b. Aug. 3, 1763; m. 1st, Daniel Alden, Dec. 18, 1786, he died Sept. 10, 1799; m. 2d, L. A. Beal, 1809.
IX. James, b. 1766. Sec. 77.

Section 38

John Cary, son of John, Sec. 17, b. Bridgewater, 1719; m. Mary Hardin, 1741; after the birth of the first two children, they removed to Mendham, Morris County, N. J. He was a carpenter and built the first place of worship in the town. He lived at the foot of the hill, east of the church, on a large farm; his wife d. Feb. 6, 1785, and he m. Elizabeth Riggs Feb. 6, 1786, and d. Aug. 20, 1793.

Children:
I. Isaac, b. Feb. 1, 1742. Sec. 78.
II. Huldah, b. March, 1744; m. Mr. Hedley in Pennsylvania.

III. Susanna, b. May 8, 1746; m. Clement Wood, of New Jersey.
IV. Eunice, b. Feb. 5, 1751; m. N. Wade, Sussex County, N. J.
V. Martha, b. Feb. 26, 1753; d. in childhood.
VI. John, b. July 25, 1757. Sec. 79.
VII. Sarah, b. Mar. 8, 1760; m. Daniel Baxter, of Pennsylvania.

Section 39

Henry Cary, son of John, Sec. 17, b. Bridgewater, 1723; m. Martha, dau. of Joseph Byrom, 1749; settled in Bridgewater, where he d. in 1762.
Children:
I. Benjamin, b. 1750; killed accidentally.
II. Eunice, b. 1758; m. William Snell, 1781.
III. Benjamin, b. 1761.

Section 40

Beriah Cary, son of John, Sec. 17, b. Bridgewater, 1729; removed to Mendham, N. J., with his brother, John, Sec. 38, 1742; m. 1st, Mary Cook, Oct. 16, 1754, at Mendham, Rev. John Dickson officiating; m. 2d, Jane Rogers. He was a Weaver, and from the organization of the church was an Elder and Trustee. The following list is taken from his Bible.
Children:
I. A son, b. July 15, 1755; d. in infancy.
II. A daughter, b. Oct., 1756; d. in infancy.
III. Joel, b. 1758.
IV. Stephen, b. 1760; was a printer in Philadelphia.
V. Thankful, b. 1764.
VI. Hannah, b. 1764; m. Thomas Homan.
VII. Experience, b. 1768; d. Dec. 7, 1869, 102 years old.
VIII. Daniel, b. 1770.
IX. Mary, b. 1771; d. 1785.
X. Samuel, b. 1773; d. Sept. 30, 1792.
XI. Reuben, b. 1774.
XII. Simeon, b. Feb. 22, 1777. Sec. 79-A.
XIII. Elizabeth, b. 1778.
XIV. Rebecca, b. 1778.

Section 41

Eleazer Cary, son of Jonathan, Sec. 18, b. Bridgewater, 1723; m 1st, Betty, dau. of Jonathan Fobes, 1745, who d. 1749; m. 2d, Mary, the widow of Nathaniel Washburne, 1753; he d. 1806.

Children:
I. Caleb, b. 1747.
II. Betty, b. 1754; m. William Perkins,. 1777.
III. Mary, b. 1756; m. Nathan Morton, Esq., 1782, and was the mother of Judge Marcus Morton.
IV. Sarah, b. 1761; d. unm.

Section 42

Jonathan Cary, son of Jonathan, Sec. 18, b. Bridgewater, 1730; m. Lois, dau. of William Hooper, Esq., 1754, and lived and d. in Bridgewater.
Children:
I. Jonathan, b. 1754; d. in the Army of the Revolution.
II. Lois, b. 1760; m. Solomon Keith, 1777; their dau., Clarissa, m. a Mr. Pratt; their dau., Christiana, m. George Washburn, who was a descendant on both his father's and mother's side of John Cary; their dau. is Lucy C. Washburn.
III. Eunice, b. 1760; m. Isaac Washburn.

Section 43

Michael Cary, son of David, Sec. 19, b. Bristol, Jan. 24, 1739; m. Patty Gunsey, Barrington, Mass.; he was a soldier in the Revolutionary War, and a pensioner at his death in 1833.
Children:
I. Ebenezer, b. about 1761. Sec. 80.
II. Nathan, b. about 1767; d. without issue.
III. Mary, b. about 1769.

Section 44

Thomas Cary, son of David, Sec. 19, b. Bristol, Jan. 19, 1735, and was a Cabinet Maker; m. at Smithfield, R. I., about 1764, Sarah, dau. of Obadiah Brown, who was a large landholder and a descendant of Elder Chad. Brown, one of the original Proprietors of the Providence Purchase, and was exiled from Massachusetts with Roger Williams.
Children:
I. Ebenezer, b. 1765; was a sailor, and near the close of the Revolution was pressed on board an English war vessel, and d. in a prison ship.
II. Chad., b. May 17, 1773. Sec. 81.
III. Asa, b. about 1775.
IV. Sally, b. about 1777.

Section 45

Joseph Cary, son of Jabez, Sec. 21, b. Windham, Ct., Sept. 28, 1723; m. Phebe Mack, July 1, 1747; lived in Windham for a time, then removed to Mansfield, Ct., and then to Williamsburg, Mass., about 1765, where he died.
Children:
I. Hannah, b. June 11, 1748; m. Thomas Meekens, July, 1767; had two sons, and d. at Williamsburg, aged 80 years.
II. Phebe, b. Jan. 6, 1750; m. Amasa Graves, July 13, 1769, and had fourteen children; d. at Middlefield, Mass., Aug. 3, 1815.
III. Mary, b. Dec. 5, 1751; m. Joel Wait, and had five children; d. in Ohio, 1836.
IV. Jemima, b. Nov. 21, 1753; m. John Ford, 1771, and had eight children; d. at Middlefield, Mass., Sept., 1849.
V. Elizabeth, b. Mar. 10, 1755; m. Anson Cheesman, 1774, and had eight children; d. in Fredonia, N. Y., Oct. 12, 1841.
VI. Joseph, b. Mar. 7, 1757. Sec. 82.
VII. Richard, b. Jan. 15, 1759. Sec. 83.
VIII. Abner, b. Jan. 21, 1760. Sec. 84.
IX. Triphena, b. Dec. 11, 1763.
X. A daughter, b. Williamsburg, Mass.
XI. A daughter, b. Williamsburg, Mass.
XII. Asa, b. April 1, 1770. Sec. 85.

Section 46

Jabez Cary, son of Jabez, Sec. 21, b. Windham, Ct., July 30, 1727; lived for some years in Mansfield, Ct., then removed to Oneida County, N. Y.
Children:
I. Jabez, b. Oct. 3, 1760.
II. Lydia, b. Sept. 10, 1762.
III. Bela, b. Dec. 2, 1764; m. and had a family in Oneida County, New York.
IV. James, b. April 22, 1766; m. Hannah Alden, May 27, 1798.
V. Martha, b. Jan. 3, 1770.
VI. Samuel, b. May 2, 1772.
VII. Lucy, b. July 5, 1774.
VIII. Olive, b. July 25, 1776; m. Elisha Hamilton, and had
1. Richard, b. June 7, 1798; d. 1884; m. Agnes Beecher, and had
(1) James.   (2) Olive.   (3) Lydia.   (4) Sophia.   (5) Reuben.
(6) Martha, b. Sept. 4, 1832; d. 1897; m. Rev. William S. Goodell, and had
1. Ella.
2. Mary, b. June 18, 1860; m. Walter S. Hartwell, and had
(1) William, b. Sept. 23, 1889.

(2) Marguerite, b. Nov. 12, 1891.
3. George.
(7) Mary.
(8) Charles.
IX. Richard, b. Nov. 22, 1778.

Section 47

Nathaniel Cary, son of Jabez, Sec. 21, b. Windham, Ct., Oct. 23, 1729; resided in Mansfield, Ct., and d. at Willimantic, Ct., at a great age. He m. 1st, Dorcas, dau. of Samuel Marcy, Woodstock, Ct., Sept. 12, 1751, who d. Dec. 13, 1766; m. 2d, Sarah, dau. of Jacob Sargent, Dec., 1767, who d. Aug. 11, 1782; m. 3d, Mrs. Tabitha Root, Willington, Ct., Mar. 18, 1784.
Children:
I. Mary, b. July 16, 1752.
II. Delight, b. Sept. 6, 1754; m. Timothy Fuller, June 14, 1774.
III. Dorcas, b. July 11, 1756.
IV. Nathaniel, b. April 18. 1758; enlisted in the Continental Army, May 12, 1777, for three years, and lost his life in the service.
V. Lucretia, b. Oct. 2, 1760.
VI. Sibbel, b. Oct. 11, 1762.
VII. Sarah, b. Oct. 1, 1764. Sec. 85-A.
VIII. Jerusha, b. Nov. 5, 1768.
IX. Hannah, b. July 5, 1770.
X. Barillai, b. Mar. 5, 1772.
XI. Asa, b. Feb. 11, 1774. Sec. 85-B.
XII. John, b. May 11, 1777.
XIII. Eleazer, b. May 15, 1779.
XIV. Prosper, b. Feb. 7, 1785.
XV. Persis, b. Mar. 15, 1786.

Section 48

Ebenezer Cary, son of Jabez, Sec. 21, b. Mansfield, Ct., 1732; m. Sarah, dau. of Walter Trumbull (b. Mar. 6, 1741; d. Aug. 18. 1830, Batavia, N. Y.), Mar. 30, 1758, and lived in Chaplin, a part of Mansfield; he was Deacon of the church for many years, and was universally esteemed for his probity and pure character. He d. Mar. 16, 1816.
Children:
I. Ebenezer, b. Dec. 27, 1758. Sec. 86.
II. Sarah, b. May 25, 1761; m. Ephraim Grant, Tolland. Ct., and had
1. Sidney.
2. Luther.
3. Calvin.

4. Lucy.

III. Walter Trumbull, b. Aug., 1762; d. in Carolina, unm., 1786.

IV. Lucinda, b. Sept. 6, 1765; d. Feb. 17, 1832; m. W. Kimberly, and had

1. Homer.
2. Ebenezer.

V. Nathan, b. 1767; was educated for the ministry at Brown University, and d. unm. in Georgia.

VI. Damaris, b. 1769; m. E. Williams, of Tolland, Ct., and d. without issue.

VII. Elizabeth, b. 1772; m. John Foote, of Tolland, Ct., and d. Dec. 13, 1852, leaving

1. Olive.
2. John.

VIII. Alfred, b. 1778, and never married; he founded the Cary Collegiate Seminary, at Caryville, N. Y., now Oakfield; he erected two fine stone buildings for the school, and gave them an endowment of $20,000. It was opened in 1844 with 196 students; in 1854 the number had increased to 287; in 1906 it became the Oakfield High School. Col. Cary d. Sept. 17, 1858.

IX. Elsie, b. 1782; d. young.

X. Trumbull, b. 1787. Sec. 87.

Section 49

John Cary, son of John, Sec. 22, b. Windham, Ct., April 12, 1717, and was a very prominent and influential man in "Scotland Parish." He m. Rebecca, dau. of Nathaniel Rudd, Nov. 13, 1740; he d. May 8, 1788, and his widow d. 1797.

Children:

I. Ezekiel, b. Dec. 7, 1741. Sec. 88.
II. Phebe, b. Nov. 14, 1743.
III. Hannah, b. Nov. 15, 1745.
IV. William, b. Oct. 25, 1747. Sec. 89.
V. Jonathan, b. June 5, 1749. Sec. 90.
VI. John, b. Aug. 9, 1751; d. 1776.
VII. Rebecca, b. Dec. 29, 1753; m. Walter Baker and reared a family.
VIII. Esther, b. May 14, 1756; d. 1777.

Section 50

Lieut. Beneijah Cary, son of John, Sec. 22, b. Scotland, Ct., Mar. 7, 1719, a very highly esteemed farmer; m. Deborah Perkins, Feb. 11, 1742; she d. Dec. 5, 1772, and he d. Mar. 11, 1773.

Children:

I. Zillah, b. Dec., 1743; m. Jonathan Kingsley, and was the mother of Prof. Luce Kingsley of Yale.
II. Anna, b. Feb. 14, 1745; d. 1763.

III. Deborah, b. Feb. 17, 1747; m. Mr. Stark, of Franklin, Ct., and had a family.
IV. James, b. Nov. 27, 1750. Sec. 91.
V. Martha, b. May 18, 1755; d. in childhood.
VI. Abigail, b. July 27, 1758; d. 1772.

Section 51

Capt. Nathaniel Cary, son of John, Sec. 22, b. Scotland, Ct., Nov. 1, 1731; was a prominent and much esteemed farmer, and a Captain in the Revolution; m. Jerusha Downer, Jan. 6, 1757, and his widow lived to be more than 90 years old; he d. Nov. 22, 1776. Children:

I. Irena, b. Oct. 2, 1757; d. 1777.
II. Roger, b. Jan. 7, 1759. Sec. 92.
III. Joseph, b. Aug. 19, 1760; was a sea captain, and engaged in the slave trade; d. unm. on the coast of Africa.
IV. Anson, b. Mar. 15, 1762. Sec. 93.
V. Martha, b. Jan. 13, 1764; m. Benjamin Greenslit, and had four children.
VI. Lavinia, b. Sept. 23, 1765; m. Asa Parish, of Vermont.
VII. Philomela, b. Mar. 2, 1767; m. Josiah Geer, and reared a family; d. in old age in Illinois.

Section 52

Dr. Samuel Cary, son of John, Sec. 22, b. Scotland, Ct., June 13, 1734; grad, at Yale, 1755, and his diploma is carefully preserved by his descendants. He was a Physician of eminent skill; m. Deliverance Grant (b. May 23, 1743, Bolton, Ct.), Jan. 7, 1762, and emigrated to Lyme, N. H., 1768; he d. there Jan., 1784, and was buried in the old burying ground on the hill, near the Connecticut River, long since abandoned as a burial place. His widow m. Capt. John Strong, of Thetford, Vt., and had two sons, John, b. Mar. 25, 1787, and Zebulon, b. Sept., 1788. Becoming a widow the second time, she emigrated to Cincinnati, O., in 1802, with her children, Christopher, Samuel, Delia, and William. She d. at the old Cary Mansion, at the junction of Main Street and Hamilton Road, in 1810, and was buried where the First Presbyterian Church now stands, at the corner of Fourth and Main Streets, Cincinnati, O. John and Zebulon Strong emigrated to Ohio in 1809, and both had large families; John d. at 83; Zebulon lived at College Hill.
Children:
I. Christopher, b. Feb. 25, 1763. Sec. 94.
II. Anna, b. May 5, 1765; m. Solomon Howard, a Revolutionary soldier, at Lyme, N. H., and removed with four children to Cincinnati, 1806, and d. at College Hill, 1854. Her descendants are very numerous, among whom are

Rev. Solomon Howard, D. D., long President of Ohio University, and the Hon. R. F. Howard, Xenia, O.

III. Phebe, b. Aug. 25, 1767. Sec. 94-A.
IV. Deliverance, b. Oct. 26, 1769; d. 1828.
V. Hannah, b. Dec. 16, 1771; d. in infancy.
VI. Samuel, b. 1773; d. in infancy.
VII. Mercy, b. Mar. 5, 1776; m. Thomas Weston, of Townsend, Mass., and had a large family. She emigrated with her family to Ohio in 1828, and d. at College Hill in 1830.
VIII. Samuel, b. Nov. 3, 1778; went to Cincinnati, 1802, and was the first Merchant Tailor in town.
IX. John, b. Dec. 26, 1780. Sec. 95.
X. William, b. Jan. 29, 1783. Sec. 96.

Section 53

Josiah Cary, son of Seth, Sec. 23, b. Windham, Ct., June 18, 1729; removed to Haddam, Ct., and m. Hannah Conklin in 1760.
Children:
I. Josiah, b. Jan. 16, 1761. Sec. 97.
II. Polly, b. 1763; m. Mr. Doan.
III. Betsey, b. 1765; m. John Strong.
IV. Thankful, b. 1767; m. Mr. Harden.
V. Hannah, b. 1769; m. 1st. Daniel Brainerd; m. 2d, W. Johnson.

Section 53-A

Moses Cary, son of Seth, Sec. 23, b. Windham, Ct., Dec. 15, 1740; m. Lucy Palmer.
Children:
I. Ebenezer; went South, and when last heard from was at Savannah, Ga.
II. Moses. Sec. 97-A.
III. Lucy.
IV. Daniel; d. in youth.
V. Elizabeth; m. Jacob Bitely, of Fort Edward, N. Y., and had 1. Stephen, b. 1793.
2. Jacob, b. 1795; m. Maudana Hitchcock, 1821, Fort Edward, N. Y., and had
(1) Melville, b. 1822.
(2) Elizabeth, b. 1824; m. Calvin Durkee, 1846, Palo, Mich., and had
1. Byron C.; d. in childhood.
2. Marian E., d. in childhood.
3. Hermione E.; m. Samuel Reeves.
4. Alice Eugenia; m. Ashley Curtis.
5. Emma A.; m. Edward A. Durkee, St. Johns, Mich.

6. Anna C.; m. Milo B. Wetmore.
(3) Almira, b. 1826.
(4) Daniel, b. 1827.
(5) Minerva, b. 1829.
(6) Stephen, b. 1831.
(7) Nancy, b. 1833.
(8) Jerome, b. 1835.
(9) Helen, b. 1837.
(10) Cyrus, b. 1839; m. Lilia Harrison.
(11) Hamilton, b. 1841.
(12) Marian, b. 1844; m Albert Rollstone.
3. Elizabeth, b. 1797.

Section 54

Eleazer Cary, son of Eleazer, Sec. 24, b. Windham, Ct., Aug. 7, 1737; m. Mercy Lathrop, widow of John Fitch, July 19, 1767, and kept a Hotel till his death, Aug. 21, 1782, and his widow continued the business many years, and d. Oct. 2, 1802.
Child:
I. Henry Lucius, b. Oct. 18, 1769. Sec. 98.

Section 55

Nathaniel Cary, son of Eleazer, Sec. 24, b. Windham, Ct., Jan. 17, 1739 m. Zervia, dau. of Thomas Storrs, of Mansfield, Ct., Dec. 5, 1765; lived for some years in Mansfield, where all his children were born, but d. in Windham, 1818; his widow lived to be more than 80 years old.
Children:
I. Clarissa, b. Jan. 1, 1767; m. Benjamin Bibbins, Dec. 31, 1789, reared a family, and d. Jan. 19, 1860.
II. Eleazer, b. Dec. 14, 1769. Sec. 99.
III. Zervia, b. Feb. 6, 1772; d. 1786.

Section 56

Phineas Cary, son of Eleazer, Sec. 24, b. Windham, Ct., Oct. 7 , 1746; m. Mary, dau. of Elisha Hurlbut, Feb. 26, 1769, and emigrated to the State of New York.
Children:
I. Mary, b. Mar. 20, 1770.
II. Anne, b. Oct. 26, 1771.
III. Elisha, b. Aug. 12, 1775.

Section 57

Olivet Cary, son of William, Sec. 25, b. Windham, Ct., Oct. 20, 1761; removed with the family to Lempster, N. H.; m. Bertha Wood, Dec. 31, 1789; he d. at Lempster, 1833, and his widow in 1845. Children:

I. Amanda, b. May 7, 1791; m. B. A. Miner, Jan. 27, 1811, and had one son and four daughters; this son became the Rev. Alonzo A. Miner, D. D., for 13 years the President of Tufft's College, Medford, Mass., and a prominent Universalist minister in Boston for nearly fifty years, and also a strong Temperance advocate.

II. Eunice, b. Aug. 17, 1793. Sec. 99-A.

III. Sophronia, b. Oct. 10, 1795; m. Anson Wheeler, and had two sons and one daughter, Croyden, N. H.

IV. Deborah, b. Jan. 26, 1798; m. John Wheeler, 1823; had one daughter; d. 1833.

V. Fanny, b. Nov. 12, 1801; m. Oliver Newell, 1847.

VI. Bertha, b. Feb. 11, 1803; m. W. S. Bools.

VII. Mary Ann, b. 1806; m. Mr. Winship of Erie county, N. Y.

VIII. Olivet, b. Nov. 6, 1810. Sec. 100.

Section 58

Elliott Cary, son of William, Sec. 25, b. Windham, Ct., Dec. 20, 1763; removed to Lempster with the family, where he was a farmer; m. Anna Roundy, Aug. 8, 1790, and d. 1844.

Children:

I. Lucinda, b. Dec. 12, 1792.

II. Elliott, b. 1794; m. Sally Fletcher, 1820, Lempster, N. H.

III. Lydia, b. Aug. 17, 1796.

IV. Nancy, b. Feb. 17, 1799; d. 1812.

V. Alden, b. 1801. Sec. 101.

VI. John, b. Feb., 1804; d. unm.

VII. Isemirah, b. 1806; d. 1812.

VIII. Willard, b. Sept. 3, 1810; d. in childhood.

IX. Susanna, b. Aug. 13, 1813; m. and left two children; d. Oct. 5, 1850.

Section 59

William Cary, son of William, Sec. 25, b. Windham, Ct., Jan. 4, 1767; went with the family to Lempster, N. H., and became a farmer; m. Jerusha Sabin, Mar. 14, 1795; d. in Lempster, Jan. 9, 1815.

Children:

I. William, b. Feb. 12, 1796. Sec. 102.

II. Jerusha, b. Sept. 9, 1797; d. 1838, Unity, N. H.
III. Byfield, b. Nov. 25, 1799. Sec. 103.
IV. Harvey H., b. May 10, 1802. Sec. 104.
V. Pamelia, b. July 10, 1804; d. 1824.
VI. Minerva, b. Jan. 15, 1807; m. John D. Wellman, M. D., Nov. 22, 1838; d. 1843, Ravenna, O.
VII. John M., b. June 12, 1810. Sec. 105.
VIII. Emeline, b. July 25, 1815; m. Nicholas E. Sargent, Oct. 17, 1832; d. July 28, 1863, Ackworth, N. H.

Section 60

John F. Cary, son of William, Sec. 25, b. Lempster, N. H., Oct. 14, 1777; grad, at Dartmouth, 1800; engaged in teaching for a number of years, then removed to Alexandria, N. Y.; m. Esther Stanton, 1804, and removed to Meadville, Pa., and finally settled on a farm in Chautauqua county, N. Y.; d. suddenly, Sept. 28, 1828.
Children:
I. Ferdinand F., b. Nov. 9, 1805.
II. William D., b. Sept. 7, 1807.
III. Daniel H., b. Aug. 13, 1809.
These sons with their families lived in Chautauqua Co., N. Y.
IV. Esther D., b. 1811; m. Mr. Fowler, and had two sons and a daughter; the sons d. in the Union Army, and the mother moved to Warrensville, Ill.

Section 60-A

John Cary, son of James, Sec. 25-A, b. Kinderhook, Columbia county, N. Y., Feb. 28, 1755, and bapt. in the old Dutch Church by Pastor Petrus Van Driesen, April 23d following. In April, 1775, at Preston, Ct., he enlisted in Capt. Ebenezer Witter's Co., "For the Relief of Boston in the Lexington Alarm," and served six days. On May 19, 1775, he enlisted in the 4th Co., Capt. Obadiah Johnson, 3d Regiment, Col. Israel Putnam. At Cambridge he was transferred to Col. Benedict Arnold's Expedition to Quebec. They left Cambridge Sept. 13, 1775, marching through Medford, Salem, Ipswich to Newburyport, where they embarked for the Kennebec river. "The troops are now at the mouth of the Kennebec, and thus far the journey of these brave men has not been an arduous one, but now is about to be commenced a march which for courage, clear grit, boldness, bravery, patience, suffering, endurance and fortitude, under the most trying and at times painful circumstances, stands, we believe, without a parallel in the world's history."

"The route of Arnold's detachment lay through an unknown wilderness. The march itself was a Campaign—a Campaign against the forest and the flood, against fatigue, sickness, and famine. The contest proved close and pitiless, and the issue remained long in doubt." Quebec was still 300 miles away; but after incredible hardships, they reach the goal of their hopes, and on the night of Nov. 13th, they crossed the St. Lawrence, and with a handful of starving and half-frozen men, they made an attack on that strongest fortification on the Continent! The great disaster came on the night of Dec. 31st, when their supreme effort was repulsed, and some were killed, others taken prisoners or wounded. The long winter passed slowly, and in early May, 1776, the British army and the new naval reinforcements swept them up the St. Lawrence and Lake Champlain.

John Cary reached home in the summer, and buys a farm at Halifax, Vt., adjoining that of his father. Perhaps too enfeebled by the effects of the Campaign of Quebec to keep in the service, he hires a man to go in his place in 1777, and this man was killed at Saratoga. But hearing in his Green Mountain home of the coming of Baum and his Hessians to attack Bennington, he shoulders his musket and trudges over the mountains, only to be just too late for the battle.

Nov. 12, 1780, he marries Mary Rude, at Preston, Ct., Rev. Levi Hart, D. D., a son-in-law of Dr. Bellamy, officiating. From Halifax, .Vt., he removed to Salem, N. Y., and bought a farm,; then, April 29, 1783, he buys another farm at Belcher, N. Y., where he settles, clearing up his farm and rearing a family. He was a good singer, and a devout man, and four of his children became school teachers.

Children:

I. Susanna, b. 1781, Halifax, Vt., who never married; a bright, intelligent woman and a school teacher; lived with her brother George, at Castile, N. Y., where she d. 1847.

II. James, b. about 1783, Salem, N. Y.; was a school teacher and a soldier in the War of 1812-14, and was in the battle of Plattsburg; removed to North Creek, N. Y., where he d. May 6, 1865, a sincere Christian; m. Abigail Leonard (b. May 21, 1790; d. Mar. 23, 1874); they had

1. Nathaniel, who went to Spartansburg, Pa.
2. Thomas, who went to Westfield, N. Y.
3. John, b. Aug. 25, 1813; m. and reared a family at North Creek, and d. July 26, 1872.
4. Alvin, b. Dec. 11, 1814; m. Mary A. —, and lived and d. at North Creek.
5. George, was a soldier in the Civil War; m. and removed to French Creek, N. Y.
6. Patty, b. June 4, 1820; m. Mr. Humes, at North Creek, and had
(1) Olive; m. George Griswold of Pottersville, N. Y.
(2) Emeline; m. Mortimer Tyrell.
(3) Mary Ann.
(4) Lilly.
7. Polly, b. 1824.

III. Catherine, b. 1785 at Belcher; m. George Liddle, and d. at Johnsburg, N.Y., May 29, 1865; they had

1. Mary.
2. Olive, m. John Ward, a Baptist minister, and had two sons and two daughters.
3. Rachel, m. Isaac Morehouse and had seven children.
4. John.
5. George.

IV. Isaac, b. Aug. 27, 1787, at Belcher; m. Anne Barton (b. Aug. 26, 1786; d. Mar. 20, 1864, at Chicago, and bu. at Erie, Pa.), July 29, 1810; he d. Aug. 24, 1830, Mt. Clemens, Mich. He was in the War of 1812-14, under Capt. Cleveland, and in the battle of Plattsburg. They lived in Troy, N. Y., and had

1. Harvey, b. July n, 1811; m. Jane Russell, and had
(1) Isaac.   (2) Anne Jane.   (3) Edward.
(4) Eliza.   (5) Ella.   (6) Harvey.
(7) Warren.   (8) Albert.   (9) Clara.
(10) Ida.   (11) John.   (12) Alice.
Five of these sons became railway men and attained distinction.

2. Phebe, b. June 8, 1813; m. Mr. Rice, and had George, a musician of the Civil War, and d. in the service.

3. Jane, b. Mar. 22, 1815; m. Dea. Daniel E. Ambrose, Co. A, 19th Illinois; d. June, 1886, and she d. Nov., 1893.

4. James Warren, b. April 24, 1818; lived at Troy and Rome, N. Y., where he d. Feb. 15, 1903; m. and had Ella J., who m. Arthur Mengel, Sylvan Beach, N. Y., and had
(1) Warren A.   (2) Ella M.   (3) Frank A.
(4) Arthur.   (5) Leo S.

5. Daniel Barton, b. April 23, 1820; m. Elizabeth Schaffer, who d. Lake Forest, Ill., Dec., 1897; he d. Feb. 21, 1898; they had
(1) Charles.
(2) Mary Elizabeth.
(3) Delia, b. Dec., 1849; m John Bowers, 1871.
(4) Jane, b. June 11, 1852; d. 1871.
(5) Martha Washington, b. Feb. 22, 1855; m. Julius Knox, Feb. 22, 1872; had
1. Elizabeth, b. Dec. 7, 1873; m. James Matson, Oct. 12, 1893.
2. Wilhelmina, b. April 9, 1874; m. Gotlieb M. Luedke.
3. George Edward, b. Dec. 10, 1876; m. Elizabeth Heiple, Nov., 1894, who d. May 12, 1895; m. 2d, Ida Wickousin, Feb. 1, 1899.
4. Julius Frederick, b. May 2, 1878; m. Catherine Meyer, Sept. 19, 1907.
5. William C., b. Dec. 18, 1880; d. in infancy.
6. Alexander Daniel, b. Nov. 20, 1881; m. Katherine Wagstaff, April 3, 1906.
7. Martha Francis, b. Sept. 20, 1883; m. Henry Sherer, Feb. 22, 1903.
8. Eva Irene, b. Feb. 11, 1889; m. Albert Boelke, June 19, 1907.
9. Clarence Harvey, b. Feb. 9, 1891.

10. Crystal Delia, b. Feb. 9, 1891.
11. Dorothy Amelie, b. May 31, 1897.
(6) Jesse, b. Jan., 1856; d. in infancy.
(7) Alice, b. Mar. 21, 1858; m. Andrew Schafifer, Oct., 1873, and had
1. Charles, b. Nov. 16, 1874; m. Gertrude McCormick, May, 1892.
2. Sylvester, b. 1876; d. in infancy.
3. Alice, b. Oct., 1879; m. John Vaughn, 1896.
The mother d. Oct. 18, 1881.
(8) Daniel Isaac, b. Dec. 21, 1860, Troy, N. Y.; m. Wilhelmena Weinburg, June, 1888, and had several children.
(9) Harvey, b. Feb. 14, 1862; m. Laura —, 1890, Mexico, Tex.
(10) Warren, b. Feb. 14, 1862; d. 1871.
(11) Carl, b. April 7, 1868; m. Ella Arnold, 1891, Waco, Tex.
6. Clarissa Olive, b. May 22, 1824, Troy, N. Y.; m. Alex. Adolph Bilinski, Feb. 4, 1857. Count Bilinski was b. in the village of Borsuki, near Balta, Province of Podalia, Poland, Jan. 1, 1814. He took part in the Polish Revolution of 1830-32, was taken prisoner, and after many months' confinement in an Austrian prison, was given the choice of death, or exile to Siberia or America. Choosing the latter, he landed in New York in 1833. In 1834 he entered the military service of the United States at the Arsenal at West Troy, N. Y., rising to the rank of Orderly Sergeant; was often detailed to work that required bravery, and performed the same with honor. Resigned in 1840, and removed to Waukegan, Ill.; in 1849 made the overland trip to California; returned two years later and settled at Diamond Lake, Ill., where he lived till his death, Aug. 13, 1886. They had
(1) Jennie Clara, b. May 28, 1858; m. 1st, John A. Singer, Nov. 1, 1876; m. 2d, Clair D. Vallette, April 14, 1885; they had
1. Jean Etta, b. Feb. 1, 1878.
2. Merritt Alexander, b. Jan. 19, 1880; m. Lillian M. Arentz, Aug. 25, 1901, and had
(1) Jean Eleanor, b. June. 6, 1902.
(2) Annah Olive, b. Dec. 25, 1859; m George N. Gridley, Sept. 27, 1883; had
1. Maud, b. Oct. 6, 1886.
2. Amy Belle, b. Sept. 21, 1888.
V. Olive, b. April 29, 1789; m. Simon Barton, moving to Moriah, N. Y., about 1820; she was a home-loving, industrious, and amiable character, coupled with great good sense and sound judgment, dying July 22, 1867; he was b. at Dudley, Mass., Oct. 30, 1782 (Timothy Stow 4, Timothy 3, Joshua 2, Samuel 1), and d. Sept. 23, 1877; they had
1. William Adams, b. Bennington, Vt., June n, 1808, and d. at Crown Point, N. Y., Jan., 1897; m. Electa Taylor and had eight children.
2. Susanna, b. July 13, 1810; d. Aug. 10, 1892; m. Benjamin Beere, 1826; had
(1) Jane, b. 1828; d. in infancy.

(2) Rosella, b. 1830; d. in infancy.

(3) George W., b. 1832; in Co. H, 34th N. Y., in Civil War; d. 1864, Red Bluff, Cal.

(4) Lyman A., b. 1834; d. 1899.

(5) Olive C., b. 1836; m. John Dolph; live in Iowa.

(6) Byron, b. 1838; d. 1852.

(7) Caroline, b. 1840; d. in infancy.

(8) Horace, b. 1842; d. 1869.

(9) Eliza D., b. 1846; m. Robert Scott, 1874; live in Iowa.

(10) Harriet, b. 1848; d. 1862.

(11) Benjamin F. B., b. 1850; m. Ada Randall; live at Port Henry, N. Y.

(12) Abbie, b. 1851; m. Edgar Lewis, 1880; live in Iowa.

(13) Seth, b. 1853, Chimney Point, Vt.

3. Lyman, M. D., b. Sept. 19, 1812, Belcher, N. Y.; d. Oct. 20, 1899; m. Minerva Lake Akin, Dec. 31, 1840, and had

(1) Elizabeth M.

(2) Abbie Olive.

(3) Ellen.

(4) Susannah Chase, b. Nov. 28, 1848; grad. Vassar, 1875; m. George A. Perry (b. Richmondville, N. Y., June 2, 1845; grad. Wesleyan University, 1874; enlisted in the 91st N. Y., and served in Virginia in the closing Campaign of the Civil War; a Teacher of Greek in New York City), July 22, 1875, and had

1. Ralph Barton, b. Poultney, Vt., July 3, 1876; grad. Princeton, 1896; Professor of Philosophy at Harvard; m. Rachel Berenson, Aug. 15, 1905, and had

(1) Ralph Barton, b. Sept. 29, 1906.

(2) Bernard B., b. Dec. 16, 1910.

2. Edward De Wolf, b. Portland, Me., Oct. 2, 1880.

(5) Sarah Stower.

(6) Lyman Guy, M. D., who is a physician at Willsboro, N. Y.

4. Elmira, b. July 27, 1816; d. 1843; m Harrison McGinnis, and their son was killed at Gettysburg.

5. Olive, b. Feb. 9, 1819; d. 1895; m. Powell C. Helms (b. July 22, 1816; d. July 12, 1889), Sept. 4, 1838, and had

(1) Caroline, b. Mar. 23, 1840; m. Theodore P. Fifield, Jan. 1, 1860, and had

1. Walter.

2. Lester.

3. Howard.

4. Lottie.

5. Loren.

6. Maud.

7. Helen.

8. Jessie.

(2) Selina, b. Dec. 8, 1841; m. Leander Case, Aug. 15, 1860, and had

1. Electa, m. Albert Hair, who was killed; had

(1) Leon.
(2) Carrie.
(3) Kenneth.
2. Charles, m. Frances Williams.
3. Carrie, m. John Wilcox.
(3) Selinda, b. April 16, 1844; d. in infancy.
(4) Jane A., b. Sept. 30, 1846; m. Zachariah S. Brewster, Nov. 22, 1873; m. 2d, Richard H. Emery, and had
  1. Katie, m. Edgar A. Aller.
(5) Charles, b. Dec. 20, 1848; m. Henrietta Arnold, and had
  1. Dora, m. Ralph Silliman.
  2. George, m. Maggie Wilson.
  3. Stellie, m. Ollie Wood.
  4. William.
(6) Barton, b. Oct. 26, 1850; d. 1881; m. Julia Case, who d. 1873.
(7) Simon Earl, b. Jan. 10, 1853; m. Nora Meyers; m. 2d, Carrie Case; they had
  1. Gertrude.
  2. Florence.
  3. Laura.
(8) Lester H., b. July 23, 1857; m. 1st, Mary Allendorf; m. 2d, Rose Arnold.
(9) Leslie, b. July 23, 1857; m Rena Keeler, and had 1. Olive.
6. Mary Ann, b. June 14, 1821; m. Charles B. Morhous, Oct. 7, 1840.
7. Phebe, b. Jan. 25, 1824; m. John Moon, April 12, 1846.
8. Albert, b. Aug. 10, 1826; d. 1896; m. Lydia Peck.
VI. Mary, usually known as "Aunt Molly," b. 1791; never married; was an invalid, lived with her brother John on the old farm; d. July 18, 1849. An earnest student of the Bible.
VII. John, b. Sept. 2, 1793. Sec. 105-A.
VIII. George, b. 1799, at Belcher, and d. Castile, N. Y., 1844; was a school teacher and something of a musician; m. Adaline Burlingham, who d. 1866; they had
1. Benjamin, b. 1828; d. Oct. 18, 1909; in his early life he rafted on the head waters of the Ohio and the Mississippi; m. Miss Marks, who d. 1907; settled at Galesburg, Ill., and had
(1) Adaline, b. 1865.
(2) William Norman, who d. at fifteen.
2. John, b. 1830; m. Mary A. Fish, Feb. 22, 1855; lived on the old farm at Castile, N. Y., and d. Dec. 23, 1906. The two brothers, aged seventy-eight and seventy-six, visited friends in Boston in 1905, to the great pleasure of all. The children of John were
(1) Addie B., who m. Thomas H. Sutherland, Feb. 5, 1880; she d. April 24, 1897, and he d. June 30, following; they had
  1. Frank.

2. Harry J.
(2) Alice M., m. William Burridge, Dec. 30, 1886.
(3) Ida F., m. H. W. Allen, Rockford, Ill.

Section 61

Joseph Cary, son of Benjamin, Sec. 26, b. Bristol, 1736; when a child removed with family to Providence, R. I.; m. 1st, Ruth Carew, 1763, who d. June 24, 1769; m. 2d, Zeruah Hutchins, Jan. 8, 1772, Killingly, Ct.; he removed to Plainfield, Ct., and afterward to Richfield, Otsego county, N. Y., where he d. 1818, and his widow in 1828. Children:
I. Elizabeth, b. Aug. 28, 1764; m. Mr. Hicks, Providence, R. I.
II. Samuel, b. Aug. 18, 1766. Sec. 106.
III. Ruth, b. June 13, 1769.
IV. Joseph, b. Aug. 18, 1773. Sec. 107.
V. Kezia, b. July 31, 1775; d. in youth.
VI. Darius H., b. Mar. 24, 1777. Sec. 108.
VII. William, b. April 12, 1778. Sec. 109.
VIII. Naba, b. April 9, 1782; d. 1813, Plainfield, Ct.
IX. Ezra, b. Aug. 25, 1785. Sec. no.
X. Augustus, b. Feb. 2, 1788; d. without issue, 1857, Middlefield, New York.

Section 62

Dr. Ebenezer Cary, son of Dea. Benjamin, Sec. 26, b. Providence, R. I., 1745; educated at Brown University, and became an eminent Physician; m. 1st, Mary Bentley, Oct. 9, 1766, and removed to Beekman, Dutchess County, N. Y.; m. 2d, Delight Champlin, Nov. 30, 1777. He was talented and of great professional skill, and represented his County in the Legislature in 1781 and 1784, and d. 1815.
Children:
I. Hepzibah, b. Jan. 9, 1767; m. John Smith, of Saratoga County, New York.
II. Lydia, b. Aug. 27, 1768; m. Rufus Sweet, Beekman, N. Y.
III. William, b. Nov. 22, 1769. Sec. 111.
IV. Taylor, b. Mar. 3, 1778. Sec. 112.
V. Lucius, b. Dec. 27, 1775; d. in infancy.
VI. Matilda; m. William Aikin, Grenbush, N. Y.
VII. Cynthia, b. Nov. 17, 1780; m. Joseph Arnold.
VIII. Delight, b. July 5, 1783; d. in childhood.
IX. Sophia, b. June 16, 1784; d. in infancy.
X. Maria, b. Oct. 20, 1787; m. Israel Cook.
XI. Egbert, b. April 12, 1789. Sec. 113.
XII. Helen, b. April 27, 1792; m. Silas German, Poughkeepsie, New York.

XIII. Sturges, b. July 25, 1794. Sec. 114.
XIV. James Rogers, b. Feb. 1, 1798.

Section 63

Nathan Cary, son of Eleazer, Sec. 29, b. Dutchess County, N. Y., 1:755; he was six feet in height, and of a muscular and powerful build; was an early emigrant with his father and brothers to the wilderness of Pennsylvania in 1772; was in the Revolutionary War, and in the memorable battle of Wyoming, but miraculously escaped without injury. He m. Jane Mann, July 11, 1782, and settled in Hanover Township in the Wyoming Valley; in 1769 removed to the headwaters of the Canisteo River, now known as Arkport, Stuben County, N. Y., where he purchased a farm covered with a heavy growth of timber, and here made a beautiful home, where he d. in 1835.

Children:
I. Johnson, b. Mar. 5, 1783. Sec. 115.
II. Eleazer, b. July 8, 1786. Sec. 116.
III. Adam, b. Jan. 1, 1789; d. unm., 1825, Natchez, Miss.
IV. William, b. Feb. 8, 1791. Sec. 117.
V. Christopher, b. June 20, 1794. Sec. 118.

Section 63-A

John Cary, son of Eleazer, Sec. 29, b. Bond's Bridge, Dutchess Co., N. Y., May 7, 1756. Went with his father to the Wyoming Valley, Pa., in 1769; and in 1772 with the family and made it their permanent home. When 18 years of age, and the settlers being in great need of food, he volunteered and went with a body of men over the mountains on foot in mid-winter to the Delaware River for flour; they had to cross the streams by first breaking the ice, stripping and wading through; the load assigned to the lad was 75 pounds.

He enlisted under Capt. Durkee in the Wyoming Company, and served with distinction through the Revolution. Was with Washington at Valley Forge. Late in 1776 the Wyoming Companies were ordered to join Washington in New Jersey with all expedition, and were with him in all his active operations until the summer of 1778. But the danger at Wyoming was so great that these Companies were ordered to the relief of the people in the Valley, but they were too late to reach the scene of action; but the Officers of the Company secured horses, and by rapid riding all night reached the Valley, and being served a hasty lunch by Mrs. Meyers, went into action, and were all killed before sunset!

By the exigencies of the service the two Wyoming Companies were reduced to one; after reaching the Valley, they remained there till Sullivan's Expedition was ordered to proceed against the Western Indians. They accompanied it, and after its return were ordered to join Washington, and remained with him till the close of the War.

John Cary was called the Samson of his Company, and it was claimed by those who knew him intimately that he resembled Washington. He was nursed through a sickness caused by these hardships by Mrs. Susanna (Mann) Green, and afterwards married her, and she became the mother of all his children; she d. in 1815, and he m. Mrs. Priscilla Chrisman, who d. in 1843, and was buried in the Hanover Burying Ground. He soon took to his bed and d. Sept. 15, 1844, and was buried in the Market Street Burial Ground with Military honors.

Children:

I. John, b. 1783; d. Dec. 28, 1808; m. Katherine Vandermark, Feb. 10, 1802; had

   1. Eleazer, d. early.

   2. Miner, d. early.

   3. Susan, m. Mr. Laird; moved to Ohio, thence to Michigan, later to Kansas.

   4. Esther, m. Mr. Jervis; moved to Ohio.

   5. Hannah, b. Dec. 20, 1808. Sec. 63-E.

II. Hannah, m. Nathan Barney; moved to Illinois.

III. Susanna, m. George Gore, son of Capt. Daniel Gore; moved to State of New York, and later to Fulton Co., Ill., where she d. June 8, 1856.

IV. Elizabeth, m. Henry Tillbury; moved to Illinois.

Section 63-B

Samuel Cary, son of Eleazer, Sec. 29, b. Bond's Bridge, Dutchess County, N. Y., 1759; went with the family to Wyoming Valley, Pa., where he enlisted in Capt. Bidlack's Co., and was taken prisoner by the Indians at the Massacre, July 3, 1778. His life was spared on account of his bravery, and he was adopted by the Chief, whose son was killed in the battle, and was given the name of Coconeunquo. He was taken to Canada and remained there four years; falling sick on account of great hardships and an almost entire lack of food, he was set on a stump to be shot, when an old squaw bought him and nursed him back to life, and also aided him to escape;, he was captured by the English and kept a prisoner till the close of the war. He reached home June 29, 1784, where for six long years he had been mourned as dead. He m. Rosanna (Cary) Bennett, his cousin (b. Aug. 22, 1755; d. Sept. 17, 1822), in 1786; m. 2d, Theressa (Gore) Clark, dau. of Capt. Daniel Gore, and widow of Aaron Clark; he d. 1843.

Children:

I. Charity, b. May 20, 1787; m. James Purdy; d. 1875.

II. John, b. Mar. 1, 1790; m. Lois Williams; d. 1856.

III. Samuel, b. April 23, 1792; m. Anna Pickett; d. 1882.

IV. George, b. July 10, 1793; m. Anna Downing, Jan. 2, 1820, and had

1. Manson; m. Abbie Colman.
2. Edmund; m. 1st, Phebe Harned; m. 2d, Elmira Cams.
3. Delilah.
4. Rosanna.
5. Freeman H.
6. Sarepta.
7. Bateman Downing, b. April 22, 1831; served with honor in the Civil War; m. Mary E. Dodder (b. April 7, 1839; d. June 6, 1908), July 6, 1856, and had
(1) Martha M., b. Sept. 26, 1858.
(2) Charles H., b. Oct. 9, 1859; m. Mary Loop,
(3) Lanah D., b. Oct. 10, 1861.
(4) Rosanna S., b. Oct. 15, 1863; m. John Martin.
(5) Alfred E., b. Aug. 27, 1866; m. Miss Loveland.
(6) Edwin E., b. April 27, 1872; m. Laura Morgan.
(7) Ellen, b. April 27, 1872; m. Earnest Evans.
(8) Ira D., b. Dec. 14, 1874.
(9) Ezra A., b. 1876; d. in infancy.
(10) Downing B., b. 1876; d. in infancy.
8. Laura.
V. William, b. Dec. 27, 1795; m.-Searle; d. April 8, 1871.
VI. Nathan, b. Oct. 1. 1797; d. April 18, 1872.
VII. Sarah, b. Oct. 1, 1797; m. Moses Williams; d. May 24, 1888.
VIII. Francis, b. Mar. 14, 1800; d. 1858.
IX. Laura, b. July, 1801; m. Martin Downing, of Wilkes-Barre, Pa.; d. 1887; had

1. Bradley, b. Sept. 2, 1824; m. Jane M. Baker, Sept., 1860; lived at West Pittston nearly 50 years, where he d. 1896; they had
(1) Edwin Martin, b. July 12, 1864; m. Kathryn Polen, Falls, Pa., Sept. 10, 1885, and had
1. Grace, b. Aug. 18, 1886; m. Henry Warren Frey, York, Pa., Aug. 4, 1908, and had Henry W., b. May 24, 1909.
2. Frances, b. Sept. 25, 1889.
3. Wilson, b. 1893.
4. Bradley Cary, b. 1897.
(2) Jessie, b. Mar. 28, 1867; m. C. F. Watrous, Jr., Forty Fort, Pa., Sept. 13, 1894, and had
1. Helen Stuart, b. Feb. 24, 1896.
2. Margaret Cary, b. Dec. 18, 1898.
3. Elizabeth, b. April 15, 1901.
4. Richard Edwin, b. Oct. 9, 1902.
(3) Norman, b. Dec. 22, 1868; m. Kate Reading, Trenton, N. J., 1890, who d. 1898; m. 2d, Lillian Van Ness, Trenton, N. J., at Hartford, Ct.; had
1. Marjorie, b. Oct. 11, 1894.

(4) Louis L., b. Sept. 22, 1870; m. Maud Robinson, Sayre, Pa., Jan. 1896, and had

1. Janet, b. Jan. 5, 1900.
2. John Cary, b. Oct. 6, 1902.
3. Carolyn, b. May 27, 1910.
(5) John T., b. Nov. 29, 1872; m. Juniatta Keefer, Scranton, June 4, 1901.
2. Lemyra.
3. Olive.
4. Martin.
5. Rosanna.

Section 63-C

Benjamin Cary, son of Eleazer, Sec. 29, b. Bond's Bridge, N. Y., 1763; went with the family to Wyoming Valley; was too young to be a soldier, but did guard duty at the Wilkes-Barre Fort during the Massacre. He m. Mercy, dau. of John Abbott; he was a very religious man, a good singer, was very hospitable, and entertained much company; was Commissioner of Luzerne County, 1813-16, and d. possessed of much coal property where the Sugar Notch Breaker now stands.

Children:

I. Nathan, b. at Hanover, 1793; m. Sally Ann Allen; he was a teacher in the public and also singing schools; in 1845 all the family went West, except Elias; they had

1. Selesta; m. John Sliker, who was killed in the Mexican War.
2. Elias, b. April 6, 1819; a carpenter, active in municipal affairs, and blind for many years; m. Sally Ann Patterson, and had
(1) Ebenezer; m. Harriet Shafer, and had
1. Jennie; m. John Wharren.
2. Anna; m. Andrew Husted.
3. Kate; m. J. H. Jones.
4. Milton; m. Gertrude Fulton.
5. Emma; m. Stewart Dunlop.
6. Gussie; d. young.
7. Charles; m. Kate Hoyez.
8. James V.; m. Crissie Simons; he is a locomotive engineer, and the President of the Wyoming and Lackawanna Branch of The John Cary Descendants, and lives at Scranton; they have
(1) James.
(2) Eleazer, who is Agent for a Tea Company.
(3) Helen G.
(4) Arthur; d. in childhood.
(5) Stella.
(6) Alice.

9. Harry; m. Agnes Dean; killed in railway accident, 1907.
10. Estella; m. Andrew Williamson, who died.
11. Elias; m. Bessie Nichols, and had Dorothy.
3. David; m. Sarah Southwick.
4. Waters.
5. Nathan.
6. Byron; m. Martha Grubb.
7. Sarah Ann.
8. Katherine.
9. Amanda.
10. Burton.
II. Nancy; m. Elijah Adams, and went West.
III. Rachel; m. Sira Landing, and went West.
IV. Elias; m. Letitia Smiley.
V. Sarah, b. 1797; m. Bateman Downing, lived in Wisconsin.
VI. Esther; m. Darius Waters.
VII. Martha; m. Peter Mensch.
VIII. Benjamin; m. Jane Smiley.
IX. Celesta; m. Harvey Holcomb.
X. John Abbott, b. 1808. Sec. 118-A.

Section 63-D

Comfort Cary, son of Eleazer, Sec. 29, b. probably at Bond's Bridge, N. Y., 1763; went to Wyoming Valley with his father in 1772; too young to be in the battle, he did duty at the Wilkes-Barre Fort, during the Massacre; m. Huldah, dau. of Phillip Weeks; Mr. Weeks, his son, and four other members of the family were in the Massacre, and all were killed. Mr. Cary was a Local Minister of the Methodist Episcopal Church, had a melodious voice, and great power over the people, and was a founder of the First Church of Wilkes-Barre; he lived at Sugar Notch, now Ashley, Pa., and d. Aug. 30, 1838.
Children:
I. John, b. Sept. 13, 1795; d. 1877; m. Hannah Dickson.
II. Benjamin; m. Katy Askum.
III. Daniel; m. Lovina Dilley.
IV. Lucy; m. Erastus Coswell.
V. Lydia; m. Jacob Worthing.

Section 63-E

Hannah Cary, daughter of John, Sec. 63-A-I, b. Carytown, Pa., now Cary Ave., Wilkes-Barre, Pa., Dec. 20, 1808; d. Dec. 3, 1888; m. Ebenezer Marble, 1830. The Marbles and Carys were of good New England stock, were moral and religious, most of them being Methodists.

Children:

I. Theodore, b. Aug. 10, 1831; d. Nov. 15, 1833.

II. John Miner Cary, b. July 27, 1833.

John Miner Cary Marble, noted above, having lost his father in infancy, with the mother made their home with his great-grandfather, John Cary of Carytown, who d. in 1844; for about two years after this he made his home in Wilkes-Barre, most of the time in school at the Academy and the Kingston Seminary. Late in the autumn of 1846, with his mother he went to Ohio, and soon entered into business, part of the time as clerk, and afterward as partner in several concerns. Soon after the passage of the National Bank Act, he established the First National Bank of Delphos, O.; later he came into control of the First National Bank of Van Wert, and the Van Wert National Bank. He also built up from nothing and managed a railway system of 346 miles in length.

He was Colonel of the Allen County Regiment of the Ohio National Guard, afterwards mustered into the United States service as the 151st U. S. I., the principal service being in the defence of Washington, as noted in the Official Records of the War of the Rebellion, Series 1, Vol. 37, Part 2.

The health of his family demanding a change of climate, he removed to California in 1888, where he established and controlled The National Bank of California, until he retired after a business career of more than fifty years. All these Banks are still in existence, having successfully withstood every financial storm. His home is at Los Angeles.

He m. 1st, Lizzie, dau. of Dr. Guilford D. and Myrilla (Skinner) Colman of Lebanon, O., 1860, who d. 1865; m. 2d, Elizabeth, dau. of Dr. Charles and Margaret (Bavman) Emerson, May 5, 1870.

Children:

I. Guilford Lionel, b. 1862; d. Nov. 22, 1902; m. 1st, Nora, dau.

of Gen. Sherwood; m. 2d, Cora May De Puy, and had

1. John McKinley.

2. William Baird, b. Feb. 4, 1901.

II. John Emerson, m. Miriam Maclaren, July 27, 1901, and had

1. John Maclaren.

2. Miriam.

III. Elizabeth Dana, b. 1874; for some years a Missionary in India.

IV. William, b. 1879; m. Jean Dickinson, 1906, at Brookline, Mass., and had

1. William Cary, b. 1908.

2. Fayette Dickinson.

Section 64

Ezra Cary, son of Ezra, Sec. 30, b. Morris County, N. J., 1735; m Lydia Thompson, and removed to Western Pennsylvania, 1777; thence with the first settlers to Marietta, O., and then to Shelby County, where he d. 1828.

Children:
I. Phebe, b. 1771; m. Mr. Harris; d. in Coshocton County, Ohio.
II. Rufus, b. 1773; m. and had a large family, living to old age; his son John lived in Putnam County, O.
III. Cephas, b. 1775. Sec. 119.
IV. Ephraim, b. about 1777, and lived in Indiana.
V. Absolom, b. about 1782, and d. young.
VI. Elias, b. about 1786, and lived in La Salle County, Ill.
VII. George, b. 1795. Sec. 120.

Section 65

Ezra Cary, son of Zechariah, Sec. 31, b. Bridgewater, April 7, 1749; m. Cynthia Brett, Stoughton, Mass.; after the birth of two children they removed to Turner, Me.; his wife d. and he m. 2d, Cynthia Tolman, about 1776; he was a highly respected Farmer.
Children:
I. Thomas, b. 1771. Sec. 121.
II. Zachary, b. 1773. Sec. 122.
III. Cynthia, b. 1775; d. in infancy.
IV. Luther, b. 1777; d. 1860.
V. Susanna, b. 1779; m. Mr. Dresser, Turner, Me.
VI. Ezra, b. 1782. Sec. 123.
VII. Daniel, b. 1785.
VIII. Cynthia, b. 1788; m. Mr. Newhall, Turner, Me.
IX. John Shepherd, b. 1790. Sec. 124.
X. Bethuel, b. 1793. Sec. 125.
XI. Tolman, b. 1796.

Section 66

Maj. Daniel Cary, son of Zachariah, Sec. 31, b. Bridgewater, June 11, 1758; m. Mehitabel, dan. of Simeon Brett, and about 1800 removed to Turner, Me.
Children:
I. Zebiah, b. July 31, 1779; m. Capt. Roger Sumner, 1801.
II. Eunice, b. Sept. 10, 1781; m. Grenfell Blake, 1804, Turner, Me. Sec. 126-A.
III. Olive, b. April 18, 1783; m. Apollas Howard, 1802.
IV. Francis, b. May 5, 1785. Sec. 126.
V. James, b. Aug. 28, 1787; d. in infancy.
VI. John, b. Aug. 28, 1787; d. in infancy.
VII. Zachary, b. April 1, 1791; d. in youth.
VIII. Daniel, b. Sept. 3, 1793; d. in childhood.
IX. Avey, b. Feb. 15, 1795; m. Dr. W. B. Bradford, July 5, 1855, Auburn, Me.

Section 67

Dr. Luther Cary, son of Zechariah, Sec. 31, b. Bridgewater, 1761; m. Abigail, dau. of Benjamin and Deliverance King, of Raynham, Mass., and removed to Oxford Co., Me., 1798; was a Physician, studied with James Freeland, Sutton, Mass., a man of distinction, and for many years a Judge; d. July 13, 1848, his wife having d. May 30, 1837. Children:

I. Cassander, b. 1782. Sec. 127.
II. William, b. Mar. 14, 1784. Sec. 128.
III. Sophia, b. Nov. 17, 1785. Sec. 128-A.
IV. Anselm, b. June 8, 1787. Sec. 129.
V. Emmelia, b. Mar. 13, 1789. Sec. 129-A.
VI. Alanson, b. Dec. 23, 1790. Sec. 130.
VII. Hugh, b. Oct. 17, 1792. Sec. 131.
VIII. Maurice, b. Nov. 15, 1795. Sec. 132.
IX. Harrison, b. 1797; d. in infancy.
X. Clara, b. Oct., 1799; m. Rev. J. P. Richardson, and d. 1831, leaving three children.
XI. Luther, b. 1801; d. in infancy.
XII. Nabby, b. 1803; d. in infancy.

Section 68

Ephraim Cary, son of Ephraim, Sec. 32, b. Bridgewater, 1748; m. Jane, dau. of John Holman, 1771; had a large family and removed to Minot, Me., where he d. 1828.

Children:
I. Jane, b. 1773; m. Zenas Keith, 1792.
II. Salome, b. 1774; m. R. Kingsley, 1794.
III. Cyrus, b. 1777; m. Nabby Keith, 1802, and went West.
IV. William H., b. May 12, 1779. Sec. 133.
V. Ephraim, b. 1782. Sec. 134.
VI. Shepard, b. 1784; d. in infancy at Dorchester, Mass.
VII. Susanna, b. 1787; m. John Eaton, 1812, Dorchester, Mass.
VIII. Francis, b. 1789; m. Harriet Hayward, 1816, East Bridgewater, Mass.
IX. Jason, b. 1791; d. in infancy.
X. Asenath, b. 1793; went to Minot, Me.; d. unm.
XI. Harmony, b. 1796; m. James Watson, 1821.

Section 69

Lewis Cary, son of Daniel, Sec. 33, b. Morris County, N. J., Oct. 23, 1742; lived on the paternal estate, and in 1777 bought 200 acres of land near

Drakesville, where he d. Sept. 27, 1817. He m. Isabel Carson (b. Jan. 14. 1757; d. May 30, 1840).

Children:

I. Daniel, b. 1770; d. in infancy.
II. Jacob, b. July 7, 1772; d. unm. 1823.
III. Jane, b. July 14, 1775; m. Mr. Drake, and d. 1854 at Princeton, Illinois.
IV. Joseph, b. Oct. 7, 1777. Sec. 135.
V. Sally, b. Dec. 4, 1779; m. Mr. Rhoades, and d. Feb. 8, 1806, Sussex County, N. J.
VI. Abel, b. June 13, 1781. Sec. 136.
VII. Lewis, b. Oct. 19, 1783. Sec. 137.
VIII. Aaron, b. Sept. 26, 1785. Sec. 138.
IX. John, b. Mar. 7, 1788. Sec. 139.
X. Ezra, b. Nov. 29, 1789; d. 1844; m. and had Lewis E., who d. unm. 1846.
XI. Daniel, b. May 29, 1791. Sec. 140.
XII. Martha, b. May 24, 1793; m. Mr. Gale and lived in Indiana; d. 1881.
XIII. Nancy, b. Aug. 26, 1795; m. 1st, Mr. McCauley; m. 2d, Mr. Mitchell, Richland Co., O.
XIV. Lurany, b. Nov. 23, 1796; m. Mr. Merriam, Wyandotte Co., O.
XV. George L., b. June 30, 1799. Sec. 141.
XVI. Ann Eliza, b. Oct. 3, 1801; m. D. P. Merchant, Morris Co., N. J., who d. Mar. 30, 1880; she d. Jan. 11, 1884.

Section 69-A

Seth Cary, son of Ichabod, Sec. 34, b. Bridgewater, 1747; m. and lived in Putney, Vt.; he was a Bible student, but does not seem to have united with any church; was by trade a Tanner, and he and his wife were buried in the little cemetery adjoining the farm of Mrs. M. M. Bacon. Mr. Edward M. Cary, Red Oak, Ia., gives the following facts: He was in Vermont with his family for a vacation, and as he went into the country store an elderly man said to him, "You are a Cary." When asked how he knew, he said that he had their hair and make-up. He then told a story that his father had told him about a Dea. Cary, of Townsend. The old Deacon had a cart, the wheels of which made a great creaking and frightened horses. A neighbor had a spirited horse that was terrified at the sight of the old cart. One night when this horseman was out, this man and another took the old cart and put it into the driveway; when the man returned the horse would not go in, and he said it must be the cart, which he found to be true. This man further said that a Cary girl married William Bacon, of Putney, and on writing to him a letter was received from his widow, as he had been dead for twenty years; and from the facts she gave him, and what he found in "Cary Memorials," he was enabled to trace his family line.

Children:

I. Seth, b. Mar. 17, 1775, Putney, Vt. Sec. 141-A.

II. George, Rochester, Vt.

III. Zenas; was a Physician, and for many years lived in Troy, N. Y., where he was burned to death in his own house.

IV. Zebulon, Haverhill, N. H.

V. Thomas G., b. Sept. 23, 1784; m. Abi Harris; was a Tanner, lived at Chesterfield, N. H., and d. at Claremont, Feb. 22, 1862; they had

1. Abia H., b. Sept. 12, 1788; d. 1868.

2. Zenas W., b. April 23, 1810; d. 1832.

3. Charles W., b. Feb. 2, 1813; m. Luthera M. Leet, and lived at Charlestown and Claremont, N. H.; d. 1862; they had

(1) Edward M., b. Oct. 5, 1843, at Haverhill, N. H., now a merchant at Red Oak, Ia.; m. Lucy Ann Clark, of Williston, N. H., and their son, Charles E., m. Carrie E. Gilman, and have one daughter; he is a merchant, Glenwood, Ia.

(2) Dora E.; m. Mr. Stone, Indianapolis, Ind.

(3) Sarah E.

4. Mary A., b. July 8, 1815.

5. Julia A., b. Sept. 29, 1819.

6. Sophia Cornelia, b. Sept. 6, 1822; m. Dr. Edward C. Dyer, Spencer, Mass., and had

(1) Carolyn E.; m. William Edward Cooper, New York City.

(2) Sarah Worcester; m. Eddy W. Prouty, Spencer, Mass. She d. Oct. 6, 1909, a noble woman.

7. Emily A., b. July 30, 1824; m. Dr. Silas Allen Sabine, Claremont, N. H., and had

(1) Grace Isabel, Claremont, N. H.

8. Charlotte H., b. Sept. 20, 1826; m and had dau., Mrs. James O'Neil, Lawrence, Mass.

9. Sarah E., b. Mar. 17, 1834.

VI. Joseph; removed to Michigan, where he died.

VII. Lydia; m. Ebenezer Perry, and lived and d. in Putney, Vt.

VIII. Harry; was Deacon of the Church at Townsend, Vt., where he lived and died.

Section 70

Aaron Cary, son of Ichabod, Sec. 34, b. Bridgewater, April 6, 1751; removed to Colrain, Mass.; m. Jemima Atwood, of Middleboro, Mass., May 31, 1781; d. on Catamount Hill, Colrain, Sept. 30, 1830, and his widow d. Feb. 19, 1837, almost 83 years old.

Children:

I. Zenas, b. Nov. 26, 1782. Sec. 142.

II. Susanna, b. June 20, 1783; m. Mr. Burns, and d. in Ohio.

III. A son, b. Jan. 23, 1785; d. in infancy.

IV. A son, b. Jan. 23, 1785; d. in infancy.
V. Hannah, b. Nov. 5, 1787; m. E. Prouty, Heath, Mass.
VI. Levi, b. May 12, 1790; killed in the battle of Tippecanoe, Ind., 1811.
VII. Charlotte, b. Nov. 15, 1797; d. in childhood.

Section 71

Capt. Howard Cary, son of Col. Simeon, Sec. 35, b. Bridgewater, 1760; m. Huldah, dau. of Samuel Packard, 1785; he was Justice of the Peace, member of the Constitutional Convention, and the first Representative of North Bridgewater, now the City of Brockton, to the Great and General Court of Massachusetts.
Children:
I. Simeon, b. 1787. Sec. 142-A.
II. Daniel Howard, b. 1788. Sec. 142-B.
III. Zenas, b. 1790, and removed to Maine; m. and had two sons, Franklin and Howard, who went to California, and d. there.
IV. William, b. 1792; m. Miss or Mrs. Alden.
V. Elbridge, b. 1794; d. in infancy.
VI. Francis, b. 1796; m. Miss or Mrs. Alden.
VII. Molly, b. 1798. Sec. 142-C.
VIII. Rhoda, b. 1800. Sec. 142-D.
IX. Ziba, b. 1802; d. in youth.

Section 71-A

Martha Cary, dau. of Col. Simeon, Sec. 35, b. Bridgewater, 1765; m. Benjamin Keith, 1788.
Children:
I. Arza; m. Marcia Kingman, and had
1. Albert, Campello, Mass.
2. Arza Benjamin; m. Mary Ann Cary. Sec. 279-A.
II. Bela; m. Mary Kingman, and had
1. Ellen Sherman, who m. Jonas Reynolds and had
(1) Abbie Keith, who m. George W. Higgins.
(2) Mary Louise.
(3) Martin E., who m. Lulu M. Sladen.
III. Ziba; m. 1st, Sally Cary; m. 2d, Polly Noyes.
IV. Polly; m. Franklin Ames.
V. Jason; m. Susie Smith.
VI. Charles; m. Mehitabel Perkins, and had
1. Charles Perkins; m. Mary Keith Williams, and had
(1) Sarah Williams, who m. Frederic W. Park, and had 1. Charles Milton.

2. Anna R.; m. Theodore Lilley.

3. Rhoda P.; m. Barnabas H. Gray.

4. Sanford; m. Maggie Harvey.

5. Damaris W.; m. Vinal Lyon, and had

(1) Ellis Vinal, who m. and had

1. Arthur Vinal Lyon, A. M., M. D., Brockton, Mass.

(2) Martha Ann; m. E. B. Fanning.

(3) Rev. Granville W.; m. Sallie Hart.

(4) Mary W.; m. Rufus E. Packard.

(5) Abbie J.; m. Sylvester O. Snyder.

(6) Chloe Richmond; m. Lysander Franklin Gurney, June 3, 1866, and had

1. Frank Lyon, b. July 2, 1867; m. Cornelia Churchill, 1892; Instructor in Bridgewater Normal School.

2. Merton Studley, b. April 14, 1869; m. Ella G. Packard, and have three children; President Gurney Bros. Cor.

3. Sanford Keith, b. Oct. 30, 1875; grad. Boston University, '97; m. Mabel Crocker and had two children; Treas. Gurney Bros. Cor.

The descendants of Col. Simeon Cary and his daughter, Martha, are naturally and genealogically descended from the old Puritan stock, in their stanch adherence to the rigid principles of their forefathers. They are almost without exception adherents of the Congregational Church, moral, religious, as well as unusually public spirited, giving liberally of time and money toward the best interests of the community in which they dwell, are filling positions requiring education, unusual executive ability, and good judgment; are shrewd, positive, and aggressive, but tempered with reason and charity, and are exerting influence for good in their day and generation.

Among these descendants of the last three generations we find five clergymen, one colporteur, seven Sunday school superintendents, seven professors and school teachers who make it their occupation, and six others who have taught at some time; two graduates of Normal School, one of West Point, about thirty from High School, one physician, one dentist, one senator, one mayor, two aldermen, eight musicians including choristers, leaders, organists, and trained singers; two postmasters, and other occupations representing tanners, farmers, carpenters, grocers, hardware merchants, watchmakers, shoemakers. These include thirteen shoe manufacturers, a singular fact being that their names are all Keith.

The territory comprising Campello, a part of Brockton, Mass., was included in the original grant set off to the Rev. James Keith, who was the first pastor, and remained 56 years, an ancient proprietor of Bridgewater; and the land upon which it is built all belonged originally to the Keith family, and descendants of the Rev. James Keith. Of the five sons and one daughter of Benjamin Keith and Martha Cary, four located in Campello, and have since been identified with the growth of the town.

Section 71-B

Rhoda Cary, dau. of Col. Simeon, Sec. 35, b. Bridgewater, 1772; m. Richard Wild, 1794.
Children:
I. Rhoda Cary; m. Ambrose Marshall, and had
1. Elizabeth L., who m. James W. Dickerman, and had
(1) Grace; grad. Boston University, 1895! m Prof. Homer Holcomb, Harvard, 1894, Fredonia, N. Y., and had
1. Lorraine, b. May 22, 1902.
2. Cary Whitney, b. Oct. 18, 1903.
(2) Sarah Elizabeth; m. Rev. Sylvester Hamilton Day, Chautauqua, N. Y.
(3) Anna L.; m. Everett Polsey, Somerville, Mass., and had
1. Hope Elizabeth.
2. Gladys Sterling.
3. Anna Joycelyn; d. in infancy.
II. Almira, b. July 13, 1806, North Easton, Mass.; d. Oct. 12, 1845; m Hayward Marshall (b. Mar. 8, 1800, North Bridgewater, now Brockton; d. April 13, 1876), Dec. 25, 1826, and had
1. Olive Hayward, b. Feb. 28, 1838; m. Fred Lucius Trow, East Bridgewater (b. Aug. 21, 1833; d. July 3, 1905), and had
(1) Frederic Stickney, b. April 25, 1849; d. i n infancy.
(2) Lizzie Florence, b. May 3, 1856; d. Jan. 20, 1884.
(3) Anna M., b. April 17, 1858; m. Henry T. Cushman, Oct. 6, 1882, and had
1. Marshall Laurence, b. Jan. 7, 1884, a Surgeon, Lansing, Mich.
(4) Eugene Torry, b. May 16, 1861; d. in infancy.
Mrs. Trow descends from the Carys on both sides of the family.
2. Eugene, b. July 10, 1832; m. Lizzie Williams, Nov. 14, 1856, who d. Oct. 22, 1895; they had
(1) Ella F., b. Sept. 15, 1858; d. in childhood.
(2) Hayward, b. July 15, 1870.
(3) Ethel, b. Mar. 18, 1880.
III. Eliza; m. Mr. Williams, and had
1. Jane; m. Mr. Warner, and had
(1) Jane Frances; m. William Edward Staples, Nov. 8, 1871, and had
1. Everett Churchill, b. July 16, 1874; m. Ila Louise Tunnicliff, 1896, and had
(1) Clarence Warren, b. 1897.
(2) Lloyd Everett, b. 1899.
2. Edward Francis, b. Oct. 14, 1876.

Section 71-C

Mehitabel Cary, dau. of Zebulon, Sec. 36, b. 1751; m. Joseph Allen, 1771, and lived in East Bridgewater; she d. 1799, and he d. 1826. Children:

I. Zebulon.
II. Susanna.
III. Mehitabel; d. young.
IV. Mehitabel; m. Ezra Phillips, 1809, South Hanson, Mass.; she d. June 22, 1812; he was killed by lightning, July 6, 1856; they had
1. Ezra, b. 1810; m. Catherine, dau. of Dr. Tilden, of Hanson, and had
(1) Calvin Tilden.
(2) Morrill Allen, a Tack manufacturer; m. Sophia Simmons, 1879, who d. 1901; they had
1. Catherine Tilden.
2. Ada Richmond.
3. Sophia Simmons.
4. Fannie Hitchcock.
(3) Catherine.
(4) Charles Follen.
(5) Alfred.
2. Mehitabel, b. 1811; m. Charles Beals, of Livermore, Me., 1836, and had
(1) Lucy Pratt; m. William Field, of Elmwood, Mass., 1876.
(2) Charles Roscoe; m. Mary Trescott, who d. 1894; he d. 1901;they had
1. Charles Elmer.
(3) Hannah Leavitt, Brockton, Mass.
(4) Nathaniel, d. 1848.
(5) Diana Phillips; m. William Stetson, of Brockton, 1875
(6) George Cary; m. Fannie Holmes, 1881, and had
1. Elton Holmes.
2. Anna Phillips.
3. Grace Hayward.

Section 72

Josiah Cary, son of Zebulon, Sec. 36, b. Bridgewater, 1754; removed to Brookfield, Mass., in youth; m. Molly Moulton, 1780, who d. 1795; m. 2d, Lydia Hale.
Children:
I. Zebulon, b. Oct. 5, 1781. Sec. 143.
II. Josiah, b. April 7, 1783. Sec. 144.
III. Polly, b. Mar. 22, 1785; m. Samuel Horrs, 1805; d. April 25, 1808.
IV. Patty, b. Mar. 16, 1787; m. Mr. Cummings, and d. Dec. 26, 1846.
V. Avery, b. Feb. 17, 1789. Sec. 145.
VI. Luther, b. Dec. 20, 1793; he was m. three times, and had a son, Luther, who d. in infancy, and a daughter, Mary Anna, who m. Timothy M. Duncan; he lived in North Brookfield, Mass., and d. Sept. 12, 1869.
VII. Lydia, b. Mar. 17, 1797; m. James Titus, 1834, and d. July 29, 1852.

VIII. Jonathan, b. Sept. 10, 1798. Sec. 146.//
IX. Mordecai, b. Oct., 1799; m. Betsey Bruce, 1832; no children; lived at West Brookfield, Mass.//
X. Thomas, b. Aug. 15, 1802. Sec. 147.

Section 73

Recompense Cary, son of Zebulon, Sec. 36, b. Bridgewater, Jan. 25, 1757; went to Ward, Mass., now Auburn; he was a mechanic, a soldier of the Revolution, engaged in mercantile pursuits, represented his town in the Legislature, and was an official member of the Congregational Church. While on a visit to a dau. in Erie Co., N. Y., he d. Dec. 13, 1836, leaving the legacy of a good name to his children. He m. Anna Drury, 1789.//
Children://
I. Zebulon, b. July 26, 1790; m. Martha Baird, and had no children; was a prominent, honored, and useful man; his widow went to Macon, Ga.//
II. Leonard, b. April 2, 1793. Sec. 148.//
III. Clarissa, b. Sept. 19, 1797; m. Rev. Isaac Oakes; lived in Livingston Co., New York.//
IV. Eliza, b. July 17, 1802; m. Rev. Mr. Cannon, of Geneva, N. Y., who was District Secretary of the American Board for 28 years; had two daughters, both of whom married.

Section 74

Moses Cary, son of Jonathan, Sec. 37, b. Bridgewater, Nov. 20, 1748; m. Susanna, dau. of Jabez Field. 1773. In 1824 he published a pamphlet containing a sketch of the families of North Bridgewater, which Gen. S. F. Cary says was useful in perfecting "Cary Memorials." He d. 1838.//
Children://
I. Lucius, b. July 28. 1776; grad, at Brown University, 1798, studied law and removed to Charleston, S. C., and d. April, 1806.//
II. Barzillai, b. Aug. 25, 1780. Sec. 149.//
III. Susanna, b. April 27, 1783; m. Rev. John Shaw, 1807.//
IV. Polly, b. Nov. 13, 1785; m. Jonathan Beals, and d. 1850.//
V. Cassandra, b. Feb. 1, 1789; d. unm. 1862.

Section 75

Jonathan Cary, son of Jonathan, Sec. 37, b. Bridgewater, Feb. 14, 1757; m. Abigail, dau. of Jonathan Perkins, 1784; he was a Revolutionary soldier, and drew a pension till his death, Dec. 25, 1852. Children://
I. Huldah, b. 1785; m. Darius Howard.

II. Caleb, b. 1788. Sec. 150.
III. Jonathan, b. 1791. Sec. 151.
IV. Luther, b. 1794. Sec. 152.
V. Martin, b. 1795. Sec. 153.
VI. Abigail, b. 1789. Sec. 153-A.
VII. Sally; m. Ziba Keith.
VIII. Mary. b. Mar. 13, 1797. Sec. 153-B.
IX. Aurelia, b. about 1802; d. in infancy.
X. Nancy, b. 1804; d. in infancy.

Section 76

Alpheus Cary, son of Jonathan, Sec. 37, b. Bridgewater, April 21, 1761; m. Ruby Perkins, Sept. 21, 1786; lived in Quincy, Mass., more than 30 years, but d. in Milton, Mass., Nov. 1, 1816; his widow d. in Boston, 1836.
Children:
I. Nancy, b. July 7, 1787; m. Lemuel Hall, and had one son, H. B. Hall, Westford, Mass., and two daughters; d. 1862.
II. Alpheus, b. Nov. 4, 1788. Sec. 154.
III. Lucy, b. April 3, 1790; m. Hazen Morse, Nov. 6, 1814, and had eleven children, and d. July 28, 1860.
IV. Charles, b. Sept. 26, 1794.
V. George, b. 1795; d. in infancy.
VI. Ruby, b. 1795; d. in infancy.
VII. George, b. Sept. 25, 1796; d. unm. in Boston.
VIII. Lewis, b. Mar. 31, 1798. Sec. 155.
IX. Ruby, b. Jan. 16, 1800; d. unm. June 17, 1847, Haverhill, Mass.
X. Isaac, b. June 25, 1802. Sec. 156.
XI. Ziba, b. June 25, 1802; d. unm. Nov. 10, 1831.
XII. Abigail, b. Mar. 1806; m. Mr. Frobisher, had a son and dau., and d. April 27, 1829.

Section 77

James Cary, son of Jonathan, Sec. 37, b. Bridgewater, April 22, 1766; m. Hannah, dau. of Samuel Alden, 1798, and had a daughter; his wife dying, he m. 2d, Hannah, dau. of Thomas Wales, and had three other children.
Children:
I. Lydia, b. 1800; m. Ephraim Howard, 1821.
II. Otis, b. June 14, 1804. Sec. 157.
III. Nancy, b. Feb. 24, 1807. Sec. 157-A.
IV. Austin, b. Oct. 1, 1809. Sec. 158.

Section 78

Isaac Cary, son of Jonathan, Sec. 37, b. Bridgewater, Feb. 1, 1742; when a child went to Mendham, N. J.; inherited half of his father's farm, and moved to Sussex Co., N. J.; m., and d. in 1791.
Children:
I. Abram, b. about 1762. Sec. 159.
II. Isaac, b. about 1764.
III. Jacob, b. about 1766.
IV. Joseph, b. about 1768.
V. Martha, b. about 1770.
VI. Phebe, b. about 1772; m. Mr. Bosley.

Section 79

John Cary, son of John, Sec. 38, b. Morris Co., N. J., July 25, 1757; m. Joanna Lyon, Dec. 28, 1778; lived on the homestead, where he d. 1824.
Children:
I. Henry, b. Jan. 6, 1780. Sec. 160.
II. Clement, b. May 22, 1782. Sec. 161.
III. Nathaniel, b. Nov. 23, 1784; d. in infancy.
IV. Nathaniel, b. Dec. 5, 1786. Sec. 162.
V. David, b. Feb. 25, 1789; d. in childhood.
VI. Mary, b. Sept. 8, 1791; m. Rev. Ezra H. Day, 1814, and moved to New Albany, Ind.; he d. 1823, and she m. Maj. Silas Miller, who d. 1855, and she returned to Morristown, N. J. There were three children by the first marriage.
VII. John, b. Sept. 3, 1794; d. in childhood.
VIII. John, b. May 27, 1797. Sec. 163.
IX. Isaac, b. Aug. 16, 1799; d. in infancy.
X. Isaac, b. Nov. 18, 1800. Sec. 164.

Section 79-A

Simeon Cary, son of Beriah, Sec. 40, b. Mendham, N. J., Feb. 22, 1777; removed to Redstone, Pa., 1795; m. Rachel Merritt, May, 1805; moved to Dodds, Warren Co., O., 1809, where he d. July 27, 1830, and was buried in the old Kirby Graveyard.
Children:
I. Joel, b. 1806; m. Rhoda, dau. of Lemuel and Osee (Drake) Gray, 1829; she was b. 1809, Essex Co., N. J., and d. Lebanon, O., 1862; he d. at the home of his son Samuel, 1879; they had
1. Simeon, b. 1830; m. Ruth Cornell; he was a Physician, in Green Co., O.
2. Osee, b. 1832; m. James C. Merritt, 1851, Springboro, O.

3. Daniel, b. 1833; d. in infancy.

4. Samuel, b. 1835; m. 1st, Hannah Earnheart, 1861; m. 2d, Mary Deulinger, 1870, and had

(1) Hallock, b. 1862; d. in infancy.

(2) Effa, b. 1863; m. David Boyer, 1884.

(3) Jacob, b. 1865.

(4) Joel, b. 1868; d. 1871.

(5) Charles, b. 1871.

(6) Edward H., b. 1874.

(7) Lizzie Almeda, b. 1876.

(8) William Stanton, b. 1879.

5. Jonathan, b. 1837; d. 1840.

6. Abraham, b. 1840; d. 1841.

7. Rachel, b. 1842; d. 1859.

8. James P.; d. in infancy.

9. Amos L., b. 1846; m. 1st, Huldah Pennywit, of Dayton, O.; m. 2d, Lydia Mercer, 1872, and had

(1) Minnie Florence, b. 1873.

(2) Elizabeth Etta, b. 1876; d. 1878.

(3) Lester J., b. 1879; d. in infancy.

(4) Chester L., b. 1879; d. in infancy.

(5) Alice M., b. 1882.

(6) Morrell Homer, b. 1887.

10. Lydia Alice, b. 1848; d. 1859.

11. Rhoda, b. 1851; d. in infancy.

II. Abraham, b. 1807; m Mary Ann, dau. of Samuel and Elizabeth Powell (b. in New Jersey, 1818; d. Lebanon, O., 1876); they had

1. John, b. 1841; d. 1843.

2. Stephen, b. 1843; d. 1866.

3. Thomas, b. 1846; m. Sally Shelly, of Dodds, O.; lived on the old farm, and had

(1) Edith, b. 1880.

(2) Herbert, b. 1882.

(3) Grace, b. 1883; d. in infancy.

(4) Pearl, b. 1886.

4. Leander, b. 1849; m. Mary Emily, 1879, and had

(1) Bertha, b. 1880.

(2) John Walter, b. 1881.

5. Rachel Jane, b. 1833; m. David Kirby, 1872.

6. Oliver, b. 1856; d. 1884.

III. Isaac, M. D., b. 1815, Utica, O.; grad. Cincinnati Med. Col., 1847; m Osee, dau. of Lemuel and Osee (Drake) Gray; d. at Dalton, Ind., 1853; they had

1. George, b. 1838; m. Laura Hastough, 1862, Lebanon, O., and had

(1) Harry Waldo, b. 1868; m. Lydia Drake, 1895, and had 1. Kathryn, b. 1902; live at Springfield, O.

2. Amzi, b. 1840; m. Ellen Bowman, 1864, and had

(1) Ada, b. 1865; m. James Moore, 1887; m. 2d, Jasper Lamb; lived at Prescott, Wash.; she d. 1906; they had

1. Miriam.
2. Lois.
3. John.
4. Reed.

(2) Frank B., b. 1871; m. Anna Surber, 1896, and had

1. Frances Louisa, b. 1906.

(3) Ralph, b. 1890.

3. Jane, b. 1842; m. Alpheus Barrett, 1869, Sioux City, Ia., and had

(1) Eda, b. 1870; d. about 1900.
(2) Mattie, b. 1873; m. Liston Alvord, Emporia, Kan.
(3) Bertha, b. 1877, and is a teacher.
(4) Harry Sylvester, b. 1881.

4. Volney, b. 1844; m. Arrilla Carter, Glasco, Kan., and had

(1) Minnie, b. 1866; m. L. M. Garman, 1883, Minnesota, Kan., and had

1. Earl.
2. Beulah.

(2) Clara, b. 1867; m Mr. Jaquis, 1887, Ottawa Co., Kan.
(3) Eva.
(4) Rolla, b. 1874.
(5) Clarence, b. 1876; d. in Kansas.
(6) Walter, b. 1877.
(7) Maud, b. 1879.
(8) Letha, b. 1882.
(9) Viola, b. 1884.
(10) Lou, b. 1886.

5. Liston D., b. 1846; m. 1st, Lizzie Ward, 1875; m. 2d, Cynthia Messimore, 1877; m. 3d, Mrs. Louisa M. Elliott, 1895; live in Minneapolis, Kan.; they had

(1) Liston D., b. 1875; m. Bertha Cook, 1898, and had

1. Robbie, b. 1899; d. in infancy.
2. Geneva H., b. 1900.
3. Fern Elizabeth, b. 1904.

(2) Mabel Anna, b. 1877; m. William H. Harper, 1895, and had

1. Lauren J.

(3) Luther Messimore, b. 1879; m. Elizabeth Rost, 1905, and had

1. Henry Stephen.

(4) Warren M., b. 1895.
(5) Milo Glen.

6. Martha, b. 1848; m. J. M. Sycks, 1873, and had

(1) Carrie Mabel, b. 1874; d. 1876.

(2) Anna Alpha, b. 1877; m. Howard Winters, of Ironton, O., 1906.
(3) Dana Dow, b. 1880; m. Daisy ___, St. Louis, 1905.
(4) Grace Cary, b. 1883.
(5) Mary Josephine, b. 1890.
7. Warren, b. 1850; m. Annie Crawford, of Dayton, O., 1879; he d. 1888; they had
(1) Earl Thresher, b. 1880; d. 1883.
(2) Eben Matlack, b. 1883.
(3) Alice.
8. Byron, b. 1852, Dayton, O.
IV. Joshua, b. 1815; m. Lydia, dau. of Henry and Amy Earnheart, 1843, a wealthy farmer living at Lebanon, O.; d. 1888; they had
1. William Henry, b. 1844; m Charlotte Kirby, of Dayton, O., 1869, and had
(1) Neta Inez, b. 1870.
(2) Anna Elizabeth, b. 1872.
(3) Trillena, b. 1875.
(4) Nancy Alice, b. 1885.
2. John Harris, b. 1850; m. Sarah Marsh, of Waynesville, O., 1874, and had
(1) Howard, b. 1875.
(2) Nannie L., b. 1880.
(3) Ivy, b. 1883
(4) Esley Ames, b. 1885.
3. Howard Ellis, b. 1855; d. 1857.
V. Jane, b. 1811; d. young.
VI. Anna, b. 1813; m. Samuel Gray, 1835; she d. Toledo, O., and he at Lebanon, O., 1870; they had
1. Martha Jane, b. 1843; m. Oliver Perry Bowman, 1863; be d. Toledo, O., 1904; they had
(1) Perla Gray, b. 1870, at Tippecanoe City, O.; Prof. of Domestic Science in Ohio State College; m. William D. Gibbs, Columbus, O., 1901; removed to Durham, N. H., where Mr. Gibbs is President of the State College, 1902; they had
1. Thomas Bowman, b. Dec. 11, 1906, Durham, N. H. (2) Walter H., b. 1874, Emporia, Kan.; grad. University of Mich., 1896; Dentist at Elmhurst, Ill.

Section 80

Ebenezer Cary, son of Michael, Sec. 43, b. Barrington, Mass.; m. about 1765; lived and d. in Barrington.
Children:
I. Nathan, b. about 1814.
II. Ebenezer, b. about 1816. Sec. 165.

Section 81

Chad. Cary, son of Thomas, Sec. 44, b. Smithfield, R. I., May 17, 1773; he was a farmer, and m. Elizabeth Smith, of Providence, R. I., Jan. 16, 1791; she was a talented woman and the author of a number of poems; he d. in North Killingly, Ct., Sept. 5, 1839.

Children:

I. Anna, b. Jan. 9, 1792; m. Amasa Olney, of Providence, Jan. 1, 1816, and had six children; d. in Weir, Mass.

II. Polly, b. April 30, 1794; m. Andrew Burlingame, a farmer, of Scituate, Mass., Mar. 22, 1821, and had six children; lived at Putnam, Ct.

III. Ebenezer, b. Aug. 6, 1797. Sec. 166.

IV. William, b. Mar. 28, 1799. Sec. 167.

V. George S., b. Sept. 6, 1801. Sec. 168.

VI. Susan T., b. Aug. 17, 1803; m. William Walker, of East 1 Woodstock, Ct., May 15, 1835.

VII. Elizabeth, b. April 21, 1805; m. Charles Hibbard, a farmer, of North Woodstock, Ct., May 25, 1834, and had two children.

VIII. Sally S., b. Nov. 7, 1806; m. Noadiah Flint, a farmer, of Thompson, Ct., Mar. 22, 1829, and had two children.

IX. Abby T., b. July 7, 1808; m. Leonard Thompson, a merchant, of Columbia, Ct., Oct. 17, 1831, and had

1. Bradford Thompson, M. D., Surgeon U. S. A. during the Civil War; later practiced in New York City.

2. Elizabeth; m. Sewell Green, a retired gentleman in New York, Oct. 28, 1863.

X. Emeline, b. Nov. 7, 1809.

XI. Almira, b. Oct. 17, 1811.

XII. Chad. B., b. April 17, 1813. Sec. 169.

XIII. John H., b. May 1, 1816. Sec. 170.

Section 82

Joseph Cary, son of Joseph. Sec.45, b. Mansfield, Ct., Mar. 7,17575 m. Rachel Thompson, Jan. 7, 1781, Canterbury, Ct.; removed to Middlefield, Mass., and later to Ontario, Wayne Co., N. Y., where he d. Feb. 3, 1848, and his widow d. Sept. 26, 1851. He was Chaplain in the Revolution.

Children:

I. Rachel, b. Mar. 31, 1782; m. Ethan Billins, of Conway, Mass., and had four children.

II. Joseph, b. Jan. 19, 1784. Sec. 171.

III. Lucy, b. Dec. 1, 1785; m. William Mott of Middlefield, Mass., and had one son and four daughters.

IV. Stephen, b. Oct. 6, 1787; m. and had one son and two daughters, and d. in New Orleans, 1814.

V. Ezekiel, b. April 1, 1789.

VI. Hannah, b. Jan. 3, 1792; m. Mr. Scott and had five children.

VII. Eunice, b. Jan. 15, 1795; m. Mr. Wright.

VIII. Phebe, b. Sept. 15, 1797; m. Mr. Frazer and had five children.

IX. Zina, b. Feb. 1, 1799; m. Mr. Gill and had four children.

X. Isaac, b. Sept. 15, 1804. Sec. 172.

Section 83

Richard Cary, son of Joseph, Sec. 45, b. Mansfield, Ct., Jan. 15, 1759; m. Susanna Ford at Williamsburg, Mass., 1782, who d. 1826; m. 2 d, Mrs. Lucy Doolittle; removed to Nelson, Madison Co., N. Y., and in 1806 to Boston, Erie Co., N. Y. For seven years he was a soldier in the Revolution; was at Monmouth with Washington, and at Valley Forge he lost the toes from both feet by being frozen. He was a religious man, and sometimes acted as minister when death came to the cabins of his scattered pioneer neighbors.

Children:

I. Susanna, b. 1784; m. Calvin Doolittle, 1803, and d. in Illinois, 1858.

II. Lucy, b. 1786; m. Nathaniel Streeter, 1804; d. in Erie Co., N. Y., 1809.

III. Phebe, b. 1788; m. Jonathan Bump, in Boston, Erie Co., N. Y., where she d. 1843 5 had

1. Lucy, b. 1814; m. Mr. Avard.

2. Alva.

3. Philander, m. Phebe Upper, and had

(1) Arktiles.

(2) Alexander.

(3) Amanda; m. Nelson Carl.

(4) Emeline; m. Mr. Brett.

(5) Margaret; m. William B. Brooks, at Boston, Erie Co., N. Y., and had

1. Egbert M.

2. Eugene.

3. Lucy Maud; m. Charles Taylor Knight, June 14, 1892, at Deadwood, South Dakota, and had

(1) Ima; at 17 is in Berlin studying Music. The family live in Denver, Colo.

4. Harry.

IV. Clarissa, b. 1790; m. Talcot Patchin, an officer in the U. S. Army, who was wounded in the battle of Chippewa, July 5, 1814; lived in Erie Co., N. Y.

V. Calvin, b. June, 1792; he was killed in a hand to hand fight with three Indians, at the burning of Buffalo, N. Y., in 1813; he was a man of giant frame, weighing 300 pounds, fine proportions, herculean in strength, and a swift runner.

VI. Richard M., b. Dec. 11, 1794. Sec. 173.

VII. Luther H., b. Feb., 1800. Sec. 174.
VIII. Relief, b. 1802; m. William Titus, 1821; d. 1838.

Section 84

Abner Cary, son of Joseph, Sec. 45, b. Williamsburg, Mass., Jan. 31, 1760; m. four times in Williamsburg; removed to Dupage Co., Ill., where he d. in 1845.
Children:
I. Lucina, b. Feb. 22, 1793; m. William W. Leonard of Middlefield, Mass.
II. Abner L., b. at Junction, Ill.
III. Alvin.
IV. Lucy.
V. Sally.
VI. Asa.

Section 85

Asa Cary, son of Joseph, Sec. 45, b. Williamsburg, Mass., April 1, 1770; m. Damaris Hickox, June 24, 1790, Conway, Mass.; removed to Erie Co., N. Y., where he d. Sept. 19, 1852; his widow d. April 17, 1863, aged 91 years.
Children:
I. Truman, b. May 31, 1791. Sec. 175.
II. Sylvia, b. June 17, 1793; m. Aaron Adams, Dec. 24, 1809; had five sons and one daughter, and lived in Boston,-N. Y.
III. Asa, b. July 18, 1795; d. in youth.
IV. Joseph, b. Dec. 24, 1797. Sec. 176.
V. Sylvester E., b. May 5, 1800. Sec. 177.
VI. Harriet, b. Jan. 13, 1803; m. Erastus Torrey, Oct. 8, 1821, Boston, N. Y.; had six children, and d. July 30, 1850, Silver Creek, Ill.
VII. Van Renssalaer, b. Jan. 5, 1805. Sec. 178.
VIII. Damaris, b. Mar. 31, 1807; m Perry J. Jencks, Sept, 9, 1823; had eight children, and lived at Wapau, Wis.
IX. Aurelia, b. Oct. 11, 1809; m Hiram Hemmenway, Sept. 6, 1827; had three children, and d. at Freeport, Ill., Mar. 30, 1858.
X. Saduska, b. Jan. 6, 1812; m. Tillinghast Vaughn; had six children, and lived in Louisiana.
XI. Almira, b. Aug. 8, 1814; m. Rev. George Wilkinson; had five children, and d. Jan. 22, 1848, Painted Post, N. Y.
XII. Asa, b. Aug. 22, 1821. Sec. 179.

Section 85-A

Sarah Cary, dau. of Nathaniel, Sec. 47, b. Oct. 1, 1764; m. 1st, Ebenezer Bush; m. 2d, Zacheus Barnum.

Children:

I. Erastus Wolcott Barnum, b. Sept. 18, 1793; d. Nov. 7, 1875; m. Sarah Julia Hand (b. June 20, 1786; d. Feb. 14, 1855), and had

1. Julia H. Barnum, b. Dec. 6, 1820; d. Sept. 21, 1907, Nevada City, Cal.; m. Dr. William Kent, Sept. 15, 1841, at Shoreham, Vt., and had

(1) Elizabeth Julia Kent, b. Nov. 1, 1844, at Shoreham, Vt.; d. May 7, 1887, Nevada City, Cal.; m. Francis Power, Atty. (b. Mar. 31, 1831; d. Mar. 18, 1902), Dec. 26, 1867, Nevada City, Cal., and had 1. E. Barnum Power, b. Nov. 22, 1869, at Nevada City, Cal.; now Assistant Attorney-General of State of California; m. Minerva Lester, Dec. 19, 1895, and had

(1) Lester Barnum Power, b. Nov. 30, 1897, Oakland, Cal. The home in San Francisco, Cal.

Section 85-B

Asa Cary, son of Nathaniel, Sec. 47, b. Mansfield, Ct., Feb. 11, 1774, and removed to Shoreham, Vt.; m. Anna Sanford, Feb. 7, 1799, and had nine children, all b. in Shoreham; his wife d. Oct. 3, 1852, Racine, Wis., and. he d. there Sept. 15, 1862.

Children:

I. Bushnell B., b. Dec. 22, 1801; d. Feb. 15, 1860, Racine, Wis.

II. Alfred, b. Jan. 25, 1804; d. Jan. 6, 1887, Racine, Wis.

III. Paulina, b. Aug. 25, 1805; d. Jan. 4, 1859, Sterling, N. Y.

IV. Nathaniel C., b. Sept. 10, 1807; removed to Mansfield, Ct., where he m. Sophia Eaton, June 14, 1829; removed to Sterling, N. Y., where were b. two sons

1. Lucius C., b. Feb. 23, 1832; removed to Racine, Wis., where he m. Emile Barton Kenea, Aug. 15, 1856; he d. Sept. 7, 1872, at La Cygnie, Kan.; they had

(1) Henry Nathaniel, b. Feb. 11, 1858, Racine, Wis.; removed to Chicago and m. Susie Louise Wustenfeldt (b. Aug. 23, 1861), Sept. 9, 1884; was connected with the "Morning Telegraph," New York, now with "The Republic," St. Louis, Mo.; they had

1. Emilie Alice, b. Dec. 8, 1892.

(2) Alfred Roswell, b. Aug. 18, 1859; d. unm. Jan. 13, 1894, La Cygnie, Kan.

2. Alfred L., b. July 23, 1835; removed to Milwaukee, Wis., where he m. Harriet Maria Van Slyck, Sept. 6, 1864, and had

(1) Robert John, b. Feb. 6, 1868; unm., Chicago.

(2) Walter, b. April 26, 1871; New York.

(3) Harriet Sophia, b. Oct. 2, 1873; m. Charles L. Jones, Milwaukee, Wis.

(4) Irving B., b. Sept. 27, 1875; Milwaukee.

V. Levi S., b. July 23, 1809; d. 1882, Springfield, Wis.

VI. Melanchton W., b. Oct. 26, 1811; d. 1885, Racine, Wis.

VII. Mary Ann, b. April 22, 1814; d. 1873.

VIII. John Watson, b. Feb. 11, 1817; m. 1st, Eliza Vilas, July 10, 1844, who d. May 12, 1845; m 2d, Isabel Brinkerhoff, June 6, 1847. Mr. Cary was grad. Union College 1842; admitted to the Bar 1844; removed to Wisconsin 1850, and elected to State Senate 1852; removed to Milwaukee, where he resided for thirty years, and became one of the leading lawyers of the State, and was regarded as one of the best equipped railway lawyers in the country, having argued many notable cases before the Supreme Court of the United States. He finally made his home at Hinsdale, Ill., where he d. Mar. 29, 1895; their children were

1. Eliza Vilas, b. May 10, 1845; m. Sherburn Sanborn. June 1, 1870.

2. Frances, b. Sept. 10, 1848; m. Charles D. Kendick, June 6, 1878.

3. Hon. Melbert Brinkerhoff, b. July 23, 1852, Racine, Wis.; moved with parents to Milwaukee 1859; grad, from Princeton 1872; practiced law, and became Asst. General Solicitor of the Chicago, Milwaukee & St. Paul Railway Co.; m. Julia Metcalf, April 28, 1880; removed to New York City in 1883, and established his home at Ridgefield, Ct., 1888; published Cyclopedia of Political Economy, and United States History in three volumes; wrote and published a volume entitled The Connecticut Constitution; was nominated for Governor by the Democratic Party in 1902; nominated for United States Senator in 1903; they had

(1) Julia Madeline, b. July 12, 1882; m. Donald Eliot Curtis, New York City, Oct. 3, 1903.

(2) Isabel Frances, b. Aug. 29, 1884; m. Henry A. Stone, New York City, May 29, 1907.

(3) Caroline, b. Nov. 22, 1887; d. in childhood.

(4) Melbert Brinkerhoff, b. Nov. 28, 1892.

4. Fred Asa, b. Racine, Wis., Mar. 25, 1857; grad. Princeton 1878, in real estate business Chicago; m. Elspeth Wilson Ferguson, Milwaukee, Dec. 7, 1881, and had

(1) Florence Ferguson, b. Milwaukee, Sept. 11, 1883.

5. John Watson, b. Milwaukee, Nov. 11, 1862; grad. Princeton 1886; in advertising business. New York City; m. Mae Alice Stone, Chicago, Oct. 2, 1889, and had

(1) Margaret Stone, b. Yonkers, N. Y., Jan. 5, 1894.

6. George Peter, b. Milwaukee, June 11, 1864; practiced law several years, now in real estate in Pasadena, Cal.; m. 1st, Margaret Lalor, Hinsdale, Ill., Oct. 12, 1898, who d. June 29, 1904; m. 2d, Florence Ross, Pasadena, Dec. 21, 1908; they had

(1) Margaret, b. Pasadena, June 25, 1904.

7. Paul Van Ettan, b. Milwaukee, Sept. 3, 1867; grad. Ann Arbor, 1887; a prominent lawyer in Appleton, Wis.; m. Caroline Madgeburg, Milwaukee, Sept. 14, 1898, and had (1) Paul Van Ettan, b. Appleton, Oct. 30, 1902.

8. Isabel Brinkerhoff, b. Oct. 30, 1869; d. in childhood.

IX. Sarah A., b. Dec. 26, 1818; d. 1887, Racine, Wis.

Section 86

Ebenezer Cary, son of Ebenezer, Sec. 48, b. Mansfield, Ct., Dec. 27, 1758; was a Revolutionary soldier, and in 1798 went with Joseph Ellicott to western New York as a Surveyor for the Holland Land Company; when over 60 years of age he m. Mrs. Elizabeth Cunningham; he d. May 16, 1825.
Children:
I. Sarah, b. 1819; m. John D. Verplanck, reared a family, and d. 1859, Brooklyn, N. Y.
II. Lucinda, b. 1824; d. unm. Jan. 5, 1849.
III. Ebenezer, b. 1826. Sec. 180.

Section 87

Trumbull Cary, son of Ebenezer, Sec. 48, b. Mansfield, Ct., Aug. 11, 1787; removed to western New York, m. Margaret E. Brisbane, June 2, 1817, Batavia, N. Y. He served as Adjutant in the War of 1812-14, and rendered honorable service in both branches of the Legislature; he was appointed Bank Commissioner by Gov. Seward in 1838, and held the position for three years. His wife d. June 22, 1863, and he d. June 20, 1869.
Children:
I. Walter, b. 1818. Sec. 181.
II. Elizabeth, b. Feb. 24, 1822; d. in infancy.
III. Elizabeth Ann, b. June 13, 1824; d. in infancy.
IV. Trumbull, b. Oct. 4, 1829; d. in childhood.

Section 88

Ezekiel Cary, son of Dea. John, Sec. 49, b. Scotland, Ct., Dec. 7, 1741; lived in Willimantic, Ct., and was a tanner and shoemaker; m. Zervia, dau. of Nathaniel Skiff, Mar. 15, 1764; his wife d. July 16, 1816, and he d. May 14, 1827.
Children:
I. John, b. June 7, 1766; was a shoemaker, removed to Baltimore, Md., where he d. in middle life, unm.
II. Diantha, b. July 14, 1768; m. Andrew Baker.
III. Waldo, b. April 3, 1772. Sec. 182.

Section 89

William Cary, son of John, Sec. 49, b. Scotland, Ct., Oct. 25, 1747; m. 1st, Irena, dau. of Josiah Manning, May 16, 1771, who d. Nov. 17, 1795; m. 2d, Celia (Darby) Bushnell, widow of Ezekiel Bushnell, Lisbon, Ct., March, 1801; he d. July 20, 1812, and his widow Oct. 12, 1844.

Children:
I. Alathea, b. Dec., 1773; d. 1795.
II. Chloe, b. Jan. 20, 1776; d. 1795.
III. John, b. Mar. 18, 1778. Sec. 183.
IV. Elijah, b. Oct. 4, 1780. Sec. 184.
V. William, b. Dec. 11, 1782. Sec. 185.
VI. Theron, b. 1786; d. 1809.
VII. Nathaniel, b. 1789; d. 1834.
VIII. Phebe, b. 1791; d. in childhood.

Section 90

Jonathan Cary, son of Dea. John, Sec. 49, b. Scotland, Ct., June 5, 1749; m. Martha, dau. of Elisha Hurlbut, Sept. 21, 1775, and in 1791 removed to Norwich, Ct., where he died.
Children:
I. Irena, b. Aug. 17, 1777; m. Capt. Elias Lord, Norwich, Ct.
II. Thomas, b. July 8, 1779; d. at sea, unm.
III. Alfred, b. June 29, 1781; d. at sea, unm.
IV. Frederick, b. Feb. 14, 1786. Sec. 186.
V. Ralph, b. June 2, 1789. Sec. 187.
VI. Fanny, b. July 26, 1791; m. Capt. James Snow, New York.
VII. Winthrop, b. 1793; m. and d. at sea.

Section 91

Capt. James Cary, son of Beneijah, Sec. 50, b. Scotland, Ct., Nov. 27, 1750; was a prominent and wealthy farmer and served with distinction in the Revolution. His estate was valued at $80,000. He m. 1st, Abigail, dau. of Joseph Kingsley, Pomfret, Ct., Aug. 12, 1773, who d. Dec. 18, 1807; m. 2d, Mrs. Anna (Spaulding) Bradford, widow of Rev. William Bradford, 1809; he d. Feb. 28, 1827.
Children:
I. Abigail, b. Jan. 28, 1775; m. Parker Morse, Oct. 6, 1798; lived in Canterbury, Ct., and had five children.
II. James, b. Dec. 9, 1777. Sec. 188.
III. Beneijah, b. Jan. 4, 1780; d. 1808.
IV. Anna, b. Feb. 21, 1782.
V. Sanford, b. July 14, 1784. Sec. 189.
VI. Sally, b. Sept. 7, 1786; m. Thomas Morse, Woodstock, Ct.

Section 92

Roger Cary, son of Capt. Nathaniel, Sec. 51, b. Scotland, Ct., Jan. 7, 1759, was a trader and speculator, and d. in the South. He m. Eunice Parish, Jan. 27, 1780.
Children:
I. Nathaniel, b. Sept. 16, 1780.
II. Joseph, b. July 4, 1783.
III. Eunice, b. Dec. 3, 1787; m. Mr. Storer, and settled at Cherry Valley, N. Y.

Section 93

Anson Cary, son of Nathaniel, Sec. 51, b. Scotland, Ct., Mar. 15, 1762; m. Hannah Carew, Norwich, Ct., and was an early settler in Oxford, Chenango Co., N. Y., where he resided till his death, May 8, 1842. He was a blacksmith, a man of unusually large and muscular frame, of great strength physically and mentally. Was a Justice of the Peace twenty years, Sheriff of the County four years, and for several years a Judge; a very prominent and useful citizen.
Children:
I. Horatio, b. Mar. 27, 1785. Sec. 190.
II. Minerva, b. Oct. 17, 1787; m. Amos A. Franklin, and removed to Grant Co., Wis.; had seven children, and d. May 25, 1859.
III. Harriet, b. July 29, 1789; m. A. B. Bennett, had two sons, and d. Aug. 9, 1863.
IV. George A., b. May 8, 1793. Sec. 191.
V. Palmer C., b. Mar. 31, 1798. Sec. 192.
VI. Zalmon S., b. Aug. 31, 1800. Sec. 193.
VII. Hannah, b. June 17, 1802.
VIII. Albert G., b. July 20, 1807; m. Melissa Madison, and had three children; lived at Oxford, N. Y.

Section 94

Christopher Cary, son of Dr. Samuel, Sec. 52, b. Windham, Ct., Feb. 25, 1763; went with the family to Lyme, N. H., then almost a wilderness. He joined the Army of the Revolution at a very early age, serving under Col. Waite of New Hampshire; was twice taken prisoner, and suffered incredible hardship. Removed to Ohio in 1802, and settled in Cincinnati. He was pre-eminently a child of misfortune; when very young he accidentally lost an eye, and a few years later, being caught under a falling tree, was made a cripple for life. Of a roving disposition he never seemed contented in any place, and an accurate sketch of his life would be more thrilling than a romance. He had a stout frame, an iron constitution, and d. Feb., 1837, near Cincinnati; m. 1st,

Elsie Terrel of Lyme, N. H., 1784; m. 2d, Leah Brokaw in Cincinnati; m. 3d, Margaret McCarty, 1825. Was a Revolutionary pensioner.

Children:

I. Lucy, b. 1784; m. James McGinnis, and had several children, one of whom, Mrs. William McCammon; d. at an advanced age.

II. Robert, b. Jan. 24, 1787. Sec. 194.

III. Beneijah, b. 1788. Sec. 195.

IV. Maria, b. 1790; m. John Loring, 1808.

V. Christopher, b. 1792; killed accidentally at Cincinnati, 1807.

VI. Irwin, b. 1826. Sec. 196.

VII. Maria, b. 1828.

VIII. Anna, b. 1831; m. Mr. Sprong, and d. in Missouri, 1864.

Section 94-A

Phebe Cary, dau. of Dr. Samuel, Sec. 52, b. Scotland, Ct., Aug. 25, 1767; went with the family to Lyme, N. H., 1768; m. John Crary of Norwich, Vt., who descended from John McCrary, but dropped the first part of the name. She was a large strong woman, with black hair and eyes, and very pious and both were Methodists. The Carys, Crarys, and Ballards together went to Cincinnati, where they settled near each other; at that time there was only the old Stone Church in the place, and was on Sycamore St. She d. 1822.

Children:

I. Benjamin.

II. John, was a grad, of Dartmouth, and a large man of fine physique, as were his sons, having dark hair and eyes; m. Roxanna Ballard (b. 1793 at Fairhaven, Vt.), Jan. 28, 1814, and had

1. John Williamson, a lawyer, who lived in Florida, where he died.

2. Oliver Beale, d. unm. in New Orleans.

3. Murray Ballard.

4. Benjamin Franklin, b. 1829; a Methodist Minister, Editor of the Central and California Christian Advocates, President of Wisconsin University, and member of many General Conferences.

5. Joseph Alexander, d. in Florida.

6. Truman Bishop, d. in Asheville, N. C.

7. Olive Jane, d. unm. at New Orleans.

8. Clarinda.

9. Loretta Cary, b. 1831, and was for many years a writer for the religious and secular press, both in prose and verse; m. Francis Sadler, 1851, and lived at Pearl River, La.; they had

   (1) Everett M., b. Feb. 28, 1853.

   (2) Olive Olin, b. July 14, 1855.

   (3) John Cary, b. Feb. 22, 1857.

   (4) Ella M., b. Feb. 11, 1860.

   (5) Hattie F., b. June 14, 1862.

(6) Alice Cary, b. Mar. 20, 1865; m. Mr. McKinney, Rushton, La., and is Editor of the White Ribboner of Louisiana.
(7) Ida Cary, b. May 16, 1874.
10. Celesta.
III. Lyman, lived on College Hill, O.
IV. Samuel.

Section 95

John Cary, son of Dr. Samuel, Sec. 52, b. Lyme, N. H., Dec. 26, 1780; removed to Hudson, N. Y., where he resided many years; thence to Ohio, and d. at Ashtabula, Mar. 23, 1863; m. 1st, Harriet Knapp of Hudson, N. Y., 1806, and late in life m. again.
Children:
I. Orrin, b. July 16, 1807. Sec. 197.
II. Harriet, b. 1809; m. Mr. Lockwood, lived in Ashtabula, had a large family, and d. 1863.
III. Franklin, b. 1811, and did not marry; went to Louisiana.
IV. Lorenzo, b. 1813. Sec. 198.
V. Delia, b. 1815; m. Dr. Jonathan W. Brooks, Norwich, Ct., had a large family, and later lived in Chicago.
VI. John, b. 1817, lived in Chicago.

Section 96

William Cary, son of Dr. Samuel, Sec. 52, b. Lyme, N. H., Jan. 28, 1783; in 1802 emigrated with his mother and brother Christopher to Cincinnati, O., and bought a farm at the head of Main Street, where he lived till 1814, when he sold his 32 acres in Cincinnati, and settled on Section 30, Millcreek Township, later called College Hill, where he resided until his death, Mar. 25, 1862. He represented Hamilton Co. in the Legislature of 1824-5, and was an active supporter of the Canal Bill, and the Free School Law of Ohio. He was remarkable for his amiability of disposition, purity of character, public spirit and benevolence; was for many years an Elder in the Presbyterian Church, and a frequent representative to the General Assembly; he originated the churches at Mt. Pleasant and College Hill; endowed a Professorship in Farmer's College, and was a patron of all the benevolent enterprises of the day. He m. Rebecca, dau. of Roswell and Deborah Fenton, Jan. 8, 1809, and d. in the full assurance of a blessed immortality.
Children:
I. Freeman Grant, b. April 7, 1810. Sec. 199.
II. William Woodward, b. Feb. 23, 1812. Sec. 200.
III. Samuel Fenton, b. Feb. 18, 1814. Sec. 201.

Section 97

Josiah Cary, son of Josiah, Sec. 53, b. Haddam, Ct., Jan. 16, 1761; m. Lydia Clark, 1783, lived in Middle Haddam, and followed the Coasting trade, and d. April 14, 1797.

Children:
I. Charlotte, b. May 30, 1784; m. Mr. Loomis.
II. Nancy, b. Aug. 11, 1787; m. Mr. Annable.
III. Josiah, b. Jan. 23, 1791. Sec. 202.
IV. Hannah, b. June 19, 1793; m. Mr. Bumphrey.
V. Lydia, b. June 26, 1795; m. Mr. Skinner.

Section 97-A

Moses Cary, son of Moses, Sec. 53-A; m. 1st, Sophronia Clark; m. 2d, Betsey Squires, and lived at Fort Edward, N. Y.

Children:
I. Clara, d. unm.
II. Ebenezer, m. Lucinda Southard, and had ten children.
III. Moses, m. 1st, Miss Clark; m. 2d, ___ ___.
IV. Annis, m. Benjamin Durkee, and had four children.
V. Daniel Clark. Sec. 202-A.
VI. Elizabeth.
VII. Zina, d. unm.
VIII. Russell, was run over in early life; an invalid ever after.
IX. Harvey, d. in infancy.
X. Roswell, d. unm.
XI. Walter, d. unm.
XII. Lucy, m. Harris Hotchkiss.
XIII. ___, d. in infancy.
XIV. ___, d. in infancy.
XV. Horace, m. unkn.
XVI. Anson, m. unkn.
XVII. Charles, m. unkn.
XVIII. Jane.
XIX. Harriet, m. James Weston.
XX. Emily, m. Joseph Barrell.
XXI. Maria, m. Mr. Goff.

Section 98

Henry Lucius Cary, son of Eleazer, Sec. 54, b. Windham, Ct., Oct. 18, 1769; m. Mary Harris, Sept. 7, 1812; d. May 3, 1848, leaving one son
I. Lucius Henry, who m. in Norwich, Ct., and had one child.

Section 99

Eleazer Cary, son of Nathaniel, Sec. 55, b. Windham, Ct., Dec. 14, 1769; he was a Goldsmith and resided in Windham most of his life, and thence removed to Norwich; he was a Musician, was specially skilled in playing the violin, and was widely known as "Eleazer the Fiddler." He m. Matilda, dau. of John Parish, Nov. 23, 1791, and d. Nov. 8, 1820; his widow d. at Willimantic, Ct., Nov. 10, 1845.

Children:

I. Thomas Storrs, b. Mar. 21, 1792; d. unm. 1823.

II. Lucia, b. Jan. 2, 1794; d. in infancy.

III. Lucia, b. June 16, 1795; m. 1st, Samuel Welch, and had three children; m. 2d, William Russell, and had three children; she lived in Buffalo, N. Y.

IV. Harriet, b. Dec. 29, 1799; m. Oliver Lathrop, lived at Willimantic, and had two children.

V. Lydia, b. 1803; m. 1st. Mr. Ware, of Hartford, Ct., and had two children; m. 2d, Mr. Gardner, and had one child, and lived at Marydosia, Ill.

VI. Eleazer, b. 1811. Sec. 203.

Section 99-A

Eunice Cary, dau. of Olivet, Sec. 57, b. Lempster, N. H., Aug. 17, 1793; m. Amasa Loveridge (b. Dec. 27, 1787, Deerfield, Mass.), Jan. 12, 1815, at Lempster; about 1816 removed to near Buffalo, N. Y., and d. Mar. 4, 1870, at Buffalo.

Their son, Dr. Edson Dexter Loveridge, b. Oct. 25, 1818, Concord, N. Y., m. Susanna Bodine Pierson, dau. of Paul Pierson and Temperance Woodruff of Buffalo, N. Y., Aug. 26, 1841, and d. at Buffalo, Jan. 12, 1902.

Their dau., May Louisa Loveridge, b. July, 1842, Buffalo, N. Y., m. Lawrence Woodruff Halsey, Jr., Milwaukee, Wis., Dec. 26, 1866.

Their dau. Louisa Ketchem Halsey, b. July 14, 1868, Oshkosh, Wis., m. Philo Clark Darrow, Western Springs, Ill., and had two children.

Section 100

Olivet Cary, son of Olivet, Sec. 57, b. Lempster, N. H., Nov. 6, 1810; m. Mehitabel Keyes, of Ackworth, N. H., Dec. 27, 1837, and lived at Ackworth.

Children:

I. Chester E., b. Mar. 11, 1839; a Printer at Montpelier, Vt.

II. Georgiana, b. Nov. 20, 1841; m. Dr. S. M. Dinsmore of Antrim, N. H., Sept, n, 1862.

III. Frank Pierce, b. 1848; a Dentist at Terre Haute, Ind.

Section 101

Alden Cary, son of Elliott, Sec. 58, b. Lempster, N. H., July 7, 1801; d. Aug. 30, 1891, and had lived 81 years on the same farm; at the age of 21 he was baptized by Rev. Wilbur Fisk, and from that time till his death was an esteemed member of the Methodist Episcopal Church; a reader and patron of *Zion's Herald* from its origin, abreast of the times in general intelligence; substantial, judicious, earnest, liberal, and faithful, retaining his official standing to the last, he exerted a helpful influence of more than ordinary potency. He m. Hannah B. Wellman, Lempster, Dec. 30, 1824, who d. April 2, 1891, a faithful member of the Church of her husband, a mother in Israel, and a helpmeet indeed. To these two saints of God, who lived in happy wedlock over 67 years, there were b. six children:

I. Abigail Angeline, b. Sept. 18, 1826; m. Orson Gee, who d. Jan. 2, 1897; they had three children.

II. Carlos A., b. Feb. 26, 1828; d. in youth.

III. Wilson Wellman, b. Aug. 24, 1831; m. 1st, Lucia P. Noyes, 1850, who d. Mar. 18, 1859; m. 2d, Ellen Augusta Hubbard, Nov. 6, 1861. He is a manufacturer of wood-working machinery, is an inventor, having taken out a dozen patents of various kinds; a man greatly respected, and a long-time resident of Lowell, Mass. They had

1. Anna F., b. Mar. 9, 1865; m. Frank J. Sherwood, and had

(1) Cary, b. Aug. 11, 1890.

IV. Rufus J., b. July 2, 1833; m. 1st, Elizabeth Gleason; m. 2d, Susan Dodge; in the boot and shoe trade, Ackworth, N. H.

V. Francis C., b. Jan. 30, 1836; m. Hannah Larabee, had five children, and is a farmer in Rockingham, Vt.

VI. Hannah T., b. Aug. 22, 1838; m. H. C. Giffen, Keene, N. H., 1859, and had

1. Fred.

2. Etta Eudora, m. Marshall Dana, Mount Holly, Vt.; they had

(1) Marian G., grad, of Simmons College, Boston, 1909; teaching in Chicago.

(2) Charles G.

(3) Burton G.

(4) Floyd G.

(5) Merritt Marshall.

(6) Doris Eudora.

Section 102

William Cary, son of William, Sec. 59, b. Lempster, N. H., Feb. 12, 1796; when 19 years old his father d. very suddenly, and he took the homestead, and by working the farm in summer and teaching in winter, paid off the heirs. He m. Sophia Hurd (b. Dec. 26, 1794; d. May 8, 1857), May 22, 1817; he was a man of commanding presence, being six feet and four inches in height;

in the military service of the State he rose to be Major-General; was Chairman of the Board of Selectmen for ten years, and in the Legislature in 1823-25; was on the Mounted Escort that received Lafayette at Concord in 1824. He removed his family to Amesbury, Mass., in 1832, and was neighbor and friend of the Poet, John Greenleaf Whittier, who once said to his son, Henry Grosvenor, "I wish we had some men in this village like thy father to stamp out this rum business." He d. May 18, 1856.

Children:

I. William Addison, b. July 23, 1818. Sec. 204.

II. Calthea Gilmore, b. Nov. 26, 1819; m. Francis C. Sweet, Amesbury, May 28, 1844; their son Frank was connected with the American Bank Note Co. for 20 years, and d. Dec. 8, 1883, Cambridge, Mass.

III. Sophia Augusta, b. Sept. 13, 1821; d. 1840, Amesbury.

IV. Milan Galusha, b. Nov. 20, 1823. Sec. 205.

V. Augustus Celanus, b. Sept. 16, 1825. Sec. 206.

VI. Henry Grosvenor, b. Dec. 4, 1829. Sec. 206-A.

Section 103

Byfield Cary, son of William, Sec. 59, b. Lempster, N. H., Nov. 25, 1799; m. Hannah Mayo (b. Oct. 29, 1802), Nov. 20, 1823, Ackworth, N. H.; removed to Ware, Mass., where he d. 1826; they had

I. Permelia Rosamond, b. Sept. 24, 1824; m. 1st, Emmons Richardson, 1842; m. 2d, William Atwood, who d. Jan. 24, 1897; they had

1. Rosetta Electa, b. 1846; m. Dean C. George, 1864; he d. Sept. 1898; they had

(1) Charles Emmons, b. June 2, 1870.

(2) Arthur Dean, b. Jan. 2, 1876.

2. Ellen Maria, b. April 10, 1852; m. William P. Chamberlain, Mar. 16, 1897, and had

(1) Elma L., b. Nov. 26, 1857; d. 1893.

(2) Emons W., b. Nov. 26, 1857; m. 1st, Nellie Bosworth, 1878; m. 2d, Dora Lang-, 1892; m. 3d, Belle Totten, 1901; they had

1. Grace Elma, b. July 7, 1881.

2. Dorris E., b. Mar. 7, 1894.

3. Norma T., b. Feb. 24, 1908.

Section 104

Harvey H. Cary, son of William, Sec. 59, b. Lempster, N. H., May 10, 1802; m. Mary Barnum, May 12, 1825, Ackworth, N. H., and had two children there; went West about 1850; he d. 1878, Union City, Mich.

Children:

I. Lucy Ann, b. July 5, 1828; m. and lived in Wisconsin.

II. Lucia Emily, b. July 15, 1836; m. William Hibb, had three children, and lived in Iowa.

Section 105

John Melville Cary, son of William, Sec. 59, b. Lempster, N. H., June 12, 1810; was a machinist, and d. May 11, 1884, Amesbury, Mass.; m. Susan Dart (b. Nov. 29, 1812; d. Nov. 4, 1870), Oct. 17, 1832, Guilford, N. H.; m. 2d, Mrs. Almira Elliott (Johnson) Devine (b. Feb. 7, 1831; d. Mar. 10, 1903).
Children:
I. Ellen Fisher, b. Oct. 4, 1834; m. Cyrus L. Shepard, Mar. 18, 1857; d. Aug. 27, 1858; they had
I. Ellen S., who m. John N. Hughes, Mar. 18, 1882, and had six children.
II. William Henry, b. April 1, 1846, and was a wood-worker; m. Emaline Fozzard, May 10, 1871; he d. Dec. 31, 1878; they had
1. Emma Louise, b. Jan. 24, 1874.
2. Susie Amelia, b. April 18, 1875.

Section 105-A

John Cary, son of John, Sec. 60-A, b. Belcher, N. Y., Sept. 2, 1793, on the farm bought by his father in 1783; his boyhood and youth were spent in helping clear up this farm, together with the usual work that comes to the sons of Pioneers. Conditions were narrow, but intelligent parents and fraternal love made the most of these. In the War of 1812-14 he was a private in the West Hebron Company, which was attached to the Hebron and Salem Regiment; in the Campaign of Plattsburg, his Company was on a slow-going sloop on the way to the battle, but was not engaged as were two of his brothers. In 1815 he bought of John Hornby a farm of no acres in Perry, Genesee Co., N. Y., which, after the division became Wyoming Co.; in 1822 he sold this to his brother George, and he returned to care for his father, and the home farm came to him by will. The winter of 1815-16 was spent in teaching school in the home District. In the State militia he became a Sergeant in 1816, and an Ensign in 1817. Like his ancestor, John Cary, he was elected a Constable of the town of Hebron in 1820-21. He m. Catherine, dau. of Seth and Anne (Smith) Cooley of Salem, N. Y., who was a descendant in the sixth generation of Benjamin Cooley, who in 1646, at the age of twenty-four, was a Selectman of Springfield, Mass. Six children grew up and all were married. He d. Sept. 19, 1865, and she d. 1869.
Children:
I. Matthew, b. Dec. 28, 1823; d. in infancy.
II. Susanna, b. Sept. 2, 1825; m. John Gould, Jan. 1, 1852; d. Jan. 14, 1854; they had

1. Katie S., b. April 7, 1853; m. Selden O. Swain, and live at Creston, Ill.; they had

(1) Blanche Cramer, b. Mar. 29, 1880; m. Bert G. Rees, Jan. 17, 1906.

(2) Charles R., b. May 4, 1883; d. July 3, 1897.

III. Anna Cooley, b. May 2, 1829; m. Joseph Merithew, Hartford, N. Y. (b. Dec. 8, 1823; d. April 4, 1902), Nov. 8, 1854, and had

1. Ira J., b. Sept. 18, 1857; m. Emma Northrup, Dec. 25, 1883, and had

(1) E. Northrup, b. May 20, 1886.

(2) Mabel E., b. July 3, 1890.

2. Hiram Rogers, b. Dec. 11, 1859.

3. Edward S., b. Dec. 18, 1861; m. Annie L. Haynes of Middletown, Vt., Sept. 1, 1897, and had

(1) Grace Geneva, b. Aug. 9, 1898.

(2) Clifford H., b. April 29, 1901.

(3) Ruth Irene, b. Oct. 9, 1909.

4. Sarah J., b. June 8, 1868; m. Charles Chapman, and had

(1) Yaleta A., b. June 28, 1892.

(2) John J., b. Aug. 28, 1895.

IV. Isaac J., b. Aug. 15, 1831; d. Dec. 3, 1868; m. 1st, Martha Jane Donaldson, Jan. 1, 1856, who d. Sept. 27, 1858; m. 2d, Mary Graham, Jan. 1, 1861; they had

1. Henrietta, who d. Oct. 3, 1874.

2. John Graham, b. Feb. 14, 1862; m. A. Belle Farwell, Nov. 11, 1885, and had

(1) Anna Graham, b. July 10, 1890.

(2) Ray, who d. in infancy.

(3) Mary Farwell, b. Mar. 16, 1894.

3. Samuel R., b. May 23, 1863; m. Miss Dinning, Nov. 19, 1902, and had

(1) Marion, b. April 19, 1904.

V. Mary Jane, b. Dec. 10, 1834; m. William Day, Jan. 15, 1856; d. May 31, 1857.

VI. Calrinda Bliss, b. Feb. 14, 1836; d. Feb. 13, 1910; m. Edward L. Coy, Sept. 21, 1858; he was b. April 4, 1831, and was for 18 years a breeder of Ayrshire cattle; and for 13 years paid attention to the Holstein-Friesian breed; he also originated 18 varieties of the potato, all of which became standard in some section; he raised more than a half million pounds of cucumber seed, and for two years the Department of Agriculture employed him to establish the type of the 250 varieties of the cucumber that were tested. They had

1. Charles Herbert, b. July 26, 1859, and is following the Seed business; m. Amelia S. Madison, Dec. 27, 1882, and had (1) Howard Winfield.

2. Seth Willard, M. D., b. May 28, 1863, a Physician in East Boston; m. Grace M. Capen, Mar. 17, 1892, and had

(1) Edward L., b. Jan. 25, 1894.

(2) Ralph, b. Oct. 31, 1899.

3. Ida Belle, b. Sept. 13, 1865; m. J. B. Sievwright, who is in business in New York City, June 19, 1889, and had
(1) Ruth, b. Feb. 3, 1891.
(2) Clara May, b. May 3, 1898.
4. Mabel, b. Aug. 28, 1873; d. Jan 10, 1895.
VII. Seth Cooley, b. June 1, 1838. Sec. 206-B.

Section 106

Samuel Cary, son of Joseph, Sec. 61, b. Providence, R. I., Aug. 18, 1766; m. Elizabeth Cornwall, Beekman, Dutchess Co., N. Y., Sept. 25, 1791, and settled at Rensselaerville, N. Y., then to Albany, where they remained till 1830, when they removed to Bethlehem, N. Y. In early life he joined the Society of Friends, and he and his wife became most acceptable Preachers, and were in the habit of attending many Yearly Meetings. They lived blameless and eminently useful lives, adorning the doctrine they professed. The savor of their good names, and the influence of their example and precept were widely felt and acknowledged. As their lives were exemplary, they died peaceful and triumphant; she d. Mar. 8, 1842, and he Feb. 16, 1845. Their Memoirs were published and widely circulated.

Children:
I. Ruth, b. Jan. 10, 1793; d. in infancy.
II. Albert, b. Feb. 23, 1794; d. in 1831.
III. Abel, b. Nov. 12, 1795; d. in childhood.
IV. Deborah, b. Nov. 18, 1797; d. in infancy.
V. Rhoda, b. Sept. 6, 1799; m. Isaac Page, 1821; d. 1848.
VI. Joseph, b. Jan. 30, 1802. Sec. 207.
VII. Mary, b. Mar. 20, 1804; d. in childhood.
VIII. David H., b. Nov. 7, 1806; m. Miss Hyde, 1833, and lived in Albany.
IX. Maria, b. May 24, 1809; m Isaac B. Briggs, Nov. 11, 1832.
X. Samuel, b. May 7, 1812; m. Jane March, Chester Co., Pa., 1840; lived at Albany.
XI. Isaac H., b. May 7, 1812. Sec. 208.
XII. George, b. Nov. 30, 1814. Sec. 209.

Section 107

Dr. Joseph Cary, son of Joseph, Sec. 61, b. Plainfield, Ct., Aug. 18, 1773; m. Ruby Ann Eaton, Killingly, Ct., and settled in Coventry, R. I. He was an eminent Physician, and d. May 15, 1815.

Children:
I. Cynthia, b. Feb. 12, 1798; m. Samuel Mowry, and d. 1823.
II. Albigense Waldo, b. May 23, 1801. Sec. 209-A.

III. Jeremiah E., b. April 30, 1803. Sec. 210.
IV. Aurelius A., b. May 20, 1806; settled in Granville, N. Y.
V. Betsey Matilda, b. July 31, 1809; m. Daniel Horton, Adrian, Michigan.
VI. Alfred X., b. Mar. 28, 1811. Sec. 211.

Section 108

Darius H. Cary, son of Joseph, Sec. 61, b. Plainfield, Ct., Mar. 24, 1777, and removed to Richfield, N. Y.; m. Patty Whitney, 1803, and d. 1863.
Children:
I. Emeline, b. 1803; d. 1805.
II. Emeline, b. 1806; m. Benjamin P. Jones, 1830.
III. Josiah Whitney, b. 1808. Sec. 212.
IV. and V. A son and daughter, b. 1810; d. in infancy.
VI. Theodore, b. 1812; d. 1827.
VII. Susan E., b. 1815; m. Isaac Gage, 1849.
VIII. Edwin, b. 1817. Sec. 213.
IX. Laura, b. 1820; d. 1867.
X. Lucy M., b. 1823; m. Mr. Judd, Cherry Valley, N. Y., 1846.

Section 109

William Cary, son of Joseph, Sec. 61, b. Plainfield, Ct., April 12, 1779; removed to New York, and m. Lydia Trask, at Paris, N. Y., 1805; d. at Mohawk, N. Y., 1854.
Children:
I. Joseph, b. 1807. Sec. 214.
II. Hannah T., b. 1809; m. 1st, A. Burpee, 1837; m. 2d, R. Brownell, 1855.
III. Alfred, b. 1813; m. Zilpha Snow, 1833, and lived at Fort Plain, New York.
IV. Harriet A., b. 1815.
V. William H., b. 1816. Sec. 215.
VI. George W., b. 1819. Sec. 216.
VII. Charles Jerome, b. 1821; m. Elizabeth Gardener, 1857, who d. 1857; he lived in Milwaukee, Wis.

Section 110

Ezra Cary, son of Joseph, Sec. 61, b. Plainfield, Ct., Aug. 25, 1785; m. and removed to Richfield, N. Y., where he died.
Children:
I. Ezra.
II. Eliza; m. William H. Hanna.
III. Zeneah; m. Mr. Eddy.

IV. Abigail.
V. Albert, Norwich, N. Y.
VI. Alanson, Troy, N. Y.

Section 111

Dr. William Cary, son of Ebenezer, Sec. 62, b. Beekman, N. Y., Nov. 22, 1769; studied medicine, and was a distinguished man and Physician; settled at Half Moon, Saratoga Co., N. Y., and was a worthy and exemplary Preacher in the Society of Friends for more than thirty years. He m. 1st, Ruth Sweet, Jan. 11, 1793; m. 2d, Hannah Cook, May 29, 1811; m. 3d, Keziah Jackson, Nov. 17, 1826. He d. Nov. 23, 1845.

Children:

I. Matilda, b. Sept. 23, 1794; m. Thomas M. Southwick, May 29, 1814; lived in New York City.

II. Seth B., b. Mar. 30, 1796; d. in infancy.

III. Ebenezer, b. Nov. 5, 1797. Sec. 217.

IV. Lucius, b. May 9, 1799. Sec. 218.

V. Jervis, b. May 23, 1801. Sec. 219.

VI. Milton, b. Sept. 6, 1803; was in business in New York City.

VII. Maria, b. Oct. 12, 1805; m. Henry Fowler, June 15, 1824, and had five children, one of whom lives at Mechanicsville, N. Y.

VIII. Katherine, b. Oct. 28, 1806; m. David Devoll, May 6, 1824, and had seven children; he was a minister among the Friends, and lived at Schaghticoke, N. Y.

IX. Lydia, b. Oct. 1, 1808; d. young.

X. William, b. Aug. 23, 1813; m. Maria Sherman; was in the Legislature, and in the New York Custom House for years.

XI. Ruth, b. June 1, 1816; m. 1st, Andrew Holmes, and 2d, Rufus Hazzard, Ferrisburg, Vt.

XII. Isaac, b. Jan. 15, 1818. Sec. 220.

XIII. Charles Jackson, b. Oct. 19, 1827; d. in young manhood.

Section 112

Taylor Cary, son of Ebenezer, Sec. 62, b. Dutchess Co., N. Y., Mar. 3, 1773; m. Betty Langdon, 1794, and settled in Clinton. Saratoga Co., for a time as a weaver, and removed to Vernon, Oneida Co., on a farm, and d. Oct. 26, 1853, at Lysander, N. Y.

Children:

I. John, b. 1796; d. 1799.

II. Lucy, b. May 9, 1798; d. 1817, Vernon, N. Y.

III. Maria, b. Jan. 18, 1801; m. Elias Cox, April 7, 1825, and had four children at Lysander, N. Y.

IV. William, b. July 12, 1803. Sec. 221.
V. Hepzibah, b. 1805; d. in infancy.
VI. Louisa, b. Jan. 7, 1808; m. Ira Mattison, Jan., 1825; removed to Worthington, O., where she d. April 14, 1838.
VII. John, b. Mar. 20, 1810. Sec. 222.
VIII. Electa J., b. Feb. 8, 1814; m. Samuel Alden, 1835, Lysander, New York.
IX. Elizabeth, b. April 2, 1817; m. Anson Smith, Feb. 17, 1835, Vernon, N. Y.

Section 113

Dr. Egbert Cary, son of Ebenezer, Sec. 62, b. Dutchess Co., N. Y., April 12, 1789; m. Tamar Flagler, 1813; was a Physician, and a member of the Legislature in 1827; lived on the old homestead, and d. 1862.

Children:
I. Sophia, b. 1814; m. George Wilkinson, Poughkeepsie, N. Y.
II. Phebe, b. 1815; m. D. H. Platt, District of Columbia.
III. Cecillia, b. 1818; m. Thomas J. Doughty, Eden, Wis.
IV. Matilda, b. 1820; m. William S. Coggshall, Brooklyn, N. Y.
V. Ebenezer, b. 1822. Sec. 223.
VI. Philip F., b. 1826.
VII. Tamar, b. 1829.
VIII. DeWitt Clinton, b. 1833; m and lived in Washington, D. C.

Section 114

Sturges Cary, son of Ebenezer, Sec. 62, b. Beekman, N. Y., July 25, 1794; m. 1st, Sarah Flagler, Dec. 17, 1818, who d. April 11, 1836, Beekman, N. Y., he moved to Binghamton, N. Y., in 1837; m. 2d, Mrs. Hannah A. Gray, Feb. 27, 1841, who d. May 5, 1898, Binghamton, N. Y., he d. May 25, 1878.

Children:
I. Solomon Flagler, b. Oct. 9, 1820. Sec. 224.
II. Cornelia Flagler, b. June 5, 1822; d. Nov. 21, 1898; m. Tracy R. Morgan, 1839, and had
  1. Jennie, who m. Wallace B. Hallock, and had
    (1) Cornelia, who m. Charles Partridge, Montclair, N. J.
  2. Sarah A.; m. David L. Brownson.
  3. Loraine T.; m. Sarah Lee.
III. Cynthia A., b. Feb. 12, 1824; d. 1851.
IV. Oliver Aikin, b. June 3, 1827. Sec. 225.
V. Phebe, b. May 10, 1829; d. in infancy.
VI. James Sturges, b. June 12, 1833; Manufacturer at Binghamton, N. Y.; m. Elizabeth Littlefair, July 12, 1862, and had
  1. Mary Littlefair, b. May 3, 1865; d. in childhood.

2. Ralph Stuart, b. Aug. 19, 1866, Binghamton, N. Y.

3. Fanny Brownson, b. July 6, 1870; m. Frederick Denton Weed, Oct. 18, 1895, and had

(1) Elizabeth Littlefair.

(2) Louise Denton.

4. Frederick James, b. May 18, 1872; d. in childhood.

VII. Abel De Forest, b. Dec. 22, 1842; d. in childhood.

VIII. Abigail, b. 1844; d. in childhood.

IX. Andrew S., b. Mar. 6, 1846, Binghamton, N. Y.; m. Hannah Ann Shaw, and had

1. Andrew Shaw; m. Catherine Barker, and had

(1) Douglass V.

(2) Dr. L. B. Cary, Douglass, Ariz.

X. Charles H., b. Nov. 12, 1849; m Louise S. Teal, June 28, 1876; d. Oct. 9, 1894; they had

1. Helen L., b. June 1, 1877; m. Frank H. Henghlen, June 26, 1899, Quincy, Ill.

2. Charles H., b. June 13, 1879.

3. Mabel E., b. May 17, 1881; m. Walter C. Clark, Aug. 16, 1905, and had

(1) Helen Louise, b. Feb. 24, 1907, Minneapolis, Minn.

Section 115

Johnson Cary, son of Nathan, Sec. 63, b. Wyoming Valley, Pa., Mar. 5, 1783; removed with the family to Steuben Co., N. Y., 1790; m. Susan Bassett, Aug. 26, 1807; was a farmer and inn-keeper, a quiet man and esteemed citizen, and d. 1862, Arkport, N. Y.

Children:

I. Jane; m. Lewis W. Dey, and d. 1835.

II. Mary Ann, b. June 22, 1813; m. William H. Hurlbut, June 26, 1839; lived in Elgin, Ill., and had

1. William.

2. Avery.

III. Elizabeth, b. June 5, 1815; m. Calvin J. Reynolds, M. D., March, 1836; lived at Cuba, N. Y., and had

1. Caroline, b. Mar. 13, 1838; m. Malcom L. Nash, Sept. 26, 1856; she d. Mar. 10, 1900, and he d. Oct. 12, 1900; they had

(1) Susan J., b. May 19, 1858; d. in infancy.

(2) Charles White, b. Mar. 22, 1862; m. 1st, Catherine Hufstader, May 3, 1884, who d. Nov. 14, 1901; m. 2d, Frances Tupper, April 6, 1904; they had

1. Robert Cary, b. Dec. 19, 1886; m. Esther Baker, Sept. 21, 1908, and live at Mechanicsville, N. Y.

(3) John C., b. Aug. 17, 1863; d. 1903.

2. Mary; m. Rufus Hufstader, Hornel, N. Y.

IV. Susan, b. July 16, 1822; m. William T. Hurlbut, Oct. 13, 1849; lived in Arkport, N. Y., and had
1. Martha E.
2. Caroline P.
3. Charles Henry.
V. Caroline, b. July 21, 1824; m. William S. Babbitt, M. D., Dec. 15, 1847; settled at Olean, N. Y., 1859, and had
1. Clarence.
2. Caroline.

Section 116

Eleazer Cary, son of Nathan, Sec. 63, b. Hanover, Wyoming Valley, Pa., July 8, 1786; m. 1st, Frances Slocum, who was the grandniece of Frances Slocum, the "lost daughter of Wyoming;" m. 2d, Mrs. Rebecca D. Chapman. He was highly respected in the city of WilkesBarre, where he resided all his life; was an Alderman, and familiarly known as 'Squire Cary; he d. Jan. 22, 1853.

Children:
I. Frances; m. Peter Osterhout, Tunkhannock, Pa.
II. Rhoda S.
III. Douglass; m. Letitia Scott, Wayne, Pa., and had
1. Lucy; d. young.
2. Frances.
3. Mary Scott; m. Herman Wendell, and had (1) Douglass Cary, b. about 1895.

Section 117

William Cary, son of Nathan, Sec. 63, b. Wyoming Valley, Pa., Feb. 8, 1791; m. Peniah Rodman, and lived near Wilkes-Barre, where he d. 1825.

Children:
I. Eleazer; became an eminent Physician, Perry, Ill.
II. Ruth; m. 1st, Calvin Stearnes; m. 2d, Jesse Gibbs, West Almond. N. Y.
III. Jane.
IV. Maria; m. Rev. Peter R. Rook, and had
1. Belle.
2. Eleazer.

Section 118

Christopher Cary, son of Nathan, Sec. 63, b. Arkport, N. Y., June 20, 1794; m. Mary Sylvester, and lived highly respected and honored; d. Jan. 1, 1844.

Children:
I. Charles, b. Nov. 15, 1829; m. Anna Mitchell, and lived at Olean, N. Y., an esteemed citizen and an able lawyer.

II. Ruth, b. 1831; d. at 16.

III. Johnson, b. July 2, 1833; m. Mary Hulbert, Livonia, N. Y., and had two children.

IV. Mary Jane, b. Nov. 1, 1835; m. Benjamin F. Wiggins, Dentist, Hornel, N. Y., and had.

1. Clarence.
2. Ida.

V. Hubbard Griswold, b. Dec. 31, 1835; d. Mar. 12, 1900. In the Civil War he was Captain in 136th New York; was patriotic, a kind father, and a Christian gentleman; m. Mary Eliza Hulbert (now living at Livonia, N. Y.), May 27, 1856, and had

1. Darwin Edward, M. D., b. Nov. 15, 1857; m. Ella D. Peck; live at Rochester, N. Y.
2. Nellie Estelle, b. April 7, 1859; m. J. Russell Stone, May 18, 1881, and had
(1) J. Albert, b. June 9, 1886.
(2) Mabel, b. June 16, 1889.
(3) Raymond, b. Sept. 22, 1896.
3. Hubbard Irving, b. Jan. 2, 1869; m. Belle Brown; live in Chicago, and had
(1) Marion, b. Oct. 25, 1896.
(2) Doris, b. Jan. 31, 1898.
(3) Winnifred, b. Sept. 17, 1904.
4. Mary Alice, b. July 5, 1872; Livonia, N. Y.
5. Charles Hulbert, b. Mar. 4, 1876; m. Alta Carman, 1895; live at Livonia, N. Y., and had
(1) Miriam, b. Feb. 2, 1897.
(2) Ethel, b. Mar. 8, 1901.
(3) Charles, b. Jan. 25, 1903.
(4) Charlotte, b. Oct, 25, 1905.

VI. John, b. June 1, 1840, and d. at 21.

Section 118-A

John Abbott Cary, son of Benjamin, Sec. 63-C, b. on the old homestead, 1808; m. Polly Bennett, dau. of Nathan, son of Ishmael Bennett, who came to Hanover from Connecticut, and one of the original settlers. He lived in Ashley most of his life, held various offices of trust, and was highly esteemed; he was a musician, and spent much of his time in his last days with his favorite violin.

Children:

I. Hiram, b. Feb. 14, 1832; m. Susan Zeigler, Jan. 28, 1858, whose ancestors were old settlers in Northampton County, and her father, Frederick, was in the War of 1812-14. He was much respected in Wilkes-Barre, where he d. July 29, 1898; they had

1. May Almeda, b. Jan. 19, 1859; m. Andrew C. Smith (grandson of Capt. Ephraim, who was a soldier and sailor in the Revolution), Jan. 13, 1881; Mrs.

Smith is the Historian of the Eleazer Cary line, and has published a book on the family; they had
  (1) Harriet Olive, b. Sept. 28, 1882; d. 1896.
  (2) Fannie Mae, b. July 19, 1883.
  (3) Andrew David, b. May 22, 1885; d. in infancy.
  (4) Adaline, b. Oct. 4, 1889; d. in infancy.
  (5) Helen; d. in infancy.
  (6) Ripple Cary, b. July 25, 1891.
  (7) Alice Cary, b. April 11, 1896.
  2. W. Franklin; d. at 23.
  3. J. Eugene, b. Oct. 3, 1862; m. Clara Kreuger.
  4. Emma.
  5. Edwin Henry.
  6. Elizabeth; m. 1st, John Cox; m. 2d, Peter Wagner; she d. Mar. 24, 1908.
  7. Rebecca E.; m. D. V. Thomas.
  8. William; d. at 19.
  9. Daisey; d. in infancy.
  10. Frederick; d. in youth.
II. Susan, b. 1834; m. 1st, Henry Stein; m. 2d, F. S. Waldeck.
III. Sarah; m. Christian Leaser.
IV. Jane; m. Charles Lehr.
V. Charles.
VI. Stewart; m. Mary McCuan.
VII. John; m. Mary Smith.
VIII. Nathan.

Section 119

Cephus Cary, son of Ezra, Sec. 64, b. in New Jersey, 1775; went with his father when a child to Western Pennsylvania, thence to Ohio in 1790, stopping for a time on the Ohio River near Wheeling, West Virginia, and thence to the wilderness of Shelby County, where he lived at Sidney till his death at the age of 94. He m. 1st, Jane Williamson, and had nine children; m. 2d, Rhoda Jerard, and had seven children; m. 3d, Elizabeth Mendenhall.
Children:
I. Lydia, b. Jan. 23, 1804; m. John Mullinger.
II. John W., b. Jan. 3, 1805. Sec. 226.
III. William A., b. Jan. 9, 1806. Sec. 227.
IV. Nancy W., b. June 16, 1807; m. William C. Dills.
V. Drusilla, b. Oct. 26, 1808; m. Marcellus Withers.
VI. David, b. Jan. 22, 1810. Sec. 228.
VII. Thomas M., b. Dec. 16, 1812. Sec. 229.
VIII. Jeremiah, b. June 7, 1814. Sec. 230.
IX. Benjamin W., b. Oct. 1, 1816. Sec. 231.
X. Stephen C., b. April 12, 1818; accidentally killed in youth.

XI. Sallie A., b. Nov. 20, 1820; m. Thomas Stevenson, Sidney, O.
XII. Simeon B., b. Dec. 20, 1822. Sec. 232.
XIII. Mary T., b. April 4, 1824.
XIV. Elarvey G., b. Aug. 18, 1826. Sec. 233.
XV. Jason S., b. Nov. 28, 1828; m. Ada Smith, 1857; their two children d. in infancy.
XVI. Milton T., b. July 22, 1831. Sec. 234.

Section 120

George Cary, son of Ezra, Sec. 64, b. Gurnsey Co., O., 1793; m. and settled in Madison Co., O., and d. 1873 in Richland Co., O. Children:
I. Henry Shorer, b. June 8, 1816. Sec. 235.
II. Simon Baker, b. Oct., 1817; m. Lucy Ann Marks, Jan., 1847, and lived at Marion, Ind.
III. John Bradford, b. Aug., 1823; d. Mar. 4, 1863, Lewis, Ia.; m. Mary Crosswait, Dec., 1858, and had
1. Jennie, b. Mar. 29, 1860.
2. Jessie, b. Jan., 1862; d. in childhood.
IV. George Washington, b. 1826; m. and lived in Lexington, O. These four brothers were giants in strength, and together weighed over 1,000 pounds.
V. Sarah A.; m. Mr. Pratt, Quincy, O.

Section 121

Thomas Cary, son of Ezra, Sec. 65, b. Bridgewater, 1771; m. Sallie Packard, Mar. 4, 1798, and settled at Enfield, Mass., where he resided till his death in 1855, aged 84 years.
Children:
I. Sarah, b. 1799; m. J. P. Stearnes, Boston, Mass.
II. Lemuel P., b. 1801; m. and removed to Princeton, Ill.; had a son, who d. in 1861.
III. Ezra, b. 1803. Sec. 236.
IV. Cynthia, b. 1805; d. 1862, Enfield, Mass.
V. Volina, b. 1807.
VI. Edward, b. 1809. Sec. 237.
VII. Zecheriah, b. 1811.
VIII. Rufus, b. Mar. 14, 1813. Sec. 238.
IX. Aurelia, b. 1817; m. Mr. Brooks.
X. Maria F., b. 1822.

Section 122

Zachary Cary, son of Ezra, Sec. 65, b. Bridgewater, 1773; went with parents to Turner, Me.; m. ____ Newhall, 1800; accidentally killed while raising a building, 1809.
Children:
I. Zachary, b. 1801. Sec. 239.
II. David, b. 1803, and lived at Fall River, Mass.
III. Ezra, b. 1804; d. in Philadelphia, Pa.
IV. Thomas, b. 1807. Sec. 240.
V. Eliza, b. 1809; m. Lewis Barry, in Florida, 1832.

Section 123

Ezra Cary, son of Ezra, Sec. 65, b. Turner Me., 1780; m. Lois Staples, and resided on a farm in Turner till his death in 1853.
Children:
I. Salmon, b. 1804. Sec. 241.
II. Seth, b. 1805. Sec. 242.
III. Daniel, b. 1806. Sec. 243.
IV. Ezra, b. 1808; d. unm.
V. Thomas, b. 1810; d. unm.
VI. Elvira, b. 1812; m. William Bradford.
VII. Lois, b. 1814.
VIII. Isabel, b. 1816.
IX. Cynthia, b. 1818.
X. Eunice, b. 1820; m. Mr. Davis, Lisbon, Me.
XI. Lydia, b. 1822.
XII. Clara, b. 1824; m. Daniel Teague, Turner, Me.

Section 124

John Sheperd Cary, son of Ezra, Sec. 65, b. Turner, Me., 1790; bought a farm in Leeds, Me., where he lived and died; m. 1st, Miss Lane, who d. 1826; m. 2d, the widow of Gen. Bolster, Paris, Me., who had one child; he was a Deacon in the Baptist church, and a prominent and influential citizen.
Children:
I. John; lived in New York.
II. James; d. at 20.
III. Ormond; d. 1852.
IV. Henry, b. 1830; lived in Franklin Co., Me.

Section 125

Bethuel Cary, son of Ezra, Sec. 65, b. Turner, Me., 1793; m. Lucy Robinson, 1817, and lived at East Sumner, Me.
Children:
I. Lucy Ann, b. 1818; m. Eleazer Ellis, 1836.
II. William, b. 1820. Sec. 244.
III. Benjamin F., b. 1822. Sec. 245.
IV. Bethuel, b. 1825; m. 1850; d. 1852.
V. Cynthia T., b. 1830; m. Charles R. Bonney, 1854.
VI. Sarah D., b. 1832; m. Isaac Bonney, 1854.

Section 126

Francis Cary, son of Maj. Daniel, Sec. 66, b. Bridgewater, May 5, 1785; m. Sallie Phillips (b. Feb. 3, 1790, of the family of the founders of Phillips Exeter and Phillips Andover Academies, and Phillips Brooks) and lived on a farm in Turner, Me.; a High School was soon formed, and a Public Library founded, and the books were for years kept in Squire Cary's house. He was greatly esteemed for his many virtues. She d. Nov. 2, 1865, and he a week later. The author of "Cary Memorials" records his great indebtedness to Francis Cary for the help he received concerning the Carys of Maine. In a letter to Gen. Cary he wrote: "I never knew a Cary extensively rich, and I never knew one supported by the town. I never knew one a drunkard, and they have been generally noted for their morality and piety."
Children:
I. Zibia, b. June 6, 1812; m. 1st, Estes W. French, Dec. 25, 1833; m. 2d, Elisha O. Drake.
II. Charles, b. June 27, 1814. Sec. 246.
III. Eunice, b. Dec. 28, 1816; m. Capt. Hiram Bryant, May 4, 1841.
IV. Ann, b. Sept. 26, 1819; d. 1843.
V. Francis, b. Sept. 29, 1824. Sec. 247.
VI. Arcy, b. Aug. 6, 1827; grad. New Hampton, N. H., and taught there afterwards; m. Rev. and Prof. Benjamin Franklin Hayes (a graduate of Bowdoin, Pastor at Olneyville, R. I.; head of Lapham Inst., North Scituate, R. I., and Professor at Bates College for thirty years), Aug. 12, 1856. She d. Jan. 22, 1804, and he Feb. 26, 1806; they had
1. Francis Little, b. Jan. 5, 1858; grad, from Bates College, Cobb Divinity School, and studied in Germany; had pastorates in Boston, Minneapolis, and now at Topeka, Kan.; m. Cora Walker, Washington, D. C., and had
(1) Cary Walker, b. Sept. 3, 1886.
(2) Doris Adelaide, b. Mar. 17, 1891; d. in infancy.
(3) Francis Little, b. Jan. 9, 1894.
(4) Elinor Guthrie, b. Sept. 25, 1900.

2. Edward Cary, b. Feb. 10, 1868, Lewiston, Me.; grad. Bates College, Cobb Divinity School, studied at Berlin, and has Ph. D. from Chicago; Prof, at Miami University, Oxford, O., and now Head of Dept, of Sociology at Illinois University, Urbana; m. Annie Lee Bean, Oct. 23, 1895, and had

(1) Edward B., b. Dec. 30, 1896.

(2) Richard Cary, b. Mar. 3, 1902.

(3) Harmon Phillips, b. Feb. 17, 1904.

3. Elizabeth Anna, b. June 18, 1860; m. Rev. Arthur Elms Cox, Pastor of the Baptist church at Poland, N. Y., and had

(1) Sidney Hayes, b. Aug. 20, 1889.

(2) Gertrude Anna, b. Nov. 20, 1890.

VII. Olive, b. Dec. 25, 1829; m. Thomas Scott Whitman, and had one child.

VIII. Chloe, b. Mar. 17, 1832; d. in childhood.

Section 126-A

Eunice Cary, dau. of Maj. Daniel, Sec. 66, b. Bridgewater, Sept. 10, 1781; m. Grenfill Blake (son of Samuel and Abigail (Richards) Blake, of Taunton, Mass., and later of Turner, Me.) at Turner, Jan. 1, 1805; he d. at Harrison, Me., 1826, and she d. 1832.

Children:

I. Harrison, b. 1805 5 m Susan Brett Cary, dau. of Dea. Alanson Cary, Oct. 3, 1836; he was a lawyer of New Brunswick, N. J., where he d. 1882, and she d. 1884; they had

1. Elizabeth Perley, b. Sept. 10, 1837; d. 1863.

2. Grenfill, b. June 2, 1839; m. Mrs. Elizabeth D. Olmstead, of New York City, May 17, 1866; d. Mar. 8, 1896, New Brunswick, N. J.

3. Zebia, b. Sept. 10, 1842; d. in childhood.

4. Susan, b. Nov. 13, 1845; m. Daniel C. English, M. D., Sept. 14, 1870, New Brunswick, N. J., and had

(1) Grenfill Harrison Blake, b. Dec. 31, 1872, and is a Civil Engineer; m. Mary B. Wilson, June 14, 1905.

Mrs. English also traces her descent from John Alden, through both Ruth and Joseph Alden.

5. Isabel Adele, b. 1853, and lives at New Brunswick, N. J.

II. Eunice Cary, b. Nov. 5, 1813, Otisfield, Me.; d. 1887.

III. Francis; m. Cornelia Elizabeth Shaw, and had

i. Cornelia Shaw, b. April 18, 1852, Lewiston, Me.; lives at Melrose, Mass.

Section 127

Cassander Cary, son of Dr. Luther, Sec. 67, b. Bridgewater, 1782; m. Sarah Clapp, Turner, Me., Oct. 12, 1808, who d. 1817; m. 2d, Joanna Jones, 1818; he d. in Turner, 1831.

Children:

I. Sophia, b. April 12, 1810.

II. Martha, b. May 5, 1812; m. Henry Roby, 1834.

III. Harriet, b. Aug. 24, 1814; m. Thomas R. Sampson, 1841, who d. Jan. 16, 1885; they had.

1. Howard L.; m. Helen L. Curtis, Freeport, Me., who d. July 10, 1878.

2. Rev. Cassander, Pastor of Congregational church, Tilton, N. H.

The good mother prized her Cary lineage, and ever held to the great principles of righteousness and religion which she received from a godly ancestry, and exemplified in her life; she d. at Harrison, Me., Sept. 27, 1906.

IV. Sarah, b. Nov. 14, 1816; m. Levi Booth, 1857.

V. Luther, b. Dec. 1, 1820. Sec. 248.

VI. Henry, b. June 12, 1823; d. Auburn, Me., Jan. 18, 1898; m. Ellen A. Sampson, Turner, Me., and had

1. Harriette Gertrude; m. Adolph G. Trimback, July 8, 1893, Campello, Mass.

2. Howard, Chicago.

3. Edward S., Lewiston, Me.

4. Cassander, Campello, Mass.

5. Alice M.; m. Freeman C. Farnham, and had

(1) Arloene.

(2) Forest Henry.

6. Nellie L.

7. Charles E., Auburn, Me.

8. Mabelle Blanche; m. Charles A. M. Sewell, 1902, and had (1) Doris, b. Feb. 9, 1904.

VII. Cassander, b. May 2, 1825; m. Mary Burrell, 1857, Turner, Me.

VIII. Clara, b. Nov. 14, 1827; m. John Martin, 1850.

Section 128

William Cary, son of Dr. Luther, Sec. 67, b. Bridgewater, Mar. 14, 1784; m. 1st, Dolly Smith, 1808, who d. 1818; m. 2d, Lucretia Reed, who d. 1826; m. 3d, Huldah Sawyer, 1828; lived to a great age at Turner, Me.

Children:

I. Nabby, b. April 23, 1809; m. J. B. Barrell, Dec. 30, 1828; d. 1858.

II. Alma, b. 1810; d. unm., Turner, Me.

III. Sophia L., b. 1812; d. 1864.

IV. Susan, b. April 18, 1813; m. Waldo A. Blossom, April 19, 1835.

V. Louisa, b. 1816; d. in infancy.

VI. Dolly, b. Aug. 13, 1818; m. Rev. J. T. Howes, Nov., 1850.

VII. William, b. Dec. 29, 1826; studied law and practiced at Galena, Ill.; m. Caroline Weston.

VIII. James A., b. Nov. 15, 1830; m. Rosetta Kimball, 1853, and had

1. James Clinton, 1854.
2. William K., b. 1858.
3. Luther Hanson, b. Oct. 11, 1867, Turner, Me.; Manager of the Congregational Pub. House, Boston; m. Mary Spencer, of Elyria, O., Aug. 20, 1892, and had
   (1) Rose Boynton, b. July 22, 1893, Elmhurst, Ill.
   (2) James Spencer, b. Aug. 10, 1894, Philadelphia, Pa.
   (3) William Kimball, b. Aug. 10, 1894, Philadelphia, Pa.
   (4) Charles Delano, b. Nov. 17, 1897, San Landro, Cal.
IX. Asa Clinton, b. May 29, 1832; m. Jessie Poestlay, 1859, and had
1. Isabella, b. 1861, Fort Fairfield, Me.
X. Ellen, b. 1834; Teacher in Portland, Me.
XI. Lucretia, b. 1835; d. 1855.
XII. Luther King. b. 1837; m. Ellen M. Bradford, Nov., 1859, and had
1. Susan, b. 1862, Fort Fairfield, Me.

Section 128-A

Sophia Cary, dau. of Dr. Luther, Sec. 67, b. Oxford Co., Me., Nov. 17, 1785; m. Dr. Silas Blake, Jan. 29, 1807.

Children:
I. Susan Cary, d. young.
II. Maria.
III. Silas, Farmer and Merchant; m. Clara C. Richardson; their son, James, is a Physician, Harrison, Me.
IV. Joseph, is a Minister; m. Hannah Clark, and had seven children.
V. Maurice Cary, a Lawyer in San Francisco, Cal.
VI. Josiah Merrill, a Physician; m. Harriet Fitch, and had
1. Silas Fitch.
2. Almira Titcomb; m. William Bradley, No. Bridgeton, Me.
3. Anne Pearson; m. Edward Humboldt.
4. Harriet Fitch.
5. Edward J.
VII. Luther Cary, a Farmer; m. Catherine Perley.
VIII. Sophia; m. Rufus Sawyer, and had seven children.
IX. Marian.

Section 129

Anselm Cary, son of Dr. Luther, Sec. 67, b. Bridgewater, June 8, 1787; m. Rhoda G. Stockbridge, Feb. 14, 1816; lived at Greene, Me., and removed to Muskingum Co., O., 1837. He lived a life of probity and usefulness, was ruling Elder in the Presbyterian church, with which denomination nearly all his family were connected; lived to a good old age.

Children:

I. Harrison Gray Otis, b. Dec. 28, 1816. Sec. 249.

II. Sarah Augusta, b. July 7, 1818; m. Morgan Lamson, a fruit grower living at Chillicothe, Mo.

III. Clara Isabella Stockbridge, b. April 24, 1820; m. Sept. 17, 1849, Alfred Barron, Druggist, Zanesville, O., and had

1. Clara Augusta, b. May 1, 1851; d. in childhood.
2. Edward Cary, b. June 28, 1853.
3. Alice Cary Stockbridge, b. Aug. 8, 1855.

IV. Frances A. Gage, b. Feb. 21, 1822; m. George W. Thompson, merchant, Jan. 22, 1845, Zanesville, O., and had

1. Alice, b. May 28, 1846.
2. Mary Helen, b. Sept. 16, 1848.
3. Julietta Eva, b. Nov. 9, 1850.
4. Frances Anna, b. Feb. 19, 1853; d. 1861.
5. Augusta Clara, b. Oct. 18, 1855.
6. George Cary, b. Jan. 2, 1858.
7. Edith Cary, b. May 7, 1860.
8. Lillian Cary, b. Aug. 27, 1862.

V. Lucretia Helen, b. Dec. 31, 1827; m. James H. Lockwood, merchant, Chillicothe, Mo.

Section 129-A

Emmelia Cary, dau. of Dr. Luther, Sec. 67, b. Turner Me., Mar. 13, 1789; m. Stephen Pollard (b. Bolton, Mass., Jan. 26, 1790), Mar. 5, 1809.

Children:

I. Luther Cary, b. 1809.

II. Lewis Johnson, b. 1811.

III. Rhoda Longley, b. 1813.

IV. Stephen, b. 1815, Belmont, N. Y.; m. 1st, Lucy B. Merrill, Dec. 3, 1846; m. 2d, Sarah A. Anderson, Oct. 26, 1856, and had

1. Julia, b. Sept. 21, 1847.
2. Olive, b. May 29, 1853.
3. Stephen, b. Dec. 26, 1858.
4. William A., b. April 26, 1862.
5. Frank, b. Nov. 6, 1864.
6. Sarah A., b. June 4, 1869.

V. William, b. 1817.

VI. Oliver, b. 1819.

VII. Alanson, b. 1821.

VIII. Emmelia, b. 1824.

IX. Nabby, b. 1826.

X. Rebecca Ann, b. 1829.

XI. Albert, b. 1832.

Section 130

Dea. Alanson Cary, son of Dr. Luther, Sec. 67, b. Bridgewater, Dec. 23, 1790; m. Susan Brett, July 4, 1816; he was Deacon of the church, and a worthy citizen of Turner, Me.
Children:
I. Susan, b. April 2, 1817; m. Harrison Blake, Oct. 3, 1836.
II. Alanson, b. Mar. 9, 1827; m. Miss Smith, Sept. 15, 1858, and lived in New York City; they had 1. Albert Alanson, b. July 16, 1859.
III. Clara E., b. May 31, 1836; m. Rev. S. G. Norcross, 1861.

Section 131

Hugh Cary, son of Dr. Luther, Sec. 67, b. Bridgewater, Oct. 17, 1792; m. Silena Phillips, July 7, 1816, and lived in Turner, Me.
Children:
I. Lucie A., b. May 14, 1818; m. Jesse Follet, July 4, 1839.
II. Emily, b. April 18, 1820.
III. Maurice, b. Nov. 23, 1821; m. Emily T. Jones, Nov. 27, 1862.
IV. Jairus, b. Sept. 25, 1823. Sec. 250.
V. Anna, b. Dec. 28, 1827; m. D. Briggs, May 31, 1853.
VI. Clara, b. Jan. 23, 1829; m. William L. Blake, May 31, 1853.
VII. Luther E., b. Jan. 16, 1834; d. in childhood.
VIII. Francis A., b. Jan. 19, 1840.

Section 132

Maurice Cary, son of Dr. Luther, Sec. 67. b. Bridgewater, Nov. 15, 1795 5 removed to Hocking Co., O.; m. Joanna Butin, Oct. 27, 1831; removed to Burlington, Ia., and thence to Jasper Co., Ia., where he resided.
Children:
I. A son, b. Aug. 4, 1835; d. in infancy.
II. Malvina, b. April 7, 1837.
III. Luther King, b. Feb. 27, 1839; was in the Union Army.
IV. John Colman, b. Dec. 6, 1841; in the 13th Iowa; engaged in the battle of Pittsburg Landing, and d. May 3, 1862.
V. Harrison, b. July 29, 1843.
VI. James, b. Dec. 21, 1845.
VII. Emily, b. May 15, 1848.
VIII. Anna Maria, b. July 4, 1850.
IX. Maurice, b. Sept. 9, 1854; d. in infancy.

Section 133

William Holman Cary, son of Ephraim, Sec. 68, b. Bridgewater, May 12, 1779; went with parents to Maine in 1822, and settled at Houlton, where he d. Jan. 27, 1859; he was a carpenter, and m. Catherine, dau. of Capt. Benjamin Haskell, 1801.

Children:

I. Jonathan Haskell, b. Nov. 23, 1802; m. Eliza Haskell, Dec. 25, 1831, at New Salem, Mass., and had 1. Henry Francis.

II. Shepard, b. July 3, 1805. Sec. 251.

III. William H., b. Oct. 23, 1812. Sec. 252.

IV. Catherine, b. June 18, 1825; m. Capt. Isaac Bowen, U. S. A., Mar. 25, 1845, and had five children; the parents d. of yellow fever at Pass Christian, N. M., and were buried at Buffalo, New York.

Section 134

Ephraim Cary, son of Ephraim, Sec. 68, b. Bridgewater, 1782; went with parents to Minot, Me.; m. Anna Hill, 1809.

Children:

I. Lucius, b. 1810; d. at Minot, 1843.

II. Horace, b. 1811. Sec. 253.

III. Anne, b. 1815; m. Dr. N. Reed, 1835; d. 1852.

IV. Jane, b. 1818; m. Mr. Wyman, 1846.

V. Catherine, b. 1822; m. P. B. Chase, 1842.

Section 135

Joseph Cary, son of Lewis, Sec. 69, b. Morris Co., N. J., Oct. 7, 1777; emigrated to Knox Co., O.; m. Susan Morris, 1800, and settled on a farm near Mt. Vernon, O., where he d. April 30, 1839.

Children:

I. Mahala, b. Dec. 15, 1801; m. James Boyle, Nov. 13, 1831; d. 1851.

II. James Bartley, b. April 10, 1804; m. Jane S. Rogers, Jan. 6, 1832, who d. Aug. 22, 1856; m. 2d, Mary Drake, Jan. 15, 1857; lived at Mt. Vernon, O.

III. Daniel Morris, b. June 17, 1806. Sec. 254.

IV. Joanna, b. Oct. 12, 1808, Mt. Vernon, O.

V. Aaron, b. July 19, 1811; went to California.

VI. Martha, b. May 6, 1816; m. Alvah Allen, Dec. 7, 1837.

VII. Nancy, b. Sept. 9, 1819; d. in infancy.

VIII. George Lewis, b. May 5, 1823; m. Margaret J. Turner, Oct. 16, 1861; Mt. Vernon, O.

Section 136

Abel Cary, son of Lewis, Sec. 69, b. Morris Co., N. J., June 13, 1781; emigrated to Indiana, where he d. about 1860; four sons went to California.
Children:
I. John.
II. William.
III. Barkley.
IV. Franklin.

Section 137

Lewis Cary, son of Lewis, Sec. 69, b. Morris Co., N. J., Oct. 19, 1783; emigrated to Kenton, O., where he lived to old age. He was an exemplary member of the Society of Friends; m. Rachel Kirk, 1807, who d. 1817.
Children:
I. Susan, b. Mar. 4, 1808; m. Mr. Merriam.
II. Abel, b. Oct. 2, 1809. Sec. 255.
III. William, b. Aug. 9, 1811; a banker in Kenton.
IV. Aaron, b. Aug., 1813. Sec. 256.
V. Edmond, b. Oct. 27, 1815. Sec. 257.
VI. Isabella, b. Sept. 14, 1817.
VII. Sarah, b. Oct. 4, 1819; d. 1841.
VIII. George, b. Aug. 4, 1821. Sec. 258.
IX. Benjamin L., b. Nov. 21, 1824; d. 1847.

Section 138

Aaron Cary, son of Lewis, Sec. 69, b. Morris Co., N. J., Sept. 26, 1785; m. Phebe Thompson, 1811; removed to Bucyrus, O., 1828, thence to Indiana, where he d. 1842.
Children:
I. Sarah W., b. Aug. 9, 1812; d. 1831.
II. Lucilla, b. Jan. 14, 1814; m. Ansel Dickinson, and lived in Wisconsin.
III. Hannah, b. Nov. 13, 1816; d. in childhood.
IV. Stephen J., b. Jan. 14, 1819; m. and removed to Council Bluffs, Ia., where he d., leaving
1. Ida.
V. Lewis, b. July 30, 1821; lived in Calusa, Cal.
VI. Hannah, b. Oct. 13, 1823; m. Mr. Clark, and lived in California.
VII. Jane W., b. June 15, 1827; m. Dr. J. Howard, San Francisco, California.
VIII. Jacob T., b. Jan. 13, 1830; d. in youth.
IX. Sarah W., b. Jan. 27, 1832; m. H. W. Williams, Calusa, Cal.

Section 139

John Cary, son of Lewis, Sec. 69, b. Morris Co., N. J., Mar. 7, 1788; removed to Ohio, and settled on a farm in Morrow Co., where he d. Dec. 2, 1860; he m. Margaret A. Snook, Jan. 30, 1811, who d. Feb. 5, 1858.
Children:
I. Lydia, b. Mar. 13, 1812; d. in infancy.
II. Lewis Henry, b. Mar. 27, 1813. Sec. 259.
III. Isabel Carson, b. Dec. 6, 1815; d. 1844.
IV. William S., b. May 16, 1818. Sec. 260.
V. John R., b. Aug. 7, 1820. Sec. 261.
VI. George C., b. May 20, 1823. Sec. 262.
VII. Ann E., b. Mar. 19, 1825; m. Alfred Beamer, Mar. 1, 1859; reared a family and lived in Chesterville, O.
VIII. Margaret J., b. May 13, 1828; m. Isaac Coleman, Oct. 12, 1848, and lived at Brandon, O.
IX. Lurany E., b. Sept. 10, 1830, Chesterville, O.
X. Charles P., b. Nov. 23, 1836; d. 1861.

Section 140

Daniel Cary, son of Lewis, Sec. 69, b. on the old farm near Drakesville, N. J., now Ledgewood, May 29, 1791; m. Eliza Wills (b. May 24, 1795; d. July 4, 1869), of Stanhope, N. J., Feb. 25, 1821. He was a successful farmer, prominent in the Presbyterian church, gentle, persevering, and d. Jan. 19, 1864.
Children:
I. William Sayre, b. Mar. 28, 1822. Sec. 263.
II. Samuel Wills, b. Mar. 1, 1824; a graduate of Princeton, and a member of the New York Bar; m. Charlotte McKenzie, Hoboken, N. J., Feb. 28, 1878, and d. May 18, 1888; they had
 1. Samuel Wills, b. Dec. 20, 1878; d. in childhood.
 2. Lyman Frederick, b. Aug. 6, 1880.
 3. William Sayre, b. Sept. 10, 1883.
III. Susan Cornelia, b. Mar. 21, 1826; m. John Riches, M. D.; d. in Suckasunna, N. J., Dec. 20, 1880.

Section 141

George L. Cary, son of Lewis, Sec. 69, b. Morris Co., N. J., June 30, 1799; emigrated to Wyandotte Co., O.; m. Lucinda Halsey, 1826, who d. Nov. 11, 1856; lived at Marseilles, O., where he d. Dec. 15, 1867. Children:
I. Henry H., b. Mar. 4, 1827; m. at Wyandotte, O., 1857.
II. Mary, b. May 16, 1837.

III. Elizabeth, b. May 6, 1841; m. John Cope, 1859.
IV. Eugenia L., b. Nov. 17, 1843.

Section 141-A

Seth Cary, son of Seth, Sec. 69-A, b. Putney, Vt., Mar. 7, 1775; m. and removed to Rochester, Vt., and thence to Ohio, stopping for a time in Pennsylvania.
Children:
I. Sarah.
II. Lyman, b. Aug. 18, 1803, Putney, Vt.; d. Aug. 8, 1846; m. Phebe Austin, and had
1. Henry.
2. Charles.
3. Jane.
4. Ransom T., b. Oct. 17, 1831, Rochester, Vt.; m. Nancy Greenfield, and had
(1) Ralph H., b. Feb. 22, 1855, Albion Pa., m. Nellie Geaney, and had
1. Lucy J.
(2) Arthur B., b. April 16, 1858, Albion, Pa.; m. Nellie Collier, May 15, 1889.
(3) Edith V., b. Jan. 14, 1871, Albion, Pa.; m. Charles O. Dayton, July 21, 1889, Burton, O., and had
1. S. Cary.
2. Robert R.
(4) Frank L., b. July 10, 1873, Albion, Pa.; m. Nellie Emerich, 1899, at Cleveland, O.
(5) Ernest R., b. Jan. 8, 1883, Burton, O.; m. Marcia Canfield, June 22, 1909, Burton, O.
III. Seth.
IV. Zebulon.
V. Lydia.
VI. Joel, b. June 1, 1814; d. Sept. 21, 1849; m. Harriet W. Ransom, Feb. 10, 1837, and had
1. Henry E., b. Jan. 14, 1838; m. Amelia Reach, Dec. 27, 1866, and had
(1) Mary.   (2) Henry.   (3) Lilly   (4) May.
2. Harlan.
3. Fidelia.
4. Glory Ann.
5. Seth.
VII. Mary.

Section 142

Zenas Cary, son of Aaron, Sec. 70, b. on Catamount Hill, Colrain, Mass., Nov. 26, 1782; m. Salome Maxam, Dec. 17, 1807. He served in the War of

1812-14, and five of the seven men from that town were from Catamount Hill. He was an enterprising and industrious man, upright in all his dealings; was dignified, religious, carefully maintained his church, and lived a long and useful life; d. Mar. 22, 1872; his widow d. April 24, 1878, nearly 93 years old.

Children:

I. Charlotte, b. Sept. 27, 1808; d. May 17, 1890; m. George V. Dunton and had

1. Mary Etta Salome, b. Sept. 28, 1834; m. 1st, Lewis S. Stacy, Manufacturer, of Colrain, Jan. 20, 1855, who d. Dec. 4, 1879; m. 2d, John Dewing, Aug. 18, 1891, who d. in 1891; resides with daughter at Portland, Me.; they had

(1) Hattie C., b. Sept. 10, 1857, a teacher of Music and in the Public Schools.

(2) Etta A., b. July 9, 1859; Matron Dana Hall, Wellesley, Mass.

(3) Sadie A., b. Sept. 29, 1862; m. F. Dana Cummings, Portland, Me., June 15, 1887, and had

1. Harold Dana, b. April 11, 1894.
2. Raymond Stacy, b. May 4, 1896.

(4) Louis Messenger, b. Sept. 6, 1864; d. 1867.

(5) Louis Bent, b. Aug. 17, 1869; d. 1889, Pasadena, Cal.

(6) Lillian S., b. Aug. 1, 1871; d. 1876.

(7) Gertrude E., b. Sept. 29, 1873; m. Arthur A. Cummings, Portland, Me., Aug. 18, 1891, and had

1. Arthur Donald, b. Sept. 28, 1903.

2. Charlotte Augusta, b. Jan. 30, 1839; educated at Wilbraham, Mass., East Greenwich, R. I.; Librarian at North Adams, 1883-1899.

3. Lydia Elvira, b. 1840; d. 1844.

4. Zenas Jesse, b. April 16, 1842; was in the 52d Mass. Infty. in the Civil War; m. Melissa D. Sweet, Dec. 31, 1865; live at Colrain, and had

(1) Bernard E., b. Feb. 3, 1867; m. Lillie M. Vaughn, of North Adams, May 7, 1894, who d. April 21, 1908; they had

1. Emily, b. Dec. 2, 1895.
2. Charlotte, b. Dec. 17, 1897; d. 1906.
3. Louis Eugene, b. June 24, 1901.
4. Orrin Bernard, b. Aug. 1, 1906.

(2) Louis Ellsworth, b. Feb. 23, 1869; m. Carrie Houghtaling, of Pownal, Vt., Nov. 5, 1900, and had

1. Eunice Augusta, b. Aug. 5, 1901.
2. Lois May, b. June 25, 1904.

(3) Mabel Augusta, b. Oct. 7, 1870; living at East Hampton, Mass.

(4) Susie Charlotte, b. June 30. 1883, East Hampton. Sarah Lindora, b. May 8, 1845; m Amasa Kenyon York, Nov. 18, 1868, who d. April 18, 1895; they had

(1) Earl Kenyon, b. Feb. 22, 1870; d. 1874.

(2) Efford Dunton, b. Oct. 22, 1871; d. 1873.

(3) Luther Amasa, b. Dec. 27, 1873; m. Helen B. Ensor, April 19, 1897; a Farmer living in Heath, Mass.; they had

1. Mary Lindora, b. Dec. 26, 1897.
2. Norman Kenyon, b. Oct. 28, 1899.
3. Gertrude Arline, b. Feb. 28, 1901.
4. Dorothy Marteil, b. Feb. 28. 1903.
5. Wayne Le Roy, b. Jan. 23, 1907.
6. Charles Ensor, b. Mar. 6. 1909.

(4) John Oland. b. Oct. 9. 1875; m Sarah E. Ashton, July 26, 1898, Adams, Mass.; they had

1. James Amasa, b. June 12, 1899; d. 1900.
2. Oland Ashton, b. Feb. 24, 1901.
3. Marjorie Vera, b. Feb. 2, 1903.
4. Gertrude Blanche, b. July 28, 1905.
5. John Heman, b. Sept. 17, 1908.

(5) Sanford Le Roy, b. July 25, 1880; m. Elvira Haischer, of Corning, N. Y., July 28, 1908; Stationer, Springfield, Mass.

(6) Walter Heman, b. Sept. 27, 1882; d. 1902.

(7) Wayne Alford, b. Sept. 18, 1885; in Third Field Artillery, U. S. A., Fort Sam Houston, Texas.

(8) Blanche Lindorah, b. Sept. 18, 1887; grad. 1907, Arms Academy, Shelburne Falls, Mass.

II. John, b. July 24, 1810. Sec. 264.

III. George, b. July 4, 1812. Sec. 265.

IV. William W., b. Feb. 24, 1815. Sec. 266.

V. David, b. July 26, 1817; m. Laura Lamb, of Heath, Mass.; went to Indiana, and after a time returned, settling at North Adams, where his wife d. July 4, 1897, and he d. in Colrain, 1907. Two of the five children survived them, George L. and Charles, who are in the West.

VI. Marietta, b. Mar. 27, 1820; d. in childhood.

VII. Levi, b. April 2, 1822. Sec. 267.

VIII. Joseph Emerson, b. May 24, 1825; d. in childhood.

Section 142-A

Simeon Cary, son of Capt. Floward, Sec. 71, b. Bridgewater, 1787; m. 1st, Roana Howard, 1806, and moved to Maine; m. 2d, Eunice Banks.

Children:

I. Dr. Nelson Howard; m. Maria Stockbridge, and had

1. William H., b. Aug. 24, 1830; d. Sept. 14, 1901; was in the 13th Mass. Vols. in the Civil War.
2. Joseph S., b. May 16, 1832; was in the 13th Mass. Vols. in the Civil War; m. Flora E. Harlow.
3. Marcia A., b. May 23, 1834; m. John Cushing Merrill, 1855, and had

(1) Maria S., a Teacher at Andover, Mass.; lives at Portland, Me.

(2) Sarah J.; m. Mr. Harlow, Woburn, Mass.

4. Ellen M., b. Oct. 11, 1837; m. 1st, John Q. Warren; m. 2d, Rev. William H. Haskell; they had

(1) Fred Morris Warren.

(2) Nelson Cary, M. D.

(3) Pearl Tenney, M. D.

(4) William Stockbridge.

(5) Harris Bigelow, M. D.

(6) Edward Kirk.

Rev. Mr. Haskell, b. at Greene, Me., son of William and Pauline Cony (Harris) Haskell; grad. Bangor, 1862; d. at Auburndale, Mass., June 11, 1905.

5. Samuel E., b. Dec. 25, 1839; he was 1st Lieut. 13th Mass. Vols., at Gettysburg, July 1, 1863, was taken prisoner, and released at Wilmington, N. C., Mar. 1, 1865, having been confined in the following prisons: Libby prison, Salisbury, and Charlotte, N. C., Augusta, Macon, and Savannah, Ga., Charleston, Columbia, and Florence, S. C., and Raleigh, N. C. He m. Catherine Lanning at Trinity church, Boston, April 11, 1871; they had

(1) Annie Louise, b. May 12, 1872, East Orange, N. J.

6. Annie Louise, b. Oct. 22, 1842; m. Charles Monson Raymond, June 29, 1882, who d. June 30, 1909.She is the widely known Contralto Singer.

7. Ada, b. Sept. 19, 1853; m. Eben H. Sturgis.

II. Daniel Williams, b. July 27, 1849, a printer, Cambridge, Mass.; m. Eldora M. Howe, Marlboro, Mass., Jan. 1, 1875, and had

1. Walter Howe, b. Dec. 13, 1876.

2. Arthur Williams, b. Aug. 26, 1880; m. Jessie E. B. Singer, and had

(1) Russell Singer.

(2) Evelyn Blanche; d. in infancy.

(3) Arthur Douglass.

(4) Robert H., b. Nov. 6, 1909.

Section 142-B

Daniel Howard Cary, son of Capt. Howard, Sec. 71, b. Bridgewater, 1788; m. Martha, dau. of Gideon Howard, Esq., 1812; he d. July 4, 1869, and his wife d. 1868, aged 75 years; they had.

I. Martha, who m. Seth Leonard, 1837; she d. 1854, leaving five children; of these, Lucia A. m. Mr. Stevens, Avon, Mass, and one m. Mr. H. H. Howard.

Section 142-C

Molly Cary, dau. of Capt. Howard, Sec. 71, b. Bridgewater, 1798; m. Ezra Dunham, who was b. at Plymouth, May 10, 1785, d. May 30, 1857; he m 1S C Abigail S. Ford, 1806, who d. Mar. 23, 1809; m. 2d. Molly Cary, 1810.

Children:
I. Gen. Henry, b. 1806, Abington, Mass.
II. Susan, b. 1810.
III. Howard Cary, b. Jan. 19, 1813. At the age of nineteen he joined the Methodist Episcopal Church, and in 1838 he entered the New England Conference, of which he remained a useful and honored member for sixty-eight years, dying Jan. 21, 1906. During the Civil War he spent two years in the Army Hospitals as the Agent of the Christian Commission. Failing health compelled him to ask to be relieved of the burdens of the pastorate, and he entered the work of the American Peace Society and for fourteen years he was thus engaged; but failing eyesight compelled him to leave that congenial service. In 1844 he m. Eliza Ann Drew, and two sons were born to them, both of whom died before him. In his blindness the family read much to him, and he was thus kept in touch with passing events. He died as he had lived, and it was well said of him, "In his translation the saintliest, sweetest, and sanest soul that many have been privileged to know has passed on to his abundant reward."
IV. Worthy C., b. 1815.
V. Charles Atwood, b. 1817, a Swedenborgian minister; m. and had Rev. Howard Cary Dunham, a minister of the same faith.
VI. Cornelius Thomas, b. 1820; a shoe merchant.
VII. Angeline H., b. 1821.
VIII. Ezra Ryder, b. 1822; a manufacturer; m. and lived in Winthrop, Mass.
IX. Elbridge Cary, b. 1828.
X. Francis Williams, b. 1829.
XI. Lydia Howard, b. 1834; m. Mr. O'Brien, Oct. 4, 1853, and had
1. Angie Frances, b. Aug. 15, 1854.
2. William S., b. Aug. 16, 1856; m. Florence Carver, and had (1) Louise Carver.
3. Delia Hammond, b. Dec. 22, 1862.
4. Robert Lincoln, b. Sept. 14, 1865; the long-time Washington Correspondent of the Boston Transcript, and now its Editor; m. Emilie Young, M. D., and have two daughters.
5. Mansfield Steede, b. June 9, 1868.
6. Charles Francis, b. Dec. 6, 1871; m. Grace Reed.
7. Helen Florence, b. July 9, 1875; m. Guy R. Cole.

Section 142-D

Rhoda Cary, dau. of Capt. Howard, Sec. 71, b. Bridgewater, 1800; m. Maj. Nathan Hayward, Nov. 17, 1818; she d. Nov. 9, 1858.
Children:
I. Nathan Cary, b. 1819; d. 1836.
II. Daniel, b. 1820; d. 1896.

III. Catherine, b. 1822; m. Edward H. Spaulding, Dec. 13, 1839, and had
1. Adelaide E., b. Feb. 27, 1841.
2. Charles Edward, b. Feb. 12, 1843; m. 1st, Eulia Hentz, Feb. 27, 1875, who d. April 10, 1878; m. 2d, Estelle Foster, Feb. 2, 1882, who d. June 22, 1885; m. 3d, Adaline Cary, Sept. 2, 1886.
3. George Elmer, b. Dec. 12, 1847.
IV. Ellen L., b. 1824; d. in infancy.
V. Ellen Louisa, b. North Bridgewater, now Brockton, Mass., April 9, 1825; m. Charles Richardson, a Boston merchant, Nov. 17, 1842, and had
1. Charles.
2. Elizabeth.
3. Arthur. All of these died early.
4. George Morey, b. July 7, 1859, at Framingham, where the family had gone for the health of their children; he grad, at Harvard, 1882, was Instructor there, Professor in University of California, and had Ph. D., from Leipsic; he then went to Greece for original research in Archaeology, but d. at Athens, Dec. 11, 1896, of typhoid fever.
5. Annah Huntington, b. June 13, 1861; m. Ansel Granville Cook, M. D., Hartford, Ct., 1891; he was Prest. of the Orthopedic Association, 1908; they had
(1) Katherine Cary, b. Aug. 21, 1894.
(2) Ellen Richardson, b. Nov. 16, 1896.
(3) Harriet Huntington, b. Mar. 31, 1898.
This family was carefully educated, traveled at home and abroad, and were workers in the church.
VI. Nathan W., b. 1827; d. 1864.
VII. Elizabeth, b. 1830; d. in youth.
VIII. Simeon, b. 1832; d. 1895.

Section 143

Zebulon Cary, son of Josiah, Sec. 72, b. Brookfield, Mass., Oct. 5, 1781; m. Polly-, 1808; he d. in Brookfield, Sept. 13, 1847, and she d. June 10, 1854.
Children:
I. Mary Ann, b. Feb. 5, 1809; m Solomon Sibley, Prescott, Mass.
II. Josiah, b. July, 1811; d. in childhood.
III. Eunice, b. Nov. 3, 1812; m. S. O. Johnson, West Brookfield, Mass.
IV. Josiah, b. Sept. 29, 1814. Sec. 268.
V. Zebulon, b. Sept. 11, 1817; d. in childhood.
VI. Susanna, b. July 5, 1819; m. Thomas Wheeler, Prescott, Mass.
VII. Calvin E., b. May 6, 1821; d. in childhood.
VIII. Zebulon E., b. April 27, 1823; m. Elizabeth Garland, West Brookfield.
IX. Harriet, b. Dec. 8, 1824, Brookfield.
X. Lucy, b. Dec. 10, 1826; m. Nelson B. Gale, Wardsboro, Vt.
XI. Sarah A., b. Sept. 11, 1828; m. E. Kent, of Vermont.

XII. Eliza S., b. Jan. 11, 1831; m. Alfred Gorham, Barre, Mass.

XIII. Ephraim C., b. Mar. 10, 1833; a member of the 34th Mass. Vols.

XIV. Lydia H., b. Sept. 10, 1835; d. Mar. 27, 1870; m. John Davis, Sept. 28, 1864, and had

1. Herbert C., b. July 1, 1860.
2. John A., b. Mar. 7, 1870.

Section 144

Josiah Cary, son of Josiah, Sec. 72, b. West Brookfield, Mass., April 17, 1783; m. Betsey Henry, May 3, 1807; he d. at St. Charles, Mo., Mar. 8, 1861.
Children:

I. Henry Watson, b. 1811; d. 1827.

II. Josiah Addison, b. 1813. Sec. 269.

III. Caroline E., b. 1815; m. Rev. A. V. C. Schenck.

IV. Charles Augustus, b. 1817; d. 1847.

Section 145

Avery Cary, son of Josiah, Sec. 72, b. Brookfield, Mass., Feb. 17, 1789; m. Abiah Spooner, of Brookfield, afterwards removed to Pittsfield, Mass.
Children:

I. Martha B., b. 1811; m. Ebenezer Dunham, Pittsfield, Mass.

II. Nathan C, b. 1814. Sec. 270.

III. Mary, b. 1816; m. Mr. Noble.

IV. Elizabeth C., b. 1820; m. S. R. Darling, Elyria, O.

V. Samuel A., b. 1823. Sec. 271.

VI. Josiah William, b. May 16, 1828, Pittsfield. In early life he entered the service of what has since become the Boston & Albany R. R.; in 1853 removed to Ohio, and in 1869 became the General Passenger Agent of the Lake Shore & Michigan Southern Ry., making his home at Elyria, O. He d. Aug. 2, 1886, having given almost fifty years to railway work. At his funeral it was said: "Pie was faithful. In all pecuniary trusts not the shadow of suspicion ever fell upon him. He was a true official because he was a true man." His children were:

1. Rollin Beach, b. Feb. 12, 1854, Elyria; m. Lillian W. Hulbert, and had

(1) Phillip Hulbert, b. July 4, 1889.

2. Mary Abiah, b. Aug. 5, 1858; m. 1st, Charles S. Hackett, Aug. 5, 1880; m. 2d, William Root, Oct. 5, 1905, and had (1) Mary Adelaide, b. May 25, 1881; m. 1st, James Simpson Sanford; m. 2d, Holden Meigs Wood, Dec. 5, 1905; they had

1. Richard J. Sanford, b. Aug. 5, 1903.

Section 146

Jonathan Cary, son of Josiah, Sec. 72, b. Brookfield, Mass., Sept. 10, 1798; m. 1st, Lucy H. Ayres, April 27, 1825; m. 2d, Betsey P. Ward, Oct. 16, 1834; lived at Worcester, Mass.
Children:
I. William Ayres, b. June 3, 1826; m. Harriet Parker, Nov., 1851, and had
1. Gertrude, b. Oct. 28, 1859.
II. Ereelove, b. April 11, 1829; m. David C. Thurston, 1854.

Section 147

Thomas H. Cary, son of Josiah, Sec. 72, b. Brookfield, Mass., Aug. 15, 1802; m. Hannah Moulton of Brookfield, Mar. 25, 1828; removed to Springville, N. Y.
Children:
I. Daniel M., b. June 25, 1831. Sec. 272.
II. Julia A., b. Dec. 20, 1833; d. 1853.
III. Charles, b. Feb. 25, 1838; m. Matilda Hanley, Dec. 1, 1862; lived at Springville, N. Y.

Section 148

Leonard Cary, son of Recompense, Sec. 73, b. Ward, Mass., April 2, 1793, a mechanic, was twice married, and had six children; d. at Boston, Mass., April 27, 1846.
Children:
I. Preston Moore, b. Aug. 15, 1816; he was at Savannah, Ga., at the beginning of the Civil War, but has not been heard from since; m. and had
1. Charles Preston, who was in the Union Army.
II. Martha E., b. Sept. 1, 1819; m. Mr. Ellis, and had a daughter who lived at Holden, Mass.
III. Caroline R., b. Dec. 17, 1822; m. William Haskell, No. Brookfield, Mass.
IV. Mary A., b. 1824; m. Mr. Johnson; lived at No. Brookfield, Mass.
V. Harriet E., b. Nov. 15, 1827.
VI. Charles Hibben, b. Oct. 5, 1829.

Section 149

Barzillai Cary, son of Moses, Sec. 74, b. Bridgewater, Aug. 25, 1780; m. Vashti, dan. of Nathan Snell, 1808; lived in his native town, which became the North Parish, and in 1821 North Bridgewater, and in 1874 the City of Brockton; he d. 1852.

Children:

I. Susanna, b. 1808; m. Luke Perkins, Auburn, Mass. Sec. 272-A.

II. Betsey, b. 1810; m. James Copeland, West Bridgewater, Mass.

III. Almira, b. 1812; m. Edward S. Packard; d. 1843.

IV. Barzillai, b. 1815; m. Augusta Gurney, lived on the Homestead, and had

1. Helen Augusta.

2. Louis Francis.

V. Nathan S., b. 1817; m. Betsey Gurney, lived in Bridgewater, and had 1. Mary Alice.

VI. Lucius, Judge, b. June 4, 1819; d. Sept. 3, 1892, Kansas City, Mo.; m. 1st, Sarah Elizabeth Gilman, April 2, 1846, who d. April 12, 1848; m. 2d, Mrs. Martha (Stone) McCoy, dau. of Daniel Stone (b. in Virginia, Dec. 29, 1830; d. April 27, 1905, Kansas City, Mo.), Dec. 15, 1853, and had

1. Robert Webster, b. Mar. 28, 1855, and lives at Kansas City, Mo.; m. Mrs. Lora (Marmaduke) Nelson, dau. of Col. Vincent Marmaduke, and had

(1) Robert Webster, b. Aug. 18, 1890; in U. S. Naval Academy, Annapolis.

2. James Stone, b. June 28, 1857; d. 1858.

3. Vesta Elizabeth, b. Jan. 20, 1860; m. Archibald G. Lackey of Kentucky, Nov. 7, 1883, and had

(1) Vesta, b. Oct. 2, 1884; m. Herbert Price of Danville, Ky.

(2) Mary Goodlow, b. June 25, 1886.

4. Martha, b. Aug. 26, 1861; m. William Stanbury Woods, April 11, 1884, and had

(1) William Clay, b. Oct. 8, 1885; m. Roxie Thompson.

(2) Martha Elizabeth, b. Sept. 29, 1887; m. Walton Holmes, Jr.

(3) Lucia Cary, b. April 27, 1890.

5. Lucius, b. Feb. 20, 1864; d. 1889.

6. Nellie, b. June 5, 1866; m. John Percy Huston of Marshall, Mo., Nov. 14, 1889, and had

(1) Lucius Cary, b. Oct. 6, 1892, in Marshall, Mo.

(2) John Percy, b. July 20, 1898, in Marshall, Mo.

(3) Mary Louise, b. Jan. 2, 1904, in Marshall, Mo.

7. Franklin Howard, b. Jan. 18, 1868.

VII. Rhoda, b. 1821; m. Daniel S. Howard. Sec. 272-B.

VIII. Mary, b. Dec. 4, 1823; m. Samuel Worcester Clapp (b. Sept. 3, 1821, Dorchester, Mass.; d. Mar. 22, 1876, Boston), April 30, 1845, North Bridgewater, and had 1. Ellen Cordelia, b. Feb. 12, 1846; d. 1869.

IX. Vesta S., b. May 1, 1827; m. Henry K. Keith. Sec. 272-C.

Section 150

Caleb Cary, son of Jonathan, Sec. 75, b. Bridgewater, 1788; removed to East Machias, Me., 1809; m. Sarah Talbot; he d. Dec. 20, 1848, and she d. 1856.

Children:

I. Charles, b. 1826. Sec. 273.

II. Lucy, d. in infancy.

III. Levi S., b. 1835; m. Lavina Simpson, 1860, and lived at East Machias; they had

1. Wales L., b. 1861.

Section 151

Jonathan Cary, son of Jonathan, Sec. 75, b. Bridgewater, 1791; while young removed to East Machias, Me.; m. Mary Handscom, 1818, and settled at Cooper, Me.

Children:

I. Elisha Caleb, b. about 1819. Sec. 274.

II. Henry Smith, b. Aug. 4, 1822. Sec. 275.

III. Mary H., b. about 1823; m. Samuel Sprague, 1844, and had eight children.

IV. Priscilla Pineo, b. about 1825; m. Nelson Bridgham, 1846; she was devoutly religious, and of a mild and trusting disposition; a true and noble mother, and much given to generosity; was optimistic and believed that "to them that love God all things work together for good." While on the way to class meeting, the horse took fright, ran, and threw her and her husband from the carriage, resulting in her death. They had

1. Emma Evelin.

2. Milton Foster, Patten, Me.

3. Embert.

4. Adra Anna.

5. Frank Lathrop.

6. Edgar Cary, b. May 18, 1861; is a member of the New England Conference, and in 1910 was appointed to Springfield, Mass.; he m. Charlotte Abbie Stratton, April 27, 1887, and had

(1) Annie Priscilla, b. April 23, 1888.

(2) Frank Nelson, b. June 18, 1890.

(3) Ralph Embert, b. June 27, 1892.

7. Mary Helen.

8. Justin Roland, b. June 8, 1865, and lives at Haverhill, Mass.; m. Nellie F. Noyes, June 6, 1891, and had

(1) Emma Florence, b. Mar. 10, 1892.

(2) Marion, b. Aug. 15, 1893.

V. Aaron H., b. about 1827, and d. young.

Section 152

Luther Cary, son of Jonathan, Sec. 75, b. Bridgewater, 1794; in youth removed to East Machias, Me.; m. Eliza W. Foster, 1818, and settled in Cooper, where he d. March, 1886.

Children:

I. James Webber, b. August, 1819. Sec. 276.

II. Eliza A., b. April, 1822; d. in childhood.

III. George Williams, b. August, 1824; m. Roxana Damon, 1855; d. 1884.

IV. Mary L., b. November, 1826; d. in infancy.

V. Delia F., b. June, 1828; m. Stephen J. Getchell, Cooper, Me.; d. at Providence, R. I., September, 1883. They had 1. Waldo L., m. and had

(1) Carroll.

(2) Helen F., d. in Providence.

(3) Jennie; m. H. I. Leith, Providence, R. I., and had

1. Fred Getchell Leith, who grad. R. I. College of Pharmacy, and is Hospital Steward in U. S. Navy.

VI. Charlotte A., b. December, 1830; m. Henry L. Foster, 1855, who d. 1875; she lives in Providence.

VII. Mary E., b. March, 1834; m. Charles Cary, son of Caleb, Sec. 273.

VIII. Martin L., b. September, 1836. Sec. 276-A.

IX. Martha E., b. April, 1838; m. William S. Humphries, 1878; d. 1894; a devout Christian woman and Temperance worker, deeply loved and greatly mourned.

X. Hiram Foster, b. Aug. 29, 1842, Cooper, Me. He was a good singer; enlisted in the 1st Rhode Island Cav., and served through the Civil War; was in business in Providence, Boston, Ballston, and Saratoga Springs, N. Y., and took out several Patents; settled at Millbury, Mass., where he m. Frances J. Harrington, June 5, 1873, and had 1. Foster Harrington, M. D., who grad. Harvard Medical School, 1898, began practice in Worcester, Mass., 1902, and has largely given himself to special work.

Section 153

Martin Cary, son of Jonathan, Sec. 75, b. Bridgewater, 1795; m Bethia, dau. of Dea. Ichabod Howard, 1822, and settled in North Bridgewater, now the city of Brockton.

Children:

I. Melinda, b. 1825; m. Benjamin C. Frobisher.

II. Henry Martin, b. 1827; d. in childhood.

III. George Clark, b. 1831; m. Harriet G. Ford, Aug. 2, 1855, and d. Sept. 12, 1896, having been a Deacon in the Porter Congregational Church, Brockton, for 27 years, and Treasurer 22 years; they had

1. Henry Martin, b. Jan. 31, 1857; d. 1865.

IV. Charles Howard, b. July 6, 1837; m. Hannah C. Alden, 1858, and had

1. Martin Alden, b. 1860.

2. Fred W.

3. George H.

Section 153-A

Abigail Cary, dau. of Jonathan. Sec. 75, b. about 1797, on Cary Hill, Bridgewater; m. Isaac Dunham of Plymouth (d. Mar. 25, 1856), Oct. 7, 1811, and removed to Maine about 1812. During the War of 1812-14, he was on a privateer; he was the first Light Keeper at Pemaquid, Me., at Nauset, Cape Cod, and at Minot's Ledge Light, off Boston; of the latter he wrote a friend, that "it would be a trap for some one;" the Minot's Ledge Light was first lighted Jan. 1, 1850; he resigned, and the next April it was washed away.

Children:

I. Henry C., b. May 25, 1814; m. Laura Brett, Sept. 8, 1838, who d. 1886, and he d. 1893.

II. Abigail, b. Aug. 31, 1817; m. Sidney Eaton of Chelsea, Mass., Dec. 25, 1860.

III. Isabella, b. April 13, 1822; m. Barnabas Snow of Eastham, Mar. 6, 1842.

IV. Mary Aurelia, b. July 11, 1824; d. Aug. 15, 1875; m. Isaac Brett, June 29, 1853.

V. Isaac Atwood, b. Mar. 6, 1827; m. Augusta L. Packard, April 29, 1849, who d. 1896.

VI. Benjamin Franklin, b. Feb. 13, 1831; m. Maria Packard, May 15, 1854, and live at Brockton, Mass.

Section 153-B

Mary Cary, dau. of Jonathan, Sec. 75, b. Mar. 13, 1797 5 d. May 8, 1869; m. James Littlefield, June 2, 1823. She had the strong characteristics of the Cary family, a woman of most excellent judgment, firm principles, warm affection, and deep religious experience—a true mother in Israel.

Children:

I. Rebecca Tucker, b. Mar. 14, 1824; d. 1879.

II. Theodore, b. Dec. 6, 1825; d. in infancy.

III. George Cary, b. Jan. 29, 1827; d. in infancy.

IV. James Austin, b. Feb. 17, 1829; d. 1903.

V. Mary Ann, b. Mar. 4, 1831; d. 1884.

VI. Edward Francis, b. Sept. 5, 1833; d. 1883.

VII. Josephine Waldo, b. Aug. 5, 1835.

VIII. Helen Maria, b. Nov. 12, 1838; d. in infancy.

Section 154

Alpheus Cary, son of Alpheus, Sec. 76, b. Quincy, Mass., Nov. 5, 1788; m. Deborah Thayer, and devoted his life to teaching; spent many years in Quincy, then removed to Boston.

Children:
I. Alpheus, b. October, 1827; d. in childhood.
II. George Washington, b. 1830; d. 1850.
III. Charles William, b. 1833; d. in childhood.

Section 155

Lewis Cary, son of Alpheus, Sec. 76, b. Quincy, Mass., Mar. 31, 1798; m. Adeline E. Billings, 1821, Boston, Mass.; he d. November, 1834
Children:
I. Lewis B., b. 1822; m. Caroline Boston, and had 1. Adeline Eliza, who d. in infancy.
II. Charles G., b. 1824. Sec. 277.
III. Thomas W., b. 1826. Sec. 278.

Section 156

Isaac Cary, son of Alpheus, Sec. 76, b. Quincy, Mass., June 25, 1802; m. Julia, dau. of Simon Willard the celebrated Clock maker (b. 1753; d. 1848, Boston), 1830; removed to Boston, and for more than thirty years was an Engraver of Bank Notes, and Manager and Treasurer of the American Bank Note Co. He was a member of the Board of Aldermen for seventeen years, besides holding various city, county, and state offices. His wife d. in 1863, and he m. Mrs. Maria White Priest, dau. of Hon. Josiah Stedman, Boston; he d. Jan. 4, 1867.
Children:
I. Abigail Perkins, b. January, 1832; d. about 1856.
II. Alexander Claxton, b. February, 1834. Sec. 279.
III. Julia Knox, b. August, 1836; studied Medicine, and was appointed on the staff of the Danvers Insane Asylum, the first woman so appointed in Massachusetts; she d. 1897.
IV. Mary Willard, b. July, 1838; m. Charles Walter Stuart, Sydney, Australia, and he d. there in 1888.
V. Isaac, b. April 13, 1840, Milton, Mass.
VI. Harriet Frances, b. April 17, 1842; m. Herman Paul Nefflen, Stuttgart, Wurtemberg, in Boston, 1884, and had
1. Pauline Willard; m. Alfred De Lisser, Brooklyn, N. Y.
2. Herman Paul, d. in infancy.

Section 157

Hon. Otis Cary, son of James, Sec. 77, b. in the North Parish of Bridgewater, now Brockton, on Cary Hill, June 14, 1804; m. Mary Dodge, dau. of Joseph Torrey of Hanson. Mass., Nov. 28, 1830, and in 1835 made his home in Foxboro, Mass., and for many years was an extensive Manufacturer and Bank President. He was public spirited, held nearly all the Town offices,.was Justice of the Peace, Representative and Senator in the General Court, and in 1844 was Chairman of the Liberty Party of Norfolk County.

Children:

I. Mary Ann, b. 1831. Sec. 279-A.

II. Sarah Thomas, b. 1834; was a Teacher in the South for some years; Foxboro, Mass.

III. John, b. 1836; d. 1862, Philadelphia, Pa.

IV. Hannah Wales, b. 1840; m. Benjamin F. Boyden, 1872, and had

1. Charles Cary, b. 1875, Newton Center, Mass.

2. Frank Learoyd, b. 1879; High School Teacher, Deerfield, Mass.

3. Ralph Howard, b. 1882.

4. Alice Cary, b. 1883; d. in childhood.

V. Charles, b. 1842; grad. Amherst; Philadelphia, Pa.

VI. Otis, b. April 20, 1851. Sec. 279-B.

Section 157-A

Nancy Cary, dau. of James, Sec. 77, b. Brunswick, Me., Feb. 24, 1807; m. Elbridge H. Packard, May 15, 1832; was at Mary Lyon's school at Ipswich, and had as schoolmate Harriet Beecher, author of "Uncle Tom's Cabin."

Children:

I. Ann Maria, b. Sept. 22, 1833; m. Benjamin F. Dunham, May 15, 1854, Brockton, Mass. He was b. in a Lighthouse on the coast of Maine, and his father was the first Keeper of the old Minot's Ledge Light, Boston. See Sec. 153-A.

II. James Alden, b. Dec. 7, 1835, and was four years in the Civil War; m. Carrie-, and had

1. Mary Cary.

2. Annie G.

3. Richard P.

4. Carrie L.

5. Ralph B.

III. Austin Cary, b. Aug. 21, 1838; m. Eliza Frances Howard, Oct. 16, 1860, and had

1. Florence L., b. July 13, 1862; m. William L. Joyce, Oct. 17, 1880, and had

(1) Bertha Frances, b. Sept. 21, 1882; m. Fred A. Leach, and had

1. Frederick Clayton, b. Mar. 2, 1904.

2. Helen Leslie, b. May 23, 1908.

2. Marion G., b. May 23, 1865; m. Howard M. Dow, June 1, 1887, and had

(1) Esther H., b. Mar. 26, 1888.

(2) Wilford Stewart, b. Jan. 5, 1894.

3. Wilford, b. Aug. 21, 1867.

4. Harold, b. Mar. 8, 1877; m. Mary E. Hollis, April 27, 1898, and had
(1) Priscilla Alden, b. June 30, 1900.
5. Robert, b. Mar. 23, 1880.
6. Robert Francis, b. Sept. 21, 1882.
7. Helen Cary, b. July 12, 1884; m. Arthur F. Reed, Aug. 9, 1906.
8. Clarence Austin, b. Oct. 26, 1886.
9. Archie W., b. May 21, 1889.

IV. Richard, b. Jan. 22, 1842; was in the Civil War, and killed at Fredericksburg, Va.

V. Hannah Persis, b. June 22, 1845.

Section 158

Rev. Austin Cary, son of James, Sec. 77, b. Bridgewater, 1809; grad, at Amherst, 1837, studied Theology, and was settled as a Congregational Minister at Sunderland, Mass., 1840-49; m. Catherine, dau. of Roger Phelps, Windsor, Ct., 1842; he d. 1849, much lamented; his widow m. Rev. M. Kingman, Claremont, N. H.

Children:
I. Austin P., b. 1846.
II. Willie C., b. 1848.

Section 159

Abram Cary, son of Isaac, Sec. 78, b. Morris Co., N. J., 1762; m. in New Jersey, removed to Pennsylvania, thence to the Northwest Territory, settling in Cincinnati, O., 1796; he owned a tract of land in Millcreek Valley, now a part of the City; afterward removed to Springfield, O., where he d. 1816.

Children:
I. Col. Samuel, b. 1784. Sec. 280.
II. Waitstill Munson, b. 1785. Sec. 281.
III. Sarah, b. 1788.
IV. Phebe, b. 1790; m. Mr. Skillman, and had five sons and three daughters.
V. Charlotte, b. 1792.
VI. Martha, b. 1794; d. Springfield, O.
VII. Francis, b. 1796; a Methodist Minister.
VIII. Martha, b. 1798.
IX. Eliza, b. 1800.

Section 160

Henry Cary, son of John, Sec. 79, b. Mendham, N. J., Jan. 6, 1780; m. Sarah Day, Feb. 9, 1802; removed to Western Pennsylvania, 1806; he was a farmer; d. 1853, and his widow in 1859.

Children:

I. Rebecca, b. Jan. 7, 1804; m JConnett, Green Co., Pa.

II. David, b. April 16, 1808; d. in childhood.

III. Bethany, b. Feb. 4, 1812; m. Mr. Jordan, Athens Co., O.

IV. John, b. Jan. n, 1815; became a Physician in Green Co., Pa., and had a daughter.

V. Isaac N., b. Mar. 22, 1816; became a Cumberland Presbyterian Minister, Carmichael's, Green Co., Pa.

Section 161

Clement Cary, son of John, Sec. 79, b. Mendham, N. J., May 22, 1792. where he lived on a farm at Suckasunna Plains; m. 1st, Phebe Jennings, and had seven children; m. 2d, Thankful Hathaway, and had one child; m. 3d, Julia King; he d. 1854.

Children:

I. Mary Ann, b. Sept. 29, 1806; m. Albert Matthews, Orange, N. J.

II. Silas Jennings, b. Jan. 1, 1808; m. Miss Dougherty, and wife and children died; settled in Clinton, Miss., where he m. and had two children; he d. of cholera on the way to New York.

III. Ebenezer, b. July 30, 1810. Sec. 281-A.

IV. Rebecca, b. Feb. 13, 1813; m. Lewis Lyon, Newark, N. J., and d. 1853.

V. Elizabeth D., b. July 9, 1815, Orange, N. J.

VI. Daniel Lyon, b. July 21, 1817; went to California.

VII. Phebe J., b. Dec. 25, 1819; m. D. G. Smith, Orange, N. J.

VIII. Ralph Hathaway, b. Mar. 8, 1827, Kenville, N. J.

Section 162

Nathaniel Cary, son of John, Sec. 79, b. Mendham, N. J., Dec. 5, 1786; m. Matilda Axtell, 1814; removed to Newark, N. J., 1856.

Children:

I. Henry Axtell, b. Nov. 4, 1816. Sec. 282.

II. Maryette, b. Feb. 3, 1819; m. F. W. Morrow, 1838, had a large family, and lived near St. Joseph, Mich.

III. Lewis, b. June 13, 1820. Sec. 283.

IV. Isaac, b. Mar. 22, 1823. Sec. 284.

V. John, b. Nov. 29, 1825; m. Martha E. Axtell, Feb. 12, 1862, Newark, N. J.

VI. Matilda, b. Feb. 11, 1828; d. in childhood.

VII. Matilda, b. Jan. 3, 1830.

VIII. Nathaniel, b. April 22, 1832; d. in infancy.

IX. Elias Riggs, b. May 25, 1833; m. Amanda Perine, Nov. 23, 1859; he was an Army Surgeon.

X. David Lyon, b. Jan. 25, 1837; d. in youth.

Section 163

John Cary, son of John, Sec. 79, b. Mendham, N. J., May 27, 1797; m. Eunice H. Babbitt, 1819, and lived on a part of the old Homestead owned by his grandfather. He wrote the following to the author of "Cary Memorials" "I have never known a Cary very wealthy, nor very poor, and never heard of one charged with crime."
Children:
I. Joanna, b. Aug. 17, 1821; m. Dr. Henry Vigor, 1815; lived in Fayette Co., O., and had ten children.
II. Elizabeth, b. Nov. 9, 1822; m. Stephen Lyon, Sept. 29, 1850; lived at Martinsville, N. J., and had two children.
III. Ezra Day, b. Feb. 11, 1824; d. in childhood.
IV. David Howell, b. Oct. 5, 1825; d. in childhood.
V. Louisa, b. April 24, 1827; d. 1854.
VI. Sarah J., b. Sept. 17, 1827; grad, at Mt. Holyoke Sem., and taught at Port Jervis, N. Y.
VII. Ezra H., b. June 25, 1830; grad, at Medical College, Cincinnati, and was a Surgeon in the Army of the Potomac.
VIII. Martha, b. July 4, 1832; d. in infancy.
IX. John H., b. April 2, 1835; d. in childhood.
X. Edwin H., b. April 24, 1837.
XI. Mary F., b. Oct. 7, 1839.

Section 164

Isaac Cary, son of John, Sec. 79, b. Mendham, N. J., Nov. 18, 1800; m. Sarah B. Hovey, Sept. 11, 1831, Richmond, Va.; he was extensively engaged in the manufacture of carriages.
Children:
I. Frances Ann, b. July 17, 1832; d. 1856.
II. Ellor Virginia, b. Oct. 17, 1838; d. in childhood.
III. Mary Julia, b. Oct. 19, 1841; d. in infancy.

Section 165

Ebenezer Cary, son of Ebenezer, Sec. 80, b. in Western New York, about 1816; m. Catherine J. Fonda; he d. November, 1863.
Children:
I. Alfred.
II. Ebenezer.
III. Lucinda.
IV. John.

Section 166

Ebenezer Cary, son of Chad., Sec. 81, b. Smithfield, R. I., Aug. 6, 1797; he was a Machinist, and m. 1st, Rhoda Burlingame, Scituate, R. I., Jan. 3, 1821; m. 2d, Adah Burlingame.
Children:
I. Hannah B., b. Oct. 14, 1821; m. John M. Barker, Providence, R. I., Nov. 24, 1856, who distinguished himself as an officer in the Union Army.
II. Elizabeth, b. Aug. 4, 1823; m. Joel G. Brown, Dec. 31, 1846, and lived in Providence.
III. George, b. Aug. 4, 1825; d. in infancy.
IV. Angeline, b. Sept. 29, 1827; m. Edward D. Leveck, May 2, 1847, Providence.
V. Abby T., b. Feb. 8, 1830; d. in infancy.
VI. Emily T., b. Feb. 8, 1831, Providence, R. I.
VII. Susan, b. May 30, 1833; m. Henry Young, Nov. 27, 1851, and had three children, Providence, R. I.
VIII. Esther A., b. May 8, 1836; m. Thomas J. Thurber, Sept., 1854, Providence, and had two children.
IX. Jerome, b. 1838; d. in infancy.
X. Ellen M., b. May 13, 1841; m. Daniel Perkins, July 25, 1864, Providence.
XI. Isabel, b. Nov. 19, 1851, Providence.

Section 167

William Cary, son of Chad., Sec. 81, b. Smithfield, R. I., Mar. 18, 1799, and was a Stonecutter; m. Elma, dau. of Olney Colwell, Johnston, R. I., Aug. 14, 1836; d. at Pine Hill, Johnston, R. I., Aug. 21, 1862.
Children:
I. William Henry, b. May 17, 1837. Sec. 285.
II. Olney C., b. July 15, 1840; d. 1842.
III. John O., b. Aug. 27, 1841; d. in childhood.
IV. Julia, b. Nov. 27, 1843; m Rufus Harris, May 11, 1862, lived at Graniteville, R. I., and had three children.
V. Sarah E., b. July 30, 1845; d. in infancy.
VI. Mary M., b. Dec. 10, 1850; d. in infancy.
VII. Ursula L., b. Dec. 10, 1850; d. in infancy.
VIII. Nathaniel S., b. Jan. 25, 1852, South Providence, R. I.
IX. George W., b. May 8, 1854, Johnston, R. I.; m. Edith V. L. Cary, Providence, April 4, 1875, and had
  1. John W., b. Jan. 26, 1876, North Providence; m. Jennie B. Whiteside, of New Bedford, Mass., Nov. 27, 1902, and had
    (1) Rebecca V., b. Nov. 8, 1903.
    (2) George W., b. July 13, 1905.

2. Elma V., b. April 9, 1883.
3. Sarah L., b. Sept. 13, 1884; d. in infancy.
X. Rodolpho F., b. Feb. 17, 1858, South Providence; m. Lillian M. Warren, Feb. 17, 1880, and had
1. Ruby W.
2. Ethel M., b. April 12, 1890.

Section 168

George S. Cary, son of Chad., Sec. 81, b. Smithheld, R. I., Sept. 6, 1801; m. Sarah, dau. of Capt. Joseph Alverson, Johnstown, R. I., Feb. 6, 1825; removed to Cleveland, O.
Children:
I. Malissa A., b. Dec. 7, 1826; m. James W. Spifield, M. D., May 10, 1846; lived in New York City, and had four children.
II. George W., b. June 11, 1829. Sec. 286.
III. William H., b. Aug. 31, 1831. Sec. 287.
IV. Edward M., b. April 28, 1834. Sec. 288.

Section 169

Chad. B. Cary, son of Chad., Sec. 81, b. Johnstown, R. I., April 7, 1813; m. Ann Field, July 14, 1831, Pomfret, Ct.; was an artistic painter, and d. Mar. 29, 1855, Oxford, Mass.
Children:
I. George A., b. June 23, 1832; d. 1858, Oxford, Mass.
II. Albert, b. Sept. 27. 1837; d. in infancy, Killingly, Ct.
III. Charles F., b. April 1, 1839; m. Emeline J. Burnett, June 10, 1862; he d. Dec. 14, 1865, Worcester, Mass.; they had
1. Gertrude L., b. July 10, 1863; d. in infancy.
IV. Frederick E., b. April 6, 1841; d. 1860, Worcester.
V. Helen E., b. February, 1843; m Joseph A. Moore, Oct. 10, 1867, Worcester.
VI. Emma J., b. May 3, 1845; m. George E. Murdock, Nov. 29, 1864; she d. 1868, Worcester.
VII. Frances A., b. Feb. 14, 1847; d. 1866, Worcester.
VIII. Edward D., b. Sept. 9, 1849; d. 1865, Worcester.
IX. Mara A., b. Jan. 7, 1852, Worcester.

Section 170

John H. Cary, son of Chad., Sec. 81, b. Johnstown, R. I., May 17, 1816; m. Sarah Livsey, of Stockport, Eng., Nov. 29, 1843; he was a Wheelwright, and lived at Providence, R. I.

Children:

I. Edward T., b. Oct. 31, 1844; d. in childhood.

II. Edwin T., b. Jan. 25, 1848; a Druggist in Providence.

III. Alfred H., b. Jan. 22, 1850; a Printer in Providence; m. 1st, Sarah, dau. of Samuel Love, Lawrence, Mass., 1873; m. 2d, Elvinia Abby, dau. of Stephen Garland, Providence, 1886; they had

  1. Helen Augusta, b. Aug., 1873; m. Robert Graham, Seattle, Wash.

  2. Grafton Everard, b. July, 1878; d. in infancy.

  3. Albert St. Clair, b. Mar. 13, 1879; m. Margaret McDonald, Providence, had

  (1) Florence, b. July 7, 1897.

  (2) Clarence, b. Sept, n, 1899.

This family live in Boston.

IV. John Leonard, b. Feb. 10, 1853, and is a Plumber; m. rst, Sarah E., dau. of John Boardman, Center Falls, R. I., May 21, 1873; m. 2d, Henrietta Jeanetta, dau, of George Dowling Flagg, Oct. 19, 1905; they had

  1. Maud Livsey, b. Mar. 10, 1874; m. Clarence O. Chase, Providence, June 21, 1897.

  2. William Leonard, b. Feb. 14, 1875; m. Carrie E. Tobey, July 8, 1902.

  3. John Henry, b. Aug. 28, 1881.

V. Sarah A., b. Feb. 1, 1856; d. in infancy.

VI. Sarah Etta, b. Sept. 30, 1862, Providence; m. Asa G. Davis, Feb. 1, 1883, had

  1. Harold G. Davis, b. July 1, 1889, Providence.

Section 171

Joseph Cary, son of Joseph, Sec. 82, b. Middlefield, Mass., Jan. 17 , 1784; m. Freelove Fuller, Jan. 20, 1803; removed to Ontario, Wayne Co., N. Y., where he d. Feb. 3, 1848.

Children:

I. Joseph, b. Sept. 6, 1805, Stowe, Vt.

II. Lyman, b. 1807, Stowe, Vt.

III. Elliott, b. 1809, Stowe, Vt.

Section 172

Isaac Cary, son of Joseph, Sec. 82, b. Williamsburg, Mass., Sept. 15, 1804; m. Sarah Wyart, 1823; who d. 1887; removed to Ontario, N. Y., thence to Stowe, Vt., where he d. 1893.

Children:

I. Sarah, b. Sept. 6, 1826; m. James Barnes, lived in Ontario, N. Y., and had six children.

II. Isaac, b. Aug. 29, 1829; m. Nancy Richardson, lived at Fort Edward, N. Y., where he d. 1895; they had one son and one daughter.

III. Olive Elizabeth, b. Mar. 28, 1833. Sec. 288-A.
IV. Mary Ann, b. July 12, 1835; m. George W. Prescott, lived at Stowe, Vt., and d. 1889; they had three daughters.
1. Satie Della, b. Aug. 22, 1871; m. John Wilson, a Railway man, Mar. 31, 1892, and live at Sumter, S. C.
V. Hudson, b. April 1, 1838; lives on the old farm, Stowe, Vt.
VI. Joseph, b. Nov. 4, 1843, Stowe, Vt.
VII. Nancy Jane, b. Mar. 19, 1845; m. George R. Stevens, Fort Edward, N. Y.

Section 173

Richard M. Cary, son of Richard, Sec. 83, b. Williamsburg, Mass., Dec. 19, 1794; m. Susanna Rice, Mar. 12, 1815; removed to Erie Co., N. Y., thence to Rock Co., Wis., where he d. Oct. 17, 1868.
Children:
I. Calvin, b. Oct. 1, 1816. Sec. 289.
II. Ephraim, b. Oct. 27, 1818. Sec. 290.
III. Benjamin F., b. Feb. 15, 1821. Sec. 291.
IV. Abraham J., b. Aug. 7, 1822; m. Elizabeth Fuller, Mar. 26, 1857, and had
I. Benjamin Franklin, b. Sept. 3, 1858, lived at Johnstown, Wis.
V. Richard M., b. Aug. 23, 1824; d. in infancy.
VI. Lydia J., b. Nov. 11, 1825; d. in childhood.
VII. Orinda P., b. Jan. 29, 1828; d. 1844.
VIII. Richard, b. April 8, 1830. Sec. 292.
IX. Lydia S., b. Feb. 12, 1832; m. F. E. Osborne, Jan. 1, 1853.
X. Melvin, b. June 28, 1834. Sec. 293.
XI. Louisa J., b. April 22, 1837; m. G. G. Clark, Janesville, Wis.
XII. Roswell, b. Jan. 13, 1839; d. 1868.

Section 174

Luther Harvey Cary, son of Richard, Sec. 83, b. Williamsburg, Mass., Feb., 1800; went to Boston, Erie Co., N. Y., 1806; was a farmer, and d. Dec. 20, 1874; m. Lucy Doolittle, Dec., 1821; they spent their lives on the farm originally taken up by the Cary family, now occupied by their descendants; in their lives they exemplified the qualities that made the New England name a synonym for intelligence and integrity.
Children:
I. Luther H., b. June 28, 1823, Boston, N. Y. Taught school; grad. Geneva Med. Col., 1846; m. Arvilla Ferguson at Boston, Sept., 1846. Removed to Greenbush, Wis., and began the practice of medicine; in which he was successful; served in the State Senate two terms, and in the lower House one; was a delegate to the Convention that nominated Abraham Lincoln. Was Surgeon of the 12th Wis., and afterwards Med. Inspector of the 16th Corps. Re-

moved to Oakland, Cal., for his health; was elected to the Legislature, and for some years was Collector of Internal Revenue; d. Sept. 16, 1888; they had

1. Florence Eugenia, b. Aug. 15, 1859; m Joseph N. Ziegenfuss, live in Oakland, and had

(1) Florence Cary, b. Mar. 13, 1884.
(2) Josephine Cary, b. Dec. 2, 1886; d. 1895.
(3) Arvilla Cary, b. Jan. 26, 1892.
(4) Kathryn Cary, b. April 16, 1896.
(5) Grace Cary, b. Oct. 13, 1900.

2. Lewis Harvey, b. Aug. 27, 1865; m. Bessie Llewellyn, live at Oakland; had

(1) Alice, b. Nov. 4, 1888.
(2) John Earl, b. July 18, 1890.
(3) Louis Llewellyn, b. Feb. 21, 1894.

II. Van Rensselaer, b. Aug. 23, 1825; m. Jane A. Skinner, Nov. 30, 1850, who d. April 23, 1810; he d. July 19, 1907. He was a school teacher and a seafarer, and held various offices in his county, where he was highly esteemed. They had

1. Cassius M., b. April 1, 1853; d. 1854.
2. Elgin Bruce, b. July 4. 1855; m. Nancy M. Cary, May 5, 1895, who d. May 8, 1907. They had

(1) Van Rensselaer, b. Mar. 1, 1896.
(2) Howard Elgin, b. Oct. 6, 1897.
(3) Esther Jane, b. Jan. 30, 1902..
(4) Nancy, b. May 5, 1907; d. 1909.

3. Luther Drysdale, b. May 19, 1857; m. Carrie B. Goodspeed, Oct. 20, 1880; was a farmer in Boston, N. Y.; d. June 25, 1909; they had

(1) David Drysdale, b. Sept. 18, 1881; m. Millicent Diver at Rusk, N. Y., 1907, and live in New York City,
(2) Frank Amzi, b. June 28, 1883; m. Helene Burkenshaw, at Troy, N. Y., Nov. 30, 1907, and live in Boston, N. Y.
(3) Robert Luther, b. Oct. 20, 1893.

III. Richard Leander, b. Feb. 11, 1827, Boston, N. Y. At 14 left home to learn printing, and became partner in the Cattaraugus Whig; m. Lucia A. Beecher, April 9, 1851, who d. 1866; m. 2d, Anna W. Matteson, who d. Feb., 1892. He was a Merchant, Postmaster under Abraham Lincoln, and Lumber Dealer, and highly respected. They had

1. Richard L., b. July 1, 1854, in Dunkirk, N. Y. He is a Newspaper Correspondent, and published a volume of Poems; m. and lives in Jacksonville, Fla.; had

(1) Hazel, b. Feb. 2, 1882; m. Charles H. Kerr, and live in Southbridge, Mass.

2. Eugene, b. Nov. 4, 1857, Dunkirk; educated at Cornell University; is a Lawyer and holds various offices; m. Mary M. Wand, July 5, 1882, and lives at Niagara Falls, N. Y.; they had

(1) Anna, b. May 26, 1883.

(2) Richard, b. Jan. 29, 1885.

3. Philip Beecher, b. May 4, 1864; m. Kate Camp Burritt of Dunkirk. June 14, 1877; reside in Buffalo; they have

(1) Barbara Alice, b. Mar. 28, 1892; d. 1893.

(2) Edward Burritt, b. Mar. 18, 1894.

(3) Winifred, b. May 22, 1898.

4. Lucia B., b. May 7, 1867.

IV. Tallcut Patchin, b. April n, 1828, Boston, N. Y. He went to California overland in 1851, and has been a successful farmer and stock raiser, lives at San Leandro; m. Elizabeth McGee, who d. May 24, 1903. They had

1. Lucy, b. Sept. 9, 1857; m. Austin Walrath, who d. some years ago; they had

(1) Avis, b. April 29, 1884; d. 1903. Mrs. W. resides with her father.

2. Margaret, b. Aug. 28, 1861; m. Edmund Perkins, and had

(1) Carolyn, b. Feb. 1, 1888.

(2) Cary, b. Nov. 18, 1889.

(3) Warren, b. May 27, 1892.

(4) Tallcut, b. Nov. 24, 1893.

3. Amzi, b. Nov. 1, 1863; m. Bessie Gibbons, is a farmer at San Leandro; had

(1) Lois, b. Mar. 11, 1891.

(2) Dorothy, b. May 29, 1894; d. 1895.

(3) Lucy, b. Sept. 16, 1898.

(4) Ruth, b. Sept. 16, 1898.

V. Amzi Beriah, b. Aug. 3, 1830, Boston, N. Y. Grad, at Oberlin, and went to Greenbush, Wis., to practice Medicine; became Surgeon of the 12th Wis., and died in the service, Sept. 14, 1862. Their children were

1. Frank, b. Oct. 21, 1857. He was educated at Cornell and Rush Med. Col., and is a Specialist and leading Physician in Chicago; m. Harriet Hyel, Aug. 13, 1885, who is also a graduate of Cornell and Blackwell Med. Col., and have

(1) Eugene, b. Nov. 11, 1886.

(2) Louis H., b. Jan. 2, 1891.

(3) Clara, b. Nov. 2, 1897.

2. Helen, b. May 21, 1860; m. Elliott Pritchard, and live at Waterman, Ill.; they have

(1) Lucile, b. Dec. 16, 1893.

(2) Elliott A., b. Mar. 14, 1896.

(3) Frank Cary, b. July 20, 1900.

VI. Eugene, b. Feb. 20, 1835, Boston, N. Y.; d. at St. Louis, Mar. 22, 1904. His early years were spent on the farm, and while still a boy taught school, and read law in Buffalo with N. K. Hall, Millard Fillmore's partner; attended Hillsdale College, and completed his legal studies at Sheboygan, Wis., and was admitted to the Bar in 1856; the next year, when only 22, was elected County Judge; m. Martha Rowe in 1858. At the beginning of the Civil War he became Captain in the 1st Wis. Vols. After the war he practiced law in Nashville,

Tenn., and served a term as State Senator, and as Judge of the Circuit Court. In 1871 went to Chicago and became the Manager of the German American Insurance Co., and was one of the most widely and favorably known insurance men in the country.

Eugene Cary was a man of the most rugged and solid qualities of body and mind; of great executive ability and business sagacity, a talented speaker. But the qualities which distinguished him among men were the integrity of his manhood, his wide benevolence, and his genial kindness of heart. His Pastor, Dr. Gunsaulus, said he was the best versed man in the Bible that he had ever known.

Section 175

Truman Cary, son of Asa, Sec. 85, b. Williamsburg, Mass., May 31, 1791; m. Fanny Alger, Nov. 4, 1813, Cazenovia, N. Y., who d. April 28, 1864; lived at Boston, N. Y.
Children:
I. Mary, b. Feb. 19, 1815.
II. Damaris, b. Feb. 18, 1817; m. Mr. Jones.
III. Fanny, b. Aug. 29, 1819.
IV. Truman, b. Nov. 27, 1821.
V. Roxania, b. Jan. 16, 1824.
VI. Danforth A., b. July 31, 1833; d. 1868.

Section 176

Joseph Cary, son of Asa, Sec. 85, b. Williamsburg, Mass., Dec. 27, 1797; m. Eliza Ayres, Oct. 5, 1823, Erie Co., N. Y.; removed to Freeport, Ill., and d. Dec. 8, 1870.
Children:
I. Wesley, b. Sept. 8, 1824; m. Hannah N. Pass, Dec. 13, 1853, Freeport, Ill., and had two sons and one daughter.
II. Erastus, b. Sept. 28, 1828; m. Priscilla Boenebright, Dec. 10, 1852, Freeport, Ill., and had two sons and one daughter; he d. Oct. 19, 1870.
III. Wealthy, b. May 16, 1839; m Austin S. Smith, Oct. 2, 1862, and lived at Webster City, Ia.

Section 177

Rev. Sylvester Cary, son of Asa, Sec. 85, b. Cazenovia, N. Y., Aug. 16, 1800; m. Cynthia Alverson, Jan. 19, 1821; a Presbyterian clergyman, and lived in Michigan.
Children:

I. Amy Ann, b. April 28, 1822; d. 1853; m. Luman Fuller, Nov. 30, 1841, Kalamazoo, Mich.; he d. June 4, 1865, Milford, Mich.; they had

1. Amelia H., b. Mar. 29, 1844; m. Darius C. Calkins, Lansing, Mich., 1864; he d. and the widow lived at Los Angeles, Cal.; they had

(1) Frederick Cary.

2. Samuel, b. Feb. 1, 1846; m. Ella E. Waterman, Aug. 4, 1868; live at Orange City, Fla., and had five children.

3. Cordelia C., b. Feb. 7, 1848; m. Benjamin Glasse, June 17, 1872, Parsons, Kan., and had five children.

4. Emory Luman, b. Mar. 7, 1850; m. Harriet Waterman, Detroit, Mich.

5. Annie Clarissa, b. Mar. 2, 1852; m. Theodore C. Link, a well-known Architect of St. Louis, Mo., Sept. 22, 1875, and had

(1) Karl Eugene, b. Nov. 28, 1876; m. Katherine R. Hall, Sept. 19, 1896, and had

1. Ella Louise, b. July 21, 1900.
2. Katherine, b. Nov. 4, 1905.

(2) Herman Theodore, d. May 29, 1902.

(3) Edwin Cary, b. May 4, 1880; m. Virginia Cabanne, Oct. 15, 1902; had

1. Virginia Cabanne, b. Aug. 16, 1903.
2. Theodore C., b. Sept. 22, 1904.
3. Edwin Cary, b. Oct. 10, 1905.

(4) Clarence Vincent, b. Oct. 30, 1882.

(5) Louise, b. June 5, 1886; d. in childhood.

II. Sylvester Emory, b. Sept. 12, 1831; m. 1st, Annie Walter; m. 2d, Cora E. Watson, Holly Springs, Miss., Feb. 24, 1870, and had

1. Arthur Lee, who d. in infancy.

2. Nellie Sheldon, b. Jan. 1, 1874; m. Lucius H. Dancy, a Pharmacist of Holly Springs, and had

(1) Cora Cary, b. Mar. 8, 1903.

(2) Nellie Mary, b. June 25, 1905.

(3) Lucius Henry, b. May 5, 1908.

3. Elizabeth Sylvester, b. July 28, 1879; m. Hamilton Johnson, C. E., and City Engineer, Jackson, Miss., Feb. 2, 1904, and had

(1) Cary, b. June 30, 1908.

Mr. Cary was Gen. Ticket and Pass. Agent of the Illinois Central R. R., and d. at New Orleans, La., Nov. 26, 1880.

Section 178

Van Rensselaer Cary, son of Asa, Sec. 85, b. Cazenovia, N. Y., Jan. 5, 1805; m. Sophia Streeter, Jan. 1, 1826, and removed to Freeport, Ill.

Children:

I. Sylvester L., b. Feb. 23, 1827. Sec. 294.

II. John W., b. Mar. 5, 1829. Sec. 295.

Section 179

Asa Cary, son of Asa, Sec. 85, b. Erie county, N. Y., Aug. 22, 1821; m. Laura Rice, Nov. 18, 1849; removed to Silver Creek, N. Y.
Children:
I. Homer A., b. May 28, 1854.
II. Almira A., b. Dec. 25, 1858.
III. Sibian G., b. Mar. 12, 1861.
IV. Laura A., b. Sept. 24, 1862.
V. Edgar H., b. Sept. 27, 1864.

Section 180

Ebenezer Cary, son of Ebenezer, Sec. 86, b. in Western New York, 1816; m. Catherine J. Fonda; he d. Nov., 1863.
Children:
I. Alfred, b. Oct. 2, 1854.
II. Ebenezer, b. Feb. 10, 1857.
III. Mary, b. Mar. 28, 1859.
IV. John, b. Oct. 26, 1861.

Section 181

Walter Cary, M. D., son of Trumbull, Sec. 87, b. Batavia, N. Y., Dec. 31, 1818; grad, at Union College, 1839, received his M. D. from University of Penna., studied at the Sorbonne, Paris; m. Julia Love, Buffalo, N. Y., April 24, 1848, where he stood high in his profession; d. Nov. 1, 1881.
Children:
I. Trumbull, b. Aug. 1, 1849; studied at Harvard, Liege, and Heidelberg; m. 1st, Grace Trescott, Aug. 12, 1874; m. 2d, Alabama Tomlinson, Dec. 8, 1887, and had
  1. Julia, b. June 10, 1875, Batavia, N. Y.; m. Ralph Plumb, June 25, 1903.
  2. Sarah, b. Aug. 6, 1877, Batavia; m. Colman Curtiss, June 28, 1905.
  3. Margaret, b. Sept. 21, 1879, Batavia; m. Edward P. Smith, July 21, 1909.
II. Thomas, b. April 27, 1851; grad, at Harvard, 1874, took LL. B. at Hamilton and Columbia; resides at Buffalo, N. Y.
III. Charles, b. Oct. 20, 1852; grad, at University of Buffalo, 1876; m. Evelyn Rumsey.
IV. Jennie, b. Dec. 23, 1854; m. Laurence D. Rumsey, Buffalo, and had
  1. Evelyn.
  2. C. Cary.
  3. Gertrude.
  4. Grace.
  5. Laurence.

V. Walter, b. Feb. 26, 1857, Buffalo; received A. B. at Harvard, 1877, and A. M., 1880.

VI. George, b. Mar. 25, 1859; grad. Harvard, 1883; m. Althea Birge, Dec. 31, 1908, and had 1. Marion, b. Oct. 22, 1909.

VII. Seward, b. Jan. 1, 1862, Buffalo; grad. Harvard, 1886; m. Emily Scatcherd, July 13, 1887, and had

1. Eleanor, b. April 23, 1888.
2. Phoebe, b. May 7, 1890.
3. Trumbull, b. Nov. 30, 1893.

Section 182

Waldo Cary, son of Ezekiel, Sec. 88, b. Willimantic, Ct., April 3 , 1772; he was a Shoemaker, and for a time lived in Vermont, but returned to his native town and settled on the farm of his maternal ancestor, which became valuable on account of its nearness to the village. He m. 1st, Fidelia, dau. of Dr. Nathan Arnold, Mansfield, Ct., 1793; she d. 1813; m. 2d, Freelove, dau. of Capt. Michael F. Durant, New Fondon, Ct., 1814.

Children:

I. Sophronia, b. Oct. 14, 1794; m. E. D. Fitch, Willimantic, Ct.

II. Julia, b. Nov. 1, 1796; d. 1813.

III. Fidelia, b. 1799; m. 1st, Reuben Safford; m. 2d, David Douglass, and had several children; went to South America, where she d. and where the family remained.

IV. Lucrctia, b. 1803; m. C. York, New York.

V. Ezekiel Waldo, b. Aug. 13, 1807; m. Harriet H. Field, Willimantic, Ct.

VI. Julia E., b. Oct. 10, 1816; m. Rev. William Wright.

VII. Dumont Ripley, b. Nov., 1819; m. and had one child, and both died.

Section 183

John Cary, son of William, Sec. 89, b. Scotland, Ct., Mar. 18, 1778; m. Sybil Gaser, 1810; lived in Scotland, and his wife d. 1845, and he in 1854.

Children:

I. Frances Harriet, b. 1811; m. B. P. Barrett, lived at Killingly, Ct.

II. Alathea, b. 1813; d. unm.

III. Edwin Wales, b. 1815.

IV. Giles, b. 1821.

Section 184

Elijah Cary, son of William, Sec. 89, b. Scotland, Ct., Oct. 4. 1780; was a farmer and m. Tabitha Bushnell, Fisbon, Ct., Sept. 22, 1813; he d. Sept. 22, 1845.

Children:

I. Esther Burnett, b. Oct. 4, 1814; m. H. Mowrv, Bozrah, Ct., and removed to Brooklyn, N. Y.

II. Alfred William, b. July 24, 1819. Sec. 296.

III. Henry Lorin, b. Nov. 21, 1824. Sec. 297.

Section 185

William Cary, son of William, Sec. 89, b. Scotland, Ct., Dec. 10, 1782; was a carpenter and farmer, and m. Lucinda Lillie, 1810; he d. in 1844, and his widow removed to Illinois.

Children:

I. Theron, b. Dec. 16, 1810. Sec. 298.

II. Frederick William, b. June 6, 1813. Sec. 299.

III. Mary L., b. Dec. 12, 1814; m. George Bass and removed to Illinois. She was a person of scholarly attainments, having been educated at the Charlestown Female Seminary; after her marriage she taught for some years, and a love of books is somewhat inherent in her descendants; showing that while the Carys were not unduly assertive, yet their characteristics are positive rather than negative. They had

1. Harriet, m. D. S. Zearing, Princeton, Ill.
2. Mary L., m. Rev. Robert Wallace, Minonk, Ill., and had (1) Louise.
3. George Cary, Emerson, Ia.
4. Judson A., Red Oak, Ia.
5. Francis W., Stennett, Ia.

IV. Horace, b. Aug. 5, 1819. Sec. 300.

V. Harriet E., b. Nov. 28, 1824; m. John Brown, St. Albans, Vt.

VI. Edwin Augustus, b. Sept. 24, 1826; d. in youth.

VII. Augustus E., b. Aug. 25, 1830.

Section 186

Frederick Cary, son of Jonathan, Sec. 90, b. Norwich, Ct., 1786; m. Anna Savage, Norwich, June 22, 1817; removed to Knox Co., O., where he settled on a farm; his wife d. Nov. 13, 1863.

Children:

I. Thomas, b. July 31, 1818; m. Cynthia Merriam, Sept. 8, 1853; had a dau. b. Mar. 18, 1855; lived in Knox Co., O.

II. Emily, b. Aug. 8, 1820; m. Isaac Merriam and lived at Mt. Gilead, O. Mrs. R. J. Seymour, Columbus, O., is a granddaughter.

III. William L., b. Sept. 25, 1822. Sec. 301.

IV. Caroline, b. Nov. 15, 1824; d. 1863.

V. George W., b. Jan. 28, 1827; m. Sarah Chambers.

VI. Frederick William, b. July 18, 1829; d. 1853.

VII. John, b. Jan. 22, 1832; d. 1856.
VIII. Charles, b. Mar. 10, 1834.
IX. James, b. May 4, 1838.

Section 187

Ralph Cary, son of Jonathan, Sec. 90, b. Norwich, Ct., 1789; m. Emily Smith, Scotland, Ct., and removed to Hartford, Ct., where he d. 1860.
Children:
I. Martha A., b. 1817; d. 1829.
II. Winthrop H., b. 1818. Sec. 302.
III. James S., b. 1820. Sec. 303.
IV. George, b. 1823. Sec. 304.
V. William H., b. 1826; went to California.
VI. Frederick A., b. 1830; m. Cordelia Church, lived in Hartford, Ct. and had
1. Emma L., b. 1861.
VII. Martha E., b. 1837; d. in childhood.

Section 188

James Cary, son of Capt. James, Sec. 91, b. Scotland, Ct., Dec. 7, 1777; he was a farmer and settled in Canterbury, Ct., and frequently represented his town in the Legislature; filled many Town offices, was honest, upright, kind, and courteous, and highly respected. He m. Phebe, dau. of William Howard, Oct. 25, 1804, who d. 1847, aged 69 years; he d. Aug. 14, 1861.
Children:
I. Phebe Howard, b. Dec. 17, 1805; m William F. Willoughby, Oct. 15, 1827. and reared a family.
II. Abigail Kingsbury, b. Aug. 22, 1807; m David F. Adams, April 13, 1832, Canterbury, Ct.
III. James Beneijah, b. Aug. 22, 1810. Sec. 305.
IV. Anna Bradford, b. Feb. 9, 1815; d. 1841.

Section 189

Sanford Cary, son of Capt. James, Sec. 91, b. Scotland, Ct., July 14, 1784; m. Caroline, dau. of Jabez Tracy, May 16, 1811, and was a much respected farmer in Scotland, where he d. May 2, 1852; his widow d. May 3, 1861, aged 74 years.
Children:
I. Henry Hudson, b. July 2, 1814. Sec. 306.
II. Dwight, b. Feb. 24, 1817. Sec. 307.
III. Wolcott, b. June 29, 1819. Sec. 308.
IV. Jane, b. Sept. 8, 1823; m. Nelson Morse.

Section 190

Horatio Cary, son of Anson, Sec. 93, b. Chenango Co., N. Y., Mar. 27, 1785; m. Elizabeth Rhodes, and removed to Madison, Wis.; he d. Feb. 10, 1855.
Children:
I. George A.   II. Horatio G.
III. Henry R.   IV. Charles P.
V. John B.   VI. Albert G.
VII. Emeline, m. Mr. Van Valkenburg, had two daughters, and d. Lockport, N. Y.

Section 191

George A. Cary, son of Anson, Sec. 93, b. Chenango Co., N. Y., May 8, 1793; m. 1st, Sarah Walters, Mar. 29, 1820, who d. June 18, 1821; m. 2d, Adeline E. Crandall, May 8, 1854; lived at Oxford, N. Y. Child:
I. Sarah W., b. 1821; m. William N. Mason, and had two children.

Section 192

Palmer C. Cary, son of Anson, Sec. 93, b. Oxford, N. Y., Mar. 31, 1798; m. Rowena Osgood, April 17, 1826, and resided in Oxford.
Children:
I. Anson L.
II. Lucy, d. at 20 years of age.
III. Rowena, m. T. Walters.
IV. Jane M.
V. Frances, m. F. Laguin, Joliet, Ill.; d. May 17, 1861, leaving two daughters.

Section 193

Zalmon S. Cary, son of Anson, Sec. 93, b. Oxford, N. Y., Aug. 31, 1800; m. Dec. 5, 1824, and d. Aug. 23, 1854.
Children:
I. Harriet M., b. Mar. 14, 1827; m. Mr. Bradley of Wisconsin, had one child, and d. May 23, 1862.
II. Sarah Elizabeth, b. April 22, 1829; m. Stephen Roripaugh, reared a family at New Bedford, Mass.
III. Helen M., b. Mar. 10, 1832; m. J. A. Wiswell, May 10, 1863, and lived in Minnesota.
IV. Mary B., b. Aug. 22, 1835.
V. John, b. Oct. 25, 1837.

ALICE CARY   PHEBE CARY

Section 194

Robert Cary, son of Christopher, Sec. 94, b. Lyme, N. H., Jan. 24, 1787; went with his father to the Northwest Territory in 1802, and lived for some years in Cincinnati, O., but settled on a farm near College Hill; was a soldier in the War of 1812-14, and was with Gen. Hull at the Surrender of Detroit. He was a quiet, unostentatious, upright man, and lived and died highly respected by all who knew him. He m. Eliza Jessup of Hamilton Co., O., in 1813; she d. July 30, 1835, and he d. Nov. 13, 1866.

Children:

I. Rowena, b. Oct. 18, 1814; m. Isaac B. Carnahan, and had several daughters of decided talent; she d. about 1868.

II. Susan, b. May 1, 1816; m. Alexander Swift, Cincinnati, and had

1. A son.

2. Alice, who became the special favorite of her distinguished aunts, Alice and Phebe, and was the legatee of their personal effects; m. George Clymer, had two children, and d. in Florida, Feb. 14, 1873.

III. Rhoda, b. 1818; d. 1833.

IV. Alice, b. April 26, 1820; her Poetry is known the world over, and many editions of her Poems have been issued. These will speak for her far better than anything that could be placed here. She d. Feb. 12, 1871, in New York City, lamented by multitudes.

V. Asa, b. May 5, 1822; m. Leah A. Woodruff, 1850; he was a farmer and lived near College Hill, a worthy and useful citizen; they had

1. Absolom, d. in infancy.

2. Walter Scott, d. in infancy.

VI. Phebe, b. Sept. 4, 1824; her Poems are known everywhere, and her "One sweetly solemn thought," is enough to enrich any literature. She d. July 31, 1871, at Newport, R. I. Both Alice and Phebe are interred in Greenwood Cemetery, N. Y.

VII. Warren, b. Oct. 16, 1826; he was twice married, and lived at Harrison, O.; they had
1. Alexander, accidentally killed, Jan. 1, 1866.
2. Robert.
VIII. Lucy, b. 1829; d. in childhood.
IX. Elmina, b. 1831; m. Alexander Swift, and d. 1862.

Section 195

Beneijah Cary, son of Christopher, Sec. 94, b. Lyme, N. H., 1788; removed to Cincinnati, O., with his father in 1802; served in the War of 1812-14; m. Polly Nichols, Hartford, Vt., 1812; settled on a farm near College Hill, and lived there many years, then removed to a farm near New Richmond, O., where he d. 1858.
Children:
I. Maria, b. 1813; m. Gilbert Hathorn, lived in Minnesota, and had several children.
II. Christopher, b. 1816; studied medicine; m. twice, lived in Indiana, and had one son.
III. Francis, b. 1819; m. and had children, and lived in New Richmond, Ind.
IV. Benjamin F., b. 1821; m. Harriet Barton, who d. 1870; a prosperous farmer in Clermont Co., O., and d. 1865 1 they had
1. William.
2. Martha, m. William McMath; lived at Foster, Ky.
3. Benjamin.
4. Susan, m. George R. Kline, and live at Des Moines, Ia.; they had
(1) Walter W., d. in childhood.
(2) Hazel, b. Mar. 23, 1886; m. Harvey S. Wagner, June 16, 1907; live at Portland, Ore.
(3) George E., b. Jan. 6, 1889.
(4) Edwin C., b. Jan. 20, 1894.
5. Albert.
6. Emorillis, lives in Chicago.
V. Martha, b. 1824; m. Mr. Hopper, Cincinnati, O.
VI. Mary, b. 1827; m. Thomas Kennedy, had two daughters, and d. 1855.
VII. Amanda, b. 1828; d. 1837.
VIII. Adaline, b. 1833; d. in childhood.
IX. Varus B., b. 1835; m Sarah Crawford, and had a son who d. in infancy; he d. in the Union Army.
X. Andrew Jackson, b. 1838; d. in childhood.
XI. Martin Van Buren, b. 1838; d. in the Union Army, much beloved.
XII. Venus, b. 1841; d. in infancy.

Section 196

Irwin Cary, son of Christopher, Sec. 94 , b. near Cincinnati, O., 1826; m. and removed to Missouri.
Children:
I. Clifton F., b. 1854.
II. Dillsworth, b. 1858.

Section 197

Orrin Cary, son of John, Sec. 95, b. Hudson, N. Y., July 26, 1807; m. Margaret E. Stever, Sept. 20, 1834; was a Carpenter, and lived at Elizabeth, N. J.
Children:
I. Lorenzo J., b. Mar. 26, 1836; m. Mary Haskins, Mar. 6, 1865; lived at Preble, N. Y.
II. Sarah A., b. Dec. 14, 1837; m. Charles W. Brown, Aug. 21, 1861.
III. Abram Stever, b. Nov. 12, 1839; a noble young man; was in the Union Army, and d. Sept. 30, 1863, New Orleans, La.
IV. John Erastus, b. Aug. 8, 1842; m. Maria D. Ball, Jan. 2, 1868; a brave soldier in the Union Army.
V. William Woodward, b. Aug. 12, 1847; m Rachel Donahue, Mar. 16, 1870.
VI. Frances Eliza, b. July 7, 1849; m Alex. C. Henry, July 20, 1868; d. 1871.

Section 198

Rev. Lorenzo Cary, son of John, Sec. 95, b. Hudson, N. Y., 1813; grad, from Yale 1835, and became a Congregational minister, and preached with great acceptance at Webster, Mass.; m. Mrs. Sarah E. Peck, 1838; was elected Professor of Languages in Farmer's College, Cincinnati, 1851; was a ripe scholar, and a good and true man; d. 1857, College Hill, O.
Children:
I. Ferdinand E., b. 1840, Chicago, Ill.
II. Sarah Josephine, b. 1842; lived in Chicago.
III. Anna Gertrude, b. 1844; lived in Chicago.
IV. Samuel Fenton, b. 1846; d. in the Union Army.

Section 199

Freeman Grant Cary, son of William, Sec. 96, b. Cincinnati, April 9, 1810; grad. Miami University 1831; devoted more than thirty years to teaching, and was eminently successful; established an Academy at College Hill, known as Cary's Academy; he also originated Farmer's College, and was its President for years; under his management the institution reached a membership of 300 students. He was an enthusiast in Horticulture and Agriculture, and established and edited the *Cincinnatus,* an agricultural periodical of great merit. He retired to his farm in Butler County, O., and devoted himself with great zeal and energy to the practical application of his scientific knowledge. He m. 1st, Malvina Macan, April 4, 1833, who d. Jan., 1872; m. 2d, Mrs. Jane Richardson, March, 1873.

Children:

I. Rebecca Fenton, b. Mar. 5, 1834; an accomplished scholar and graduate of the Wesleyan Female College, Cincinnati; m. Dr. William B. Ludlow, Hamilton, O., and had

1. Freeman Cary, who m. and had a dau. Wanda; Cincinnati, O.
2. John Niles, who m. and had five sons; Denver, Colo.
3. Mary, m. Harry Bowman, College Hill, O.
4. Rebecca, m. Frank E. Walker, College Hill, O.

II. Elizabeth, b. April 29, 1836; d. in childhood.

III. Maria, b. Mar. 15, 1838; d. in childhood.

IV. Malvina Estella, b. Jan. 13, 1841; m. George S. Rail, and had 1. William Cary, m. and had dau. Pearl; Los Angeles, Cal.

2. Ella, m. Davis Harbeson, and have three sons.
3. Albert George, Fort Worth, Tex.
4. Edward.
5. Guy, Fort Worth.
6. Anna.
7. Cary.

V. Anna Ramsay, b. Feb. 16, 1844; grad. Ohio Female College; a successful Teacher; m. John M. Henderson, a lawyer of East Cleveland, O.; they have

1. William Cary, who m. and has John M.; Los Angeles, Cal.
2. Grace, m. Charles C. Johnson, Cannonsburg, Pa.
3. Anna, Cleveland.
4. Rebecca, m. Rev. Edward S. Claflin, and have
(1) James M., b. Nov. 29, 1905.
(2) Anna E., b. July 9, 1906. The home is at Cleveland.
5. Janet M.; m. Carl F. Adams, and have (1) Janet, b. Aug. 24, 1908.
6. Florence.
7. Ruth.

VI. William, b. Mar. 7, 1847.

VII. Samuel Fenton, b. June 2, 1849.

VIII. Mary, b. Mar. 2, 1855; m. Daniel Cook, and have
1, Simeon L.
2. Lila I.

Section 200

William Woodward Cary, son of William, Sec. 96, b. Cincinnati, O., Feb. 23, 1812; pursued a Scientific course in Miami University, and was distinguished for his acquirements in mathematics; chose farming for his profession, settled on a portion of the paternal estate at College Hill, and was a quiet, useful, and honored citizen; m. Eleanor Smith, Poughkeepsie, N. Y., April 30, 1835; he d. July 25, 1848, and his wife d. of ship-fever, Oct., 1854, Poughkeepsie.

Children:

I. Helen M., b. June 11, 1836; d. of ship-fever, Oct. 25, 1854.

II. Adalyn S., b. Dec. 9, 1838.

III. Emily Ione, b. Dec. 14, 1840; m. Alonzo Horton, Sept. 27, 1860; d. Sept. 11, 1863.

IV. Maria, b. June 2, 1844; m. David Carnahan, Sept. 19, 1861, and d. Nov. 12, 1867; they had

    1. William Woodward.

Section 201

Gen. Samuel Fenton Cary, son of William. Sec. 96, b. Feb. 18, 1814, Cincinnati, O.; grad. Miami University 1835; grad, at Cincinnati Law College, 1837, practicing his profession in Cincinnati until 1844, when he abandoned this to devote his time and energies to the promotion of the Temperance Reform. He lectured in all parts of twenty-seven States of the Union, in all the British Provinces of North America, and in all the leading cities and towns of England, Ireland, Scotland, and Wales; he edited several papers and magazines, and was elected to the chief office of

HON SAMUEL FENTON CARY
AUTHOR OF
"CARY MEMORIALS"

the Sons of Temperance in North America, at Baltimore, Md., 1847. He had some celebrity as a political speaker, and was elected to the Fortieth Congress, from the Second Ohio District. In January, 1873, he returned to the practice of the law in Cincinnati. For some years he devoted his leisure time in gathering up the history of the Carys, which was issued in 1874, as the "Cary Memorials." This work is the Cary classic, and practically has been the only work representing the line of John Cary. All Carys owe to him a debt of gratitude that can only be repaid by as earnest work for the Family as he himself gave to it.

He m. 1st, Maria Louise Allen, Oct. 18, 1836, who d. Sept. 25, 1847; m. 2d, Lida J., dau. of J. G. Stillwell, Esq., May 29, 1849, who d. Aug. 1, 1903. He resided at College Hill, Ohio, where he d. Sept. 29. 1900. Children:

I. Martha Louisa, b. Sept. 16, 1837; m. Charles B. Huber, Williamsburg, O., Oct. 16, 1855, and d. Dec. 16, 1856; they had 1. Charles Woodnutt, b. Aug. 2, 1856; he was educated at Earlham College and Cincinnati Law School, graduating in the Class with President Taft. His health not being firm, moved to a farm at Connersville, Ind.; m. 1st, Ida May Murphy, Dec. 7, 1882, who d. Feb. 8, 1898; m. 2d, Rozzie Brown, Feb. 22, 1900; they had

(1) Frances Woodnutt, b. Oct. 6, 1887.
(2) Louisa, b. Sept. 21. 1890.
(3) Ella May, b. Nov. 3, 1892.
(4) Charles Albert, b. Jan. 12, 1902; d. in infancy.
(5) Mary Florabel, b. Sept. 19, 1903.
(6) Edward Brown, b. Feb. 10, 1906.

II. Ella Woodnutt, b. Feb. 13, 1841; m. Edward D. Sayre, Nov. 14, 1871, and reside at College Hill, O.

III. Lou Allen, b. May 24, 1847; d. in infancy.

IV. Olive, b. Aug. 12, 1851; d. in infancy.

V. Samuel Fenton, b. Mar. 22, 1857; he is a Journalist and connected with the Daily Enquirer; m. Cornelia Goodrich, June 1, 1886, and had

1. Ethelwyn, b. Jan. 20, 1890.

VI. Jessie, b. Oct. 13, 1858; has traveled extensively, and resides in Cincinnati, O.

Section 202

Josiah Cary, son of Josiah, Sec. 97, b. Haddam, Ct., June 23, 1791; m. Eunice Tripp, Dec. 25, 1817.

Children:
I. Anna M., b. Oct. 20, 1818; m. Edward E. Anable.
II. Clark S., b. Feb. 2, 1821; d. in infancy.
III. Jonathan T., b. Mar. 31, 1823. Sec. 309.
IV. Clark W., b. Jan. 28, 1825. Sec. 310.
V. Lydia, b. Mar. 28, 1827; m. James M. Newton, Oct. 21, 1844.
VI. Mary J., b. Dec. 19, 1830; m. Myron H. Peck, June 7, 1853.
VII. Jedediah T., b. Feb. 13, 1833. Sec. 311.
VIII. Benjamin H., b. Jan. 26, 1835. Sec. 312.

Section 202-A

Daniel Clark Cary, son of Moses, Sec. 97-A, b. Fort Edward, N. Y., April 17, 1794, and d. at Marila, N. Y., Dec., 1884; m. Hannah Marvin Love (b. Oct. 13, 1802, Hartford, N. Y.; d. Feb. 14, 1891, Marila, N. Y.), Oct. 8, 1826.
Children:
I. Ann Eliza, b. July 5, 1827, Sodus, N. Y.; m. Lorenzo Martin (b. Jan. 17, 1824; d. Jan. 10, 1904, Bath, N. Y.), of Castile, N. Y., 1846; d. Dec. 13, 1901, Bath, N. Y.; they had 1. Oscar D., b. Sept. 24, 1848; d. May 31, 1889, Syracuse, N. Y.

II. Almira, b. Nov. 21, 1829, Hartford, N. Y.; d. unm. Mar. 15, 1907, Marila, N. Y.

III. Albert H., b. Aug. 30, 1831, Sodus, N. Y.; m. Cynthia Warner (b. Oct. 14, 1838, Collins, N. Y.); d. May 23, 1870; they had

1. Albert Warner, b. May 3, 1868; d. 1881.
2. William Harvey, b. Nov. 21, 1870; m. Caroline Roogey (b. Aug., 1875), Oct. 7, 1896, and had

(1) William Horace, b. June 20, 1898, Buffalo, N. Y.
(2) Alice Warner, b. May 7, 1900, Buffalo, N. Y.

IV. Horace Daniel, b. Sept. 19, 1835, Castile, N. Y.; m. Adele R. Preston (b. Mar. 30, 1838), Jan. 28, 1858; he was in the 27th N. Y. Light Battery in the Civil War; removed to Buffalo in 1870, and became the head of the Cary Safe Co., and d. Jan., 1909; they had

1. Sherman Lucius, b. Mar. 5, 1859, Marila, N. Y.; m. Capitola Eastwood (b. June 29, 1859), Dec. 24, 1879, and had

(1) Libyan Dorothy, b. April 22, 1883; m. John Herbert Bradley (b. June 25, 1882, Hoosac Falls, N. Y.), June 16, 1909, at Buffalo, N. Y., where they reside.
(2) Ethel, b. Aug. 6, 1895.

2. Alta Blanche, b. May 13, 1866, Marila, N. Y.; m. Harry Allison Brundage (b. Mar., 1864, Sodus Bay, N. Y.), Aug. 13, 1885, Buffalo.
3. Myrtle Adele, b. Oct. 8, 1872; m. Edwin Francis Crane (b. Sept. 21, 1857, Centerville, N. Y.), June 22, 1898.

V. Lucius May, b. July 21, 1837; d. Feb. 21, 1910; m. Amanda Maud Dean, Grand Rapids, Mich., Mar. 8, 1871, and had

1. Maud Louise, b. Oct. 10, 1876; m. Comstock Konkle (b. May 3, 1873), April 23, 1902, and had

(1) Elizabeth, b. Aug. 5, 1905.
2. Walter Dean, b. Nov. 12, 1880.

VI. Julia Maria, b. Sept., 1839, Castile, N. Y.; m. James Case (b. 1840, Sheldon, N. Y.; d. 1884, Marila, N. Y.), 1862.

VII. George Harlow, b. Sept. 13, 1844; d. Feb. 10, 1907; m. Emma Van Benschoten (b. Feb. 17, 1853), Sept. 11, 1875, and had 1. Mable Lulu, b. April 21, 1877, Saratoga Springs.

VIII. La Verne, b. Castile, N. Y.; d. 1899, Marila, N. Y.

Section 203

Eleazer Cary, son of Eleazer, Sec. 99, b. Windham, Ct., 1811; was a Carpenter in Willimantic, Ct., and at times went to sea; d. 1850. Children:
I. Lucius Henry, b. 1838, and became a Sea Captain.
II. Imogene, b. 1840; d. 1855.
III. Lydia, b. 1842; d. 1859.
IV. George Thomas, b. 1843; d. 1860.
V. Julian, b. 1845; d. i n the Union Army.

Section 204

William Addison Cary, son of Gen. William, Sec. 102, b. Lempster, N. H., July 23, 1818; m. Lydia Gould at Northfield, Vt. (b. Mar. 3, 1815; d. Aug. 24, 1900), Sept. 8, 1839; he d. Feb. 23, 1885, Malden, Mass.
Children:
I. Emma Augusta, b. June 3, 1840; d. Dec. 8, 1900, Newark, N. J.
II. Anna Maria, b. July 16, 1842; d. in childhood, Amesbury, Mass.
III. Ann Sophia, b. Feb. 27, 1846; d. in infancy, Amesbury.
IV. Mary Alice, b. May 30, 1849.
V. Harriet Elizabeth, b. Oct. 8, 1850; d. in childhood, Amesbury.
VI. Winnifred, b. Feb. 16, 1856.
VII. William Addison, b. Feb. 25, 1857, Malden, Mass.

Section 205

Dr. Milan Galusha Cary, son of Gen. William, Sec. 102, b. Lempster, N. H., Nov. 20, 1823; m. Emily M. Dennett (b. Nov. 21, 1821; d. Sept. 24, 1893), May 4, 1847, Salisbury, Mass.; studied medicine and took his degree at Harvard, 1847, and finally settled at Medford, Mass., where he stood high in his profession; d. Mar. 10, 1854, greatly lamented.
Children:
I. Thesta Sophia, b. May 14, 1848; m. James S. Bennett, June 1, 1870, and had
 1. Milan F., b. July 28, 1872; d. Dec. 15, 1905.
 2. Lester, b. Aug. 3. 1879; m. and lives at Melrose, Mass.
II. Henry Frank, b. June 29, 1851; m. 1st, Mary Elizabeth White,
Newburyport, Mass., Nov. 25, 1875, who d. Sept. 26, 1876; m. 2d, Sarah Elizabeth Seavey, York, Me., Feb. 22, 1882, and had
 1. Frank Smith, b. Sept. 20, 1876; d. in infancy.

Section 206

Augustus Celanus Cary, son of Gen. William, Sec. 102, b. Lempster, N. H., Sept. 16, 1825; m. Harriet E. Folsom (b. Dec. 16, 1827; d. Jan. 28, 1903), Aug. 17, 1846, at Amesbury, Mass. In 1856 when the "Know Nothing" party arose, he was elected Representative to the General Court, and in 1857 became Senator from Essex Co., Mass.; for fifty years he was Justice of the Peace and Notary Public. He took out a hundred Patents, and recently invented an appliance for preventing collision of railway trains. His home was in Boston, where he d. January, 1910.

Children:

I. William Augustus, b. June 12, 1848. Sec. 313.

II. George Roswell, b. Dec. 31, 1850; d. Nov., 1908; was a Civil Engineer and Mathematician, and was in the Engineering Dept, of the City of Boston for many years; he m. but had no children.

III. Annie Susan, b. April 8, 1853; d. 1892, Malden, Mass.

IV. Nellie Lee, b. Sept. 23, 1856.

Section 206-A

Henry Grosvenor Cary, son of Gen. William, Sec. 102, b. Lempster, N. H., Dec. 4, 1829; d. April 4, 1905; m. Mary Kendrick Bagley (b. Jan. 23, 1833), Aug. 15, 1854, Amesbury, Mass. In early life he developed a fine musical taste, and his father had a pipe organ put into the home; this was supplemented by a piano, which the lad was allowed to pay for. At sixteen lie was teaching a District .school, and soon after was teaching Singing schools in halls and church vestries, having taken a few piano lessons, which was the only musical instruction received during his minority. He joined the village Brass Band, and played at "Musters" and such like occasions. He was Instructor in music at Cotting Academy, Arlington, and in Harvard, 1879-1883, and was church Organist for more than forty years. His work in teaching music in the Public schools had a wide range: Malden, Medford, Melrose, Reading, Watertown, Brookline, and Milton. Possibly his great work may be said to have begun when he entered the Public schools of Boston, first as Instructor, and in 1884 as Director, continuing until his resignation in 1900.

In the midst of these labors, he was an active member and an official in the Handel and Hayden Society, being a Director six years; the Librarian of the Cecillia Club, and for a number of years an examiner of voices in the Apollo Club. He visited Europe four times; after his death, his two books were issued, "The Cary Family in England," in 1906, and "The Cary Family in America," in 1907. The home of his later years was "Clovelly," facing the ocean at Winthrop, Mass.

Section 206-B

Seth Cooley Cary, son of John, Sec. 105-A, b. Belcher, N. Y., June 1, 1838, on the old Homestead which sheltered four generations of Carys. In early life he taught school; entered the Union Army of the Civil War as 2d Lieutenant in Co. E, 123d New York Infantry; was in the Campaigns of Chancellorsville and Gettysburg, in the Army of the Potomac, and in the Campaign of Atlanta, under Gens. Thomas and Sherman, and was twice promoted in the field; at the battle of Peach Tree Creek, in front of Atlanta, he was severely wounded, July 20, 1864; after this did special duty in Nashville, Tenn., in the winter of 1865, and was mustered out with his regiment, as Adjutant, June 8, 1865, at Washington, D. C. In 1869 graduated from what is now the Boston University School of Theology, and in 1870 joined the New England Conference of the Methodist Episcopal Church. He m. 1st, Mrs. Sarah (Wing) Bouton, Oct. 7, 1873, who d. Sept. 21, 1875; m. 2d, Hattie Landon Bouton, April 17, 1878, who d. April 13, 1882; m. 3d, Jennie S. Dunn, M. D., Nov. 20, 1895.

Child:

I. Knibloe Bouton, b. Mar. 26, 1882, Beverly, Mass. Sec. 318.

Section 207

Joseph Cary, son of Samuel, Sec. 106, b. Albany Co., N. Y., Jan. 30, 1802; m. Lydia, dau. of Cornelius Chase, Chatham, N. Y., 1825. A worthy member of the Society of Friends, and highly respected by all who knew him; lived at Albany, N. Y.

Children:

I. Mary Ann, b. 1826.
II. Lucia, b. 1828; m. George Brown, Brooklyn, N. Y., 1852.
III. Elizabeth, b. 1829; d. in childhood.
IV. Eliza, b. 1833.
V. Albert, b. 1835; m. Emma Server, Albany, N. Y., 1859.
VI. Maria, b. 1837.
VII. Edward, b. 1840.
VIII. Egbert, b. 1840; m. Amelia Wolford, 1861; lived at Albany.

Section 208

Isaac H. Cary, son of Samuel, Sec. 106 , b. Albany Co., N. Y., May 7, 1812; m. Emily Hyde, 1844 , Rensselaerville, N. Y.; and was a member of the Society of Friends in Albany, N. Y.

Child:

I. Edwin H., b. 1846.

Section 209

George Cary, son of Samuel, Sec. 106, b. Albany Co., N. Y., Nov. 30, 1814; m. Caroline, dau. of Nathaniel Sawyer, 1842; a member of the Society of Friends, and lived in Albany, N. Y.
Children:
I. Elizabeth, b. 1843.
II. George, b. 1848; d. in infancy.
III. Joseph Albert, b. 1852.

Section 209-A

Albigense Waldo Cary, son of Dr. Joseph, Sec. 107, b. Coventry, R. I., May 23, 1801; removed to Brockport, N. Y., about 1820, where he established himself in the hardware business. He invented and manufactured a Rotary Pump, which was extensively used in mills, factories, etc. He m. and had Child:
I. Joseph Clinton, b. 1829, Brockport, N. Y. About 1850 he went to New York City, and exhibited the Rotary Pump in the "Crystal Palace," where it attracted wide attention and interest. With this Pump ag a basis he designed a Steam Fire Engine, about 1860, which propelled itself. It proved to be very effective at fires in the city, and helped to save a great amount of property. It was the forerunner of the later Steam Fire Engine, and was probably as effective, but the idea was too novel and strange for adoption at that time, and no great financial success came of it. He entered Wall Street about 1865, and became a factor on the Stock Exchange, of which he was a member till his death in August, 1884. He was instrumental in getting the Cross-Town R. R. through the City. He m. and had 1. Ada; m. Mr. Vaughan.

Section 210

Hon. Jeremiah Eaton Cary, son of Dr. Joseph, Sec. 107, b. Coventry, R. I., April 30, 1803; his father d. in 1815, and after the death of his mother, which took place before 1820, he removed to Cherry Valley, N. Y., and entered the law office of James Bracket, Esq.; m. his dau., Mary Elizabeth, was admitted to the Bar, and practiced there till 1848; in the meantime he had been elected Sheriff of Otsego County, and also to Congress. He then removed to New York City, entered into public affairs, became a member of the School Board, and introduced various reforms; by diligence he reached a position in the legal profession where it was known that he was fitted to draft any legal paper, and was considered "one of the best read men in the profession." The last ten years of his life he was a "Reference Lawyer." He was an omnivorous reader, and when others asked him what they ought to read, was wont to reply, "The Bible and Shakespeare; read them, mark, learn, and inwardly digest them."

He was a quiet man of high character, and d. in 1881.
Children:
I. Mary, b. 1831; m. George M. Allen, Brockport, N. Y.
II. John Ely, b. 1833; a Surgeon in the Army.
III. Margaret Louise, b. 1835; m Frederick H. Van A leck. New York City, Nov. 21, 1860; he is an Attorney, and of the old Knickerbocker stock, one of his ancestors having been active in New Amsterdam in Peter Stuyvesant's time; he is prominent in the reform political movements in Brooklyn, and the Deputy Tax Commissioner of New York City. They had
  1. Mary Elizabeth, b. Jan. 14, 1862, Hollis, L. I.
  2. William Cary, b. Feb. 25. 1864.
  3. Ida Curtis, b. 1866; d. 1867.
  4. Katherine Frederika, b. Mar. 26, 1868; m. Alfred D'Arcy Pearce, June 17, 1899.
  5. Durbin Bartholomew, b. April 16, 1870; m. Elizabeth Hart, June 5, 1903, and had
    (1) Durbin Hart, b. June 8, 1905.
  6. Frederick Easton, b. Sept. 16, 1872.
  7. George Allen, b. Oct. 18, 1874, Liberty, N. Y.
  8. Alice Kip, b. Mar. 16, 1877; m. William H. Geiger, Aug. 1, 1907.
  9. James Bracket, b. Dec. 23, 1879; m. Halle Bayle, May 15, 1907.
IV. Eliza M., b. 1837.
V. William Bracket, b. 1841. Sec. 314.
VI. Joseph L., b. 1843.
VII. Charles A., b. 1845.
VIII. Anna Eaton, b. 1849; m Francis S. Hoyt.
IX. Helen Ida, b. 1851; m. Charles Louis Condit, Brooklyn, and had
  1. Elizabeth Cary.
  2. Helen Cary.
  3. Louis Cary.
  4. Laura Chapin.
  5. Victoria Lathrop; d. in infancy.
X. Katherine A., b. Jan. 10, 1854; m. Donald Stuart Cameron (b. Jan. 7, 1854), Jan. 8, 1878, and had
  1. Mary Cary, b. Oct., 1879; d. in infancy.
  2. Louise Cary, b. Oct., 1879; d. in infancy.
  3. Elizabeth, b. Oct. 12, 1882; d. in 1897.
  4. Marjorie Groves, b. Feb. 14, 1888.

Section 211

Alfred X. Cary, son of Dr. Joseph, Sec. 107, b. Coventry, R. I., Mar. 28, 1811; m. Sarah Musdirk, 1833; removed to Brockport, N. Y., and thence to Grand Rapids, Mich., where he was a Merchant.

Children:
I. Sarah Jane, b. 1835; d. 1843.
II. Elizabeth D., b. 1836; m. Robert M. Collins.
III. Charles Henry, b. 1838; was 1st Lieutenant in the U. S. Signal Corps, and d. in the service in Mississippi, July, 1863.

Section 212

Josiah Whitney Cary, son of Darius H., Sec. 108, b. Richfield, N. Y., 1808.; m. Miss or Mrs. Ward, 1835, at Rochester, N. Y.; d. at Albany, 1842.
Children:
I. Henry W., b. 1836; d. in infancy.
II. Emeline, b. 1838; d. in childhood.
III. Louisa E., b. 1840, Ontario Co., N. Y.
IV. Calista, b. 1842; d. in childhood.

Section 213

Edwin Cary, son of Darius H., Sec. 108. b. Richfield, N. Y., 1817; m. Adele M. Gaige, 1849, and lived in Richfield.
Children:
I. Fanny, b. 1850.
II. Rhoda, b. 1851; d. in 1852.
III. Martha J., b. 1853.

Section 214

Joseph Cary, son of William, Sec. 109 , b. Herkimer Co., N. Y., 1816; m. Caroline Eames, 1840; removed to Milwaukee, Wis.
Children:
I. William Henry, b. 1841.
II. Charles Joseph, b. 1843.
III. Edward Lester, b. 1846.
IV. Caroline Eames, b. 1850.

Section 215

William Hutchins Cary, son of William, Sec. 109, b. Herkimer Co., N. Y., 1816; m. Mary B. Taylor, Milwaukee, Wis., 1853; removed to Hastings, Minn.
Children:
I. George Hutchins, b. Feb. 7, 1854, Milwaukee; removed with parents to Hastings, Minn., 1860; grad, from High School, 1870, and finally settled at

Lapeer, Mich., where he has been Station Agent, Merchant, and active in public affairs; m. Lilia Bell Mark, Imlay City, Mich., Aug. 14, 1877, and had

1. Alice, b. June 9, 1879, Imlay City, Mich.
2. Mark, b. Mar. 9, 1881; m. Jane Bernice Beecher, Batavia, N. Y., 1907; in business at Lapeer; they have
(1) Beecher Bancroft, b. Oct. 18, 1908.
3. George Hutchins, b. Aug. 10, 1900, Lapeer.

II. Frederick William, b. 1857, Milwaukee; m. Amy Davenport, Lapeer, 1885 1 removed to Glens Falls, N. Y., where he d. 1905.

III. Walter, b. 1859, Milwaukee; removed to Zumbrotta, Minn.; m. Ida Weatherhead, 1880, and d. 1889; they had

1. Margaret, b. 1882, Zumbrotta.
2. Walter B., b. May 8, 1885; in 1910 organized The Detroit Gear and Machine Co., of which he is Secretary.

Section 216

George W. Cary, son of William, Sec. 109, b. Herkimer Co., N. Y., 1819; m. Sarah Ann Dickson, of Paris, N. Y., 1846; he d. 1850, and the family lived at Fly Creek, N. Y.

Children:
I. Ann Elizabeth, b. 1847.
II. Alfred D., b. 1849.

Section 217

Ebenezer Cary, son of Dr. William, Sec. in, b. Saratoga, Co., N. Y., Nov. 5, 1797; m. Hannah Hammond, and lived in Sandy Hill, New York.

Children:
I. Maria, b. April 24, 1821; d. 1845.
II. Amy, b. April 23, 1826.
III. Lydia, b. Feb. 2, 1828.
IV. Mary, b. July 5, 1829.
V. Samuel, b. April 9, 1831; d. 1860.
VI. Ruth, b. April 25, 1838; d. 1860.

Section 218

Lucius Cary, son of Dr. William, Sec. 111, b. Half Moon, N. Y., May 9, 1799; m. Cynthia Merritt; lived at Moreau, Saratoga Co., N. Y., where he d. 1856.

Children:
I. Ruth Sweet, b. Moreau, N. Y., Aug. 1, 1821, and d. at Rome, N. Y., 1909; m. Joseph Hill (b. Dec. 3, 1804; d. June 6, 1896), Nov. 11, 1852; he was son of

Zacheus and his wife, Mary Hawkins, who was a Minister in the Society of Friends; they removed to Western, Oneida Co., N. Y., and settled at Quaker Hill; they had

1. Mary C., b. Oct. 21, 1853; m. George Griffith, of Western, Jan. 2, 1880, and had

(1) Mabel E., b. Dec. 17, 1880; a Missionary at Allahabad, India.

(2) Clarence H., b. Nov. 27, 1883; New York City.

2. Amelia, b. June 19, 1856; m. George B. Olney, Dec. 10, 1879, Westernville, N. Y., and had

(1) George J., b. April 28, 1890.

(2) Max H., b. June 25, 1894.

3. Emma, b. Dec. 20, 1857; m. Orson L. White, Skaneateles, N. Y., and had

(1) Clara M., b. May 9, 1884.

(2) Harold O., b. Nov. 2, 1886.

(3) Margaret R., b. Aug. 17, 1900.

4. Carrie M., b. Mar. 21, 1860; d. in childhood.

II. Joseph M., b. April 30, 1823; m. Sarah Ann Clements, and had

1. Phebe C., b. June 24, 1851; m. Emons S. Austin, Glens Falls, N. Y.

2. Isaac J., b. May 5, 1859; m. Mary A. Eddy, Dec. 10, 1880, and had

(1) Edith, a Teacher at Westtown, Pa.

(2) Clarence, Glens Falls, N. Y.

III. Mary Anne, b. Nov. 3, 1824; d. 1869.

IV. Jervis, b. Mar. 5, 1827, Moreau, N. Y.; m. Sarah Eddy, Feb. 4, 1852, and had

1. George Lucius, b. Dec. 31, 1857; lives on the old Homestead, and is a Farmer and Beekeeper; m. Anna M. Carpenter, Dec. 25, 1879, and had

(1) Mabel A., b. Feb. 1, 1881; grad, at Earlham Col. 1903; a Teacher and Y. W. C. A. Secretary; m. Rev. Homer J. Coppeck, Prin. Corinth Acad., Ivor, Va., June, 1906, and had

1. Paul R.

2. Anna E.

(2) Grace L., b. Jan. 9, 1884; d. 1891.

(3) Sarah E., b. May 23, 1886; m. Lester M. Whitney, Nat. Bank of Glens Falls, and had

1. Maurice Cary.

(4) William E., b. Nov. 17, 1888; in Earlham College.

(5) A. Heywood, b. June 2, 1891; grad. Oakwood Acad., 1910.

(6) George Lucius, b. Feb. 9, 1905.

2. Cynthia H., b. Jan. 12, 1861; m. Edson W. Haviland, 1879; live at Bentley Manor, Staten Island, N. Y., and had

(1) William J., b. July, 1883; m. Bertha M. Esten, June, 1910; live at Benton Harbor, Mich.

(2) Edna C., b. July 1, 1888; studied at Earlham College.

(3) Ernest C., b. Oct. 31, 1890; Staten Island, N. Y.

(4) Katherine A., b. May 31, 1898.

3. Arthur W., b. Feb. 5, 1864; Truck-farmer and Beekeeper; m. Louisa Haviland, Jan. 18, 1888, Glens Falls, N. Y.

4. Alice L., b. Sept. 30, 1866; m. Edward S. Scales, Draftsman, June, 1893, Staten Island, N. Y., and had

(1) Harold, b. Mar. 25, 1894.

(2) Margaret C., b. Feb. 5, 1897.

(3) Cynthia A., b. Jan. 15, 1908.

5. William J., b. Nov. 20, 1868; d. 1871.

V. Egbert, b. Nov. n, 1828; d. at Baltimore, Md.; m. Martha Snell, and had

1. Charles J., b. Feb. 10, 1855, Moreau, N. Y.; m. 1st, Sue B. Reed, Aug. 23, 1877, Baltimore, who d. Feb., 1886; m. 2d, Minnie C. Wing, Oct. 25, 1888, Brooklyn, N. Y.; they had

(1) Charles Reed, b. Dec. 26, 1881, Baltimore; grad, at Haverford, Col. and Mass. Inst. Technology.

(2) Herbert, b. Jan., 1882; d. in infancy.

(3) Eleanor J., b. June 19, 1890; grad, at Goucher College.

(4) Frank W., b. Oct., 1894.

(5) Margaret S., b. Jan. 9, 1899.

2. John R., m. Mary E. Bush; Secy. Provident Savings Bank, Baltimore; they had

(1) Richard L.

(2) Donald B.

3. Egbert Snell; m. Elizabeth M. Allen, and had

(1) Dorothy.

(2) Egbert.

VI. James Richardson, b. Oct. 13, 1831; grad, at University of Michigan, 1859; was a highly respected Teacher, Editor, and Telephone Manager, and d. at Neligh, Neb., 1906; m. Mary Matthews, of Monroe, Wis., also a Teacher, Oct. 13, 1874, and had

1. Earnest, b. Feb. 25, 1879; grad, at Gates College, took the degrees A. B., A. M., and Ph. D. at Harvard, from which he had a Traveling Fellowship, and where he afterwards taught Greek; in 1908 became Instructor at Smith College, and in 1910 became Instructor at Princeton.

2. Merritt, b. Dec. 21, 1880, and is in the Biological Survey, Dept, of Agriculture; m. Eirene I. Young, Oct., 1905, and had

(1) Harold J., b. Sept. 11, 1906.

(2) Walter M., b. Oct. 1, 1909.

3. Grace, b. April 13, 1884.

VII. Matilda, b. Aug. 11, 1833; d. 1863; m. Charles Devoll, and had 1. Carrie; m. Charles Numan, and had

(1) Herbert O., a Singer, of Glens Falls, N. Y.

VIII. John Milton, b. April 21, 1835; d. 1860; m. Josephine Ferris, who d. 1909.

IX. Kezia, b. June 16, 1837; m. Silsby Scovel, Grimes, Ia., who d. 1900.

X. William, b. May 17, 1839; m. 1st, Amanda Mott, Fort Edward, N. Y.; m. 2d, Lydia Mott, a Minister in the Friends Society; he is Prest. of the Cary Association, at Lake George, New York.

XI. Lucius Falkland, b. May 21, 1841; d. in infancy.

XII. Cynthia M., b. Dec. 1, 1843; an enthusiastic worker for Missions; m. William T. Heywood, Des Moines, Ia., and d. June 20, 1909; they had

1. Fred Cary; m. Ada Whitmer, Los Angeles, Cal.
2. John William; m. Virginia Allen, Denver, Colo.

Section 219

Jervis Cary, son of Dr. William, Sec. 111, b. Half Moon, N. Y., May 23,0801, where he lived and died; m. Clarissa Dillingham.

Children:

I. John M., b. May, 1827, and went to California.

II. Joseph W., b. Dec. 16, 1828; d. in infancy.

Section 220

Isaac Cary, son of Dr. William, Sec. ill, b. Half Moon, N. Y., Jan. 15, 1818; m. Melissa Noxon, and lived at Half Moon, about four miles from Mechanicsville, N. Y.

Children:

I. Hannah C., b. Jan. 8, 1857; m. Walden L. Haskins, and had

1. Florence.
2. Marion.
3. Leon.

II. Charles, b. June 16, 1860; d. 1874.

III. William N., b. Sept. 13, 1862; he is Prest. of the Cary Brick Co., with main office at Mechanicsville, and branches at Boston and New York; m. Alice L. Hall, and had

1. Mabel; m. Herman F. Sholtz, C. E., and live at Bremerton, Wash.
2. Gertrude M.
3. Mildred.
4. William.
5. Charles Howard.
6. Alice.

IV. Edward D.; m. Ella Bailey, who d. 1910; lives at Mechanicsville, N. Y.

V. Marie S., grad, of Syracuse; m. Burdette Cleveland, Albany, New York.

VI. Ruth; with the mother at Mechanicsville.

Section 221

William Cary, son of Taylor, Sec. 112, b. Saratoga Co., N. Y., July 12, 1803; m. Celesta Gridley, April 7, 1831; was a Farmer, and lived at Sheridan, Chautauqua Co., N. Y.
Children:
I. Celesta, b. Mar. 29, 1835; d. in infancy.
II. Maria, b. Dec. 19, 1839.

Section 222

John M. Cary, son of Taylor, Sec. 112, b. Oneida Co., N. Y., Mar. 20, 1810; m. 1st, Fanny Hopkins, April 20, 1833, who d. May 26, 1864, aged fifty-one years; m. 2d, Louisa M. Baldwin, Nov. 24, 1864; removed to Hamilton Co., O., thence to Adrian, Mich.; an intelligent and respected Farmer.
Children:
I. Elizabeth, b. Sept. 4, 1835; m. B. F. Latham, 1855.
II. Ira H., b. Jan. 3, 1838; m. Elizabeth Logan, Aug. 19, 1870, Montgomery, O.
III. Minerva, b. July 28, 1844; d. in childhood.
IV. William H., b. July 28, 1844; d. in childhood.
V. Levi J., b. May 24, 1849; d. in infancy.
VI. Fanny Jane, b. Mar. 17, 1851.
VII. Bessie M., b. Sept. 6, 1870.

Section 223

Ebenezer Cary, son of Egbert, Sec. 113, b. Beekman, N. Y., 1822; m. Mary E. DeGroff, 1844, and lived at Poughkeepsie, N. Y.
Children:
I. Egbert J., b. 1847.
II. Harriet E, b. 1848.
III. Sophia W., b. 1850; d. 1851.
IV. Lauetta C., b. 1856.
V. Mary E., b. 1860.

Section 224

Solomon Flagler Cary, son of Sturges, Sec. 114, b. Beekman, N. Y., Oct. 9, 1820; m. Sarah M. Jarvis, 1852, and lived at Binghamton, N. Y., where he d. Feb. 25, 1896. She was descended from William and Esther, who were in Huntington, L. I., in 1696. There were three generations of Sea Captains; then Capt. Samuel Jarvis removed to Norwalk, Ct. In the Revolutionary War the family was divided: Stephen Jarvis and his son Samuel (ancestor of Mrs. Cary) were patriots, while Stephen, a brother of Samuel and son of Stephen, remained loyal to the King, removed to Canada, and later became its Governor-General. Abraham Jarvis, brother of Stephen, Sr., and great-uncle of Mrs. Cary, became the second Episcopal Bishop of Connecticut, succeeding Bishop Seabury, both of whom were consecrated in England. She d. Sept. 26, 1900.

Children:

I. William Ely, b. Dec. 15, 1852; m. Louise Eaton (whose Gt. Grandfather, Gen. Joshua Whitney, founded Binghamton, N. Y.), Nov. 11, 1897, and had 1. Constance, who d. in childhood.

II. Marietta Jarvis, b. April 30, 1855; m. Frederick Hyde Foote (whose Grandfather, Col. Isaac Foote, was on Washington's Staff), Mar. 10, 1896.

III. Sarah Flagler, b. Nov. 3, 1866; m. Charles Lyon Corbin, Metuchin, N. J., Jan. 17, 1907, who is a leading member of the New Jersey Bar.

Section 225

Oliver Akin Cary, son of Sturges, Sec. 114, b. Beekman, N. Y., June 3, 1827; removed with his father to Binghamton, N. Y., 1837; m. 1st, Sarah Maria Newell (b. Mar. 14, 1826; d. May 4, 1857), Oct. 1, 1850; m. 2d, Virginia D. Hart, May 7, 1872, and removed to Corning, New York.

Children:

I. Cornelia Maria, b. Mar. 7, 1852; d. 1876.

II. Tracy Morgan, b. Jan. 17, 1854, Binghamton, N. Y.; removed to Chippewa Falls, Wis., 1873; m. Mary Gertrude Cruttenden (b. Dec. 7, 1853, Morris, N. Y., whose ancestor, Abraham of Cranbrook, Eng., came to Guilford, Ct., 1639), Sept. 26, 1877, and had

1. Clara Maria, b. Oct. 20, 1879; d. 1905.
2. Walter Edward, b. Mar. 22, 1885; m. Bertha Schneider, June 17, 1908, and had

(1) Alice Gertrude, b. May 27, 1909.

3. Evan Falkland, b. Feb. 16, 1896.

Mr. Cary is a public-spirited citizen, Cashier of the First National Bank, Alderman, and Church official.

III. Edward, b. Oct. 16, 1855, Binghamton, N. Y., and removed to Chippewa Falls, Wis., 1874, and has been largely interested in the handling and investment in lands, and is a Vestryman in the Episcopal Church; m. Mrs. Ardelle I. (Knapp) Hoffman, Oct. 16, 1885.

IV. Myra Ford, b. Oct. 4, 1873; m. John A. Sanders, Feb. 17, 1903, and had

1. John Oliver, b. at Albany, N. Y., Dec. 28, 1903.
2. Kenneth Cary, b. at Albany, April 17, 1906.
3. Susan Virginia, b. at Corning, N. Y., Aug. 24, 1907.

V. Edith Harriet, b. May 30, 1875.

VI. Elizabeth Hart, b. July 18, 1878.

VII. Sturges Flagler, b. Feb. 5, 1880.
VIII. Flora Virginia, b. Mar. 2, 1882; d. 1884.
IX. Jesse Oliver, b. July 22, 1886.
X. Harold Shaw, b. April 26, 1888.
XI. Leigh Randolph, b. April 4, 1890.

Section 226

John W. Cary, son of Cephas, Sec. 119, b. Shelby Co., O., Jan. 3, 1805; m. Miss or Mrs. Kenard, and lived at Sidney, O., a man held in high esteem.
Children:
I. Elizabeth M., b. 1827; m. in 1859, Sidney, O.
II. Clara B., b. 1829; m. in 1854, Sidney, O.
III. Hattie R., b. 1833; m. in 1857, Sidney, O.
IV. Anna K., b. 1835; m. in 1855, Sidney, O.
V. John W., b. 1837; d. 1839.
VI. B. Franklin, b. 1842; m. and lived at Sidney, O.
VII. Jane, b. 1843; d. in infancy.
VIII. Edward, b. 1846.
IX. John S., b. 1848.
X. Ella, b. 1851.
XI. John W., b. 1855; d. 1858.
XII. Tom Corwin, b. 1860.

Section 227

William A. Cary, son of Cephas, Sec. 119, b. Sidney, O., Jan. 9, 1806; m. Miss or Mrs. Vandermark.
Children:
I. Catherine J., b. 1835.
II. William T., b. 1837.
III. Henry Clay, b. 1840.
IV. Josephine, b. 1844.
V. Clementine, b. 1848.

Section 228

David M. Cary, son of Cephas, Sec. 119, b. Shelby Co., O., Jan. 22, 1810; m. Isabella Gerard, Jan. 22, 1832.
Children:
I. Cephas S., b. Nov. 25, 1832.
II. William C., b. July 22, 1834.
III. George W., b. Aug. 8, 1836; d. in infancy.
IV. T. J., b. Aug. 8, 1836; d. in infancy.

V. Finley W., b. July 25, 1838.
VI. Alena A., b. July 25, 1838.
VII. Celestina C., b. May 1, 1841; m. James B. Beach.
VIII. Mary E., b. April 1, 1843; d. in infancy.
IX. Rhoda J., b. Dec. 1, 1845.
X. Hester C., b. Sept. 1, 1847; d. in childhood.
XI. David A., b. Sept. 1, 1849.
XII. Clara S., b. Dec. 1, 1851.
XIII. Julia M., b. July 1, 1857.

Section 229

Thomas M. Cary, son of Cephas, Sec. 119, b. Sidney, O., Dec. 16, 1812; m. Miss or Mrs. Cole, and lived at Sidney, O., where he d. 1873. Children:
I. Marcellus, b. 1831.
II. John W., b. 1833.
III. Stephen, b. 1836; d. 1838.
IV. John N., b. 1838.
V. Loretta, b. 1841.
VI. Tamar Ann, b. 1843
VII. Harry G., b. 1846.
VIII. Nancy A., b. 1852.
IX. William T., b. 1856.
X. Ida M., b. 1857.

Section 230

Jeremiah Cary, son of Cephas, Sec. 119 , b. Sidney, O., June 7 , 1814; m. and lived at Sidney.
Children:
I. Sarah J., b. 1838; d. 1859.
II. David R., b. 1840; d. in infancy.
III. Elmore Y., b. 1847; d. in childhood.
IV. John H., b. 1850; d. in infancy.
V. Flora H., b. 1853.
VI. Mary A., b. 1861.
VII. Lizzie T., b. 1863; m. Mr. Wigton, and had
1. Ethel Cary; m. Albert Morgan, Sioux City, Ia.
VIII. Edith.

Section 231

Benjamin Wesley Cary, son of Cephas, Sec. 119 , b. Sidney, O., Oct. 1, 1816; m. Miss or Mrs. Cole, and lived at Sidney.

Children:
I. William Raper, b. 1838.
II. Stephen H., b. 1841.
III. Laura Caroline, b. 1843.
IV. Jane Wesley, b. 1850.

Section 232

Simeon B. Cary, son of Cephas, Sec. 119 , b. Sidney, O., Dec. 30 , 1823; m. and lived in Brooklyn, N. Y.
Children:
I. Ida F., b. May 3, 1857; d. in infancy.
II. Nellie, b. July 14, 1859; d. in infancy.
III. Jennie, b. Oct. 15, 1860.
IV. Samuel C., b. Dec. 16, 1861.

Section 233

Harvey G. Cary, son of Cephas, Sec. 119, b. Sidney, O., Aug. 18, 1826; m. Miss Newman and lived in Indianapolis, Ind. He was widely known, and highly esteemed.
Children:
I. Gertrude N., b. 1851.
II. John Newman, b. 1853.
III. Peter Lowe, b. 1856.

Section 234

Dr. Milton T. Cary, son of Cephas, Sec. 119 , b. Sidney, O., July 22 , 1831; m. Cornelia Burnett, 1856; studied Medicine, had a large practice, and stood high in the profession in Cincinnati, O., where he lived; was also a Surgeon in the Union Army.
Children:
I. Burnett, b. Oct. 21, 1856; d. in childhood.
II. Mollie, b. May 8, 1860.
III. Lydia K., b. Mar. 26, 1862.

Section 235

Dr. Henry Shorer Cary, son of George, Sec. 120, b. Shelby Co., O., June 8, 1816; m. Margaret Ewing Chapman, Sept. 28, 1837, in Union Co., O.; remained in Shelby and Champaign counties for some time, when he removed to Lewis Cass Co., Ia., 1855, where he d. Sept. 16, 1867; his widow d. Nov.,

1897, Pender, Neb. He was a very large man, weighing 330 pounds; was the first Physician in Cass Co., and his practice extended over a wide extent of country.

Children:

I. Sophia Aurora, b. Aug. 30, 1839; m. James M. Hart, who d. Feb., 1906; they had

1. George Cary Hart, Topeka, Kan., with whom the mother lived.

II. Mary Barbara, b. April 12, 1842; m. William H. Bailey, Sept. 16, 1861, and had

1. Ira M., May 12, 1863, who lived near Merced, Cal.

III. Ellena Ardelia, b. June 14, 1844; d. 1907.

IV. Sarada, b. Feb. 16, 1846; d. in infancy.

V. Hugh Thompson, b. Sept. 14, 1847; d. in infancy.

VI. John Calvin Williamson, b. Dec. 31, 1848; lives at Atlantic, Ia., and travels for a Drug firm at Omaha; m. Clara Joy, and had

1. Henry S.

2. John Raymond.

VII. Clara Bell, b. Mar. 15, 1851; d. in infancy.

VIII. Charles Henry Warden, b. July 10, 1854; m. Mary Iowa Davis, Modesto, Cal., Oct. 20, 1878; he d. Mar., 1896, and his widow m. W. A. Shinn, and lived at Lodi, Cal.; had

1. Frank.

2. Melvin.

IX. David Chapman, b. Oct. 2, 1856, d. 1866.

X. George Thompson, b. Oct. 2, 1856; m. Ellen G. Gifford, Nov. 2, 1881, and is a Druggist at Grant, Ia.

XI. Carrie Eugenia, b. Sept. 8, 1859; d. 1863.

Section 236

Ezra Cary, son of Thomas, Sec. 121, b. Enfield, Mass., 1803; m. Lucretia P. Jenny, 1832, and lived at Enfield.

Children:

I. Thomas, b. 1833.

II. Aurelia, b. 1835.

III. Lucretia, b. 1837.

Section 237

Edward Cary, son of Thomas, Sec. 121, b. Enfield, Mass., 1809; m. Eliza Tucker.

Children:

I. Charles.

II. Harvey.
III. George.
IV. Rufus.

Section 238

Rufus Cary, son of Thomas, Sec. 121, b. Enfield, Mass., Mar. 14, 1813; m. Mary K. Ferry, April 26, 1837, who d. Mar. 19, 1900; settled in Princeton, Ill., where he d. Aug. 7, 1873. When twenty years old he taught school in Pelham and Granby, Mass., and at twenty-one removed to Princeton, which was sparsely settled, and the Indians were still there. He bought the farm which afterwards became the County Farm, and in 1855 removed to town and built for himself a brick house, and became the County Treasurer.

Children:
I. Francis, b. Aug. 15, 1840; d. 1895.
II. Eliza, b. Oct. 24, 1842; d. 1844.
III. Amelia, b. Mar. 23, 1848; d. 1869.
IV. Warren, b. Dec. 13, 1849, and was a Physician; m. Frances Ives Crawford, May 2, 1874, and had

1. Edward F., b. Feb. 13, 1875; m. 1st, Lora G. Simmons, who d. 1905; m. 2d, Miriam Platt, Sept. 6, 1907. He grad, at University of Michigan, and Andover Theo. Sem.; was Missionary at Plarpoot, Turkey, and was Head of their Theological School.

2. Amelia L., b. July 28, 1876, and grad, at University of Michigan; m. Dr. Oscar M. Duncan, Bridgeport, Ill., July 2, 1902, and had

(1) Dorothy, b. Jan. 22, 1909.

3. Edith M., b. Aug. 18, 1878; m. Walter S. Rogers, Esq., who grad, at University of Chicago and Kent Law School, June 17, 1903, and had

(1) Lora Elizabeth, b. Nov. 2, 1906.

4. Alice, b. Aug. 20, 1880, a grad, of University of Illinois; m. Alexander D. Bailey, University of Michigan.

Section 239

Zachary Cary, son of Zachary, Sec. 122, b. Sterling, Mass., 1801; m. Miriam Morse, 1823, and lived in Norway, Me.

Children:
I. James Henry, b. 1824; d. Portland. Me., 1851.
II. Albert Quincy, b. 1826, and was killed by the blowing up of the steamer Princess, on the Mississippi River in 1859.
III. Lydia Ann, b. 1829; d. in infancy.
IV. Martha Jane, b. 1832; m. W. B. Harman.
V. George Francis, b. 1837; m. Harriet N. Flood, 1866.
VI. Lewis Clark, b. 1843.

Section 240

Thomas Cary, son of Zachary, Sec. 122, b. Sterling, Mass., 1807; m. 1st, Miss Walker, 1834; m. 2d, Miss Waterhouse, 1838; lived in Gray, Me.
Children:
I. Sarah C., b. 1835.
II. Theda, b. 1841.
III. Cephas, b. 1843.
IV. Gustavus, b. 1845
V. Cynthia, b. 1851.

Section 241

Salmon Cary, son of Ezra, Sec. 123, b. Turner, Me., 1804; m. Anna Turner, 1830, and lived at Turner, Me.
Children:
I. Lorana F., b. 1832; m. Frank Whitman, 1860.
II. Lois Staples, b. 1834; d. in infancy.
III. Thomas, b. 1836, and was in the Union Army.
IV. Susanna D., b. 1838; d. in infancy.
V. Lydia A., b. 1841; d. in infancy.
VI. Salmon W., b. 1843.
VII. Ezra D., b. 1848.

Section 242

Seth S. Cary, son of Ezra, Sec. 123, b. Topsham, Me., Feb. 5, 1810; m. Susanna F. Hildreth (b. May 30, 1809; d. May 5, 1886), April 22, 1834; lived in Topsham, where he d. May 23, 1857.
Children:
I. Susan Perkins, b. Feb. 21, 1835.
II. Henry S., b. May 7, 1837.
III. George A., b. May 7, 1837.
IV. Priscilla Purington, b. June 8, 1839.
V. Seth Franklin, b. Mar. 10, 1841.
VI. Frances Jane, b. Jan. 12, 1843.
VII. Samuel Page, b. Mar. 18, 1845.
VIII. Hosea Hildreth, b. Aug. 9, 1847; m Harriet A. Pray, Gardiner, Me., July 26, 1873, and had
  1. Susan Augusta, b. Gardiner, Me., Jan. 2, 1876.
  2. Mary Hildreth, b. Gardiner, Me., April 16, 1878.
  3. Eliphalet Pray, b. East Pittston, Me., Oct. 9, 1880.
  4. Gilbert Gowell, b. East Pittston, Me., Feb. 20, 1886.

IX. Mary Ella, b. Oct. 21, 1849.
X. Daniel Herbert, b. Aug. 21, 1852.
XI. Lucy Patten, b. Oct. 13, 1856.

Section 243

Daniel Cary, son of Ezra, Sec. 123, b. Turner, Me., 1806; m. Temperance Waterman, 1833, and lived in Maine.
Children:
I. Augustus, b. 1834.
II. Ellen, b. 1836; m. Augustus Carter, 1855.
III. Lois Amelia, b. 1841.
IV. Daniel Frederick, b. 1848; d. in childhood.
V. Herbert, b. 1851; d. 1853.
VI. Clara Isabella, b. 1854.

Section 244

William R. Cary, son of Bethuel, Sec. 125, b. Sumner, Me., 1820; m. Mary E. Clark, 1841, and lived in East Sumner, Me.
Children:
I. Sarah, b. 1844.
II. Mary E., b. 1852.
III. Lydia, b. 1856.

Section 245

Benjamin F. Cary, son of Bethuel, Sec. 125, b. Sumner, Me., 1822; m. Sophia Robinson, 1846.
Children:
I. Bethuel, b. 1852.
II. Leonard, b. 1860.

Section 246

Charles Cary, son of Francis, Sec. 126, b. Turner, Me., 1814; m. Sallie Bradford, 1837, and lived in Turner.
Children:
I. Charles Knowlton, b. Dec. 26, 1838; m. Florence E. Potter, Sept. 26, 1866, and lived in Boston, Mass.
II. Mary B., b. Sept. 27, 1840; m. Wallace Clark, Esq.

Section 247

Francis Cary, son of Francis, Sec. 126 , b. Turner, Me., 1824; m. Lois Allen, 1851, and lived in Turner.
Child:
I. Daniel, b. 1854.

Section 248

Luther Cary, son of Cassander, Sec. 127, b. Turner, Me., Dec. 1, 1820; m. Dora Spencer, 1852.
Children:
I. Sarah, b. 1856.
II. Clara, b. 1861.

Section 249

Harrison Gray Otis Cary, son of Anselm, Sec. 129, b. Greene, Me., Dec. 28, 1816; removed with family to Zanesville, O.; m. 1st, Emma V. Bateman, Oct. 13, 1842, who d. April 27, 1847; m 2d, Matilda A. Ingalls, Nov. 16, 1854. He was a popular Druggist of Zanesville, and an active philanthropist.
Children:
I. Elizabeth Cox, b. 1843; d. in infancy.
II. Edward Russell, b. Jan. 2, 1845 5 a Druggist at Des Moines, Ia.
III. Emma, b. April 10, 1847; d. in infancy.

Section 250

Jairus Cary, son of Hugh, Sec. 131, b. Turner, Me., Sept. 25, 1823; m. Sophronia M. Foster, 1848, and lived in Turner.
Children:
I. Julia F., b. 1850.
II. Edward F., b. 1855.
III. Ada G., b. 1861.

Section 251

Shepard Cary, son of William H., Sec. 133, b. New Salem, Mass., July 3, 1805; at the age of seventeen, went to Houlton, Me., with his parents; m. Susanna Whitaker, at New Salem, Mass., Dec. 25, 1832, and d. at Houlton, Aug. 9, 1866. In early life he engaged in storekeeping, and as he came to manhood, developed the capacity for large enterprises, which gave employment to hundreds of men. He carried on extensive lumbering operations on the waters of the Upper St. John and Allagash Rivers; he was also owner of large tracts of timber land in those regions, and in other parts of Aroostook County; he also engaged extensively in agriculture, built and operated a foundry and machine shop at Houlton, and grist and lumber mills, besides a profitable mercantile business. In addition to these great undertakings, he took an active part in politics, serving sixteen terms in the House and Senate of Maine; was a member of Congress in 1842, and in 1854 was candidate for Governor on the ticket of the Liberty Party.

Children:

I. Theodore, b. April 9, 1835; m. 1st, Althea M. Dodge, Nov. 14, 1861; m. 2d, Phebe S. Plummer, Belfast, Me., Dec. 24, 1874; his education was secured in the public schools and Houlton Academy; in 1860 he established The Aroostook Times, the first newspaper printed in Houlton, and continued to edit and publish it for nearly forty years; he was public-spirited, and a useful citizen; they had

1. Alice, who d. in infancy.
2. Eugene, who d. in infancy.
3. Walter, b. Aug. 7, 1865; fitted for College at Houlton Academy, and grad, at Colby, 1890; was admitted to the Bar in 1892, and to the U. S. Circuit Court in 1893; is a practicing Lawyer, and Prest. of the Board of Trustees of the Cary Library, founded by his uncle, George Cary; m. Florence Emerson, Lincoln, Me., Jan. 22, 1895, and have

(1) Catherine, b. Nov. 17, 1899.

II. George, b. Aug. 29, 1837; grad, at Bowdoin, 1860, in the Class with Hon. Thomas B. Reed; enlisted as a private in the 1st Maine Cav., and was promoted to a Captaincy; was in the Battles of Cedar Mountain, Second Bull Run, Fredericksburg, and others, but failing health compelled him to resign in 1863. Received his M. D. from the College of Physicians and Surgeons, New York, and practiced his profession till his death, Nov. 29, 1899, bequeathing to his native Town a considerable estate to establish and maintain a Free Public Library, known as the Cary Library.

III. Jefferson, b. Sept. 4, 1841; he also is a practicing Physician, at Caribou, Me., and has been thrice married.

IV. John H., b. July 18, 1844; d. in infancy.

V. Bion B., b. July 18, 1844; d. in infancy.

Section 252

William Holman Cary, son of William Holman, Sec. 133, b. New Salem, Mass., Oct. 23, 1812, and d. at St. Paul, Minn., Mar. 19, 1884; m. 1st, Cordelia Matthews, 1844, who d. April 29, 1849; m 2(h Adelaide Currier, Nov., 1858. For many years he was engaged with his brother, Shepard, in the management of lumbering operations in Northern Aroostook, where native pine lumber, then much in demand in England for ship timber, was cut and floated down the rivers to St. John's, N. B., for export.

Children:
I. Sylvester, b. Jan. 8, 1845.
II. William H., b. April 2, 1849, Boston, Mass.
III. Catherine H., b. May 15, 1860.
IV. Annie A., b. Nov. 25, 1861; d. in infancy.

Section 253

Horace Cary, son of Ephraim. Sec. 134, b. Minot, Me., 1811; m. Miss Bradford, Turner, Me., 1835.
Children:
I. Charles, b. 1836; d. 1859.
II. Zoe Jane, b. 1839; m H. Haskell, 1863.
III. Lucius, b. 1843.
IV. Lyman, b. 1847.

Section 254

Daniel Morris Cary, son of Joseph, Sec. 135, b. Knox Co., Me., June 17, 1806; m. Dorcas Price, Dec. 28, 1830; removed to Millersburg, Ia., where he d. April, 1874.
Children:
I. Sarah W., b. Oct. 27, 1831; m. A. Ackers, 1855; d. 1856.
II. William, b. Fcb. 2, 1833. Sec. 315.
III. James B., b. June 24, 1835; m.. Clara E. Penn, Millersburg, Ia., May 14, 1867, and had
 1. James H., b. Aug. 2, 1868, and lived at Victor, Ia.
IV. John A., b. May 24, 1838; he was in the 28th Iowa Regt.; m. Ellen C. Sherwood, June 23, 1861, and had
 1. Charles A., b. June, 1862.
 2. Samuel D., b. Jan., 1869.
 3. Sherman G., b. Dec. 8, 1873.
V. Samuel P., b. May 18, 1840; d. Feb. 20, 1866; m. Sarah B. Young, June 28, 1863, and had 1. Alice, b. April 18, 1864.
VI. Martha, b. Feb. 11, 1843; m. Dr. J. S. Gaines, June, 1862.
VII. Alvah A., b. Nov. 17, 1845.
VIII. Emily J., b. Aug. 2, 1852; m. Allen Thompson, Aug. 19, 1872.

Section 255

Dr. Abel Cary, son of Lewis, Sec. 137, b. in Ohio, Oct. 2, 1809; studied Medicine, and stood high as a Physician and as a man; settled in Salem, O.; m. Maria P. Miller, May 5, 1843.

Children:
I. Isabella, b. June 20, 1844; d. in childhood.
II. Ashbel, b. Jan. 6, 1846.
III. Barclay, b. Mar. 20, 1847; d. in childhood.
IV. David M., b. Jan. 26, 1849.
V. James R., b. April 17, 1851.
VI. Charles M., b. May 14, 1853.
VII. Lewis, b. May 14, 1855; d. in childhood.
VIII. Alice, b. Sept. 17, 1857.
IX. William B., b. Dec. 9, 1860.

Section 256

Aaron Cary, son of Lewis, Sec. 137, b. in Ohio, Aug. 17, 1813; m. Nancy Myers, of Bucyrus, O., Sept. 22, 1840, and lived at Defiance, O. Children:
I. Lewis M., b. Oct. 7, 1841; m. Hattie C. Scott.
II. Melancthon, b. May 21, 1844.
III. Abram M., b. Dec. 15, 1846.
IV. William H., b. June 14, 1850.

Section 257

Edmond Cary, son of Lewis, Sec. 137, b. in Ohio, Oct. 27, 1815; m. Delia Bartlett, Oct. 27, 1840; removed to Rockton, Ill.
Children:
I. Sarah, b. Oct. 12, 1841; d. in childhood.
II. Pamelia, b. Nov. 10, 1843; d. in childhood.
III. Daniel B., b. April 8, 1845; d. in Union Army, Mar. 19, 1864.
IV. Thomas J., b. Aug. 27, 1847.
V. Lucretia, b. Mar. 29, 1850.
VI. Esther, b. Jan. 29, 1852.
VII. Charles W., b. July 8, 1854.
VIII. Kate M., b. Mar. 4, 1856.
IX. Susan B., b. Dec. 30, 1857.
X. George E., b. Feb. 25, 1864.

Section 258

George Cary, son of Lewis, Sec. 137, b. in Ohio, Aug. 4, 1821; m. Catherine G. Gordon, April 10, 1849; removed to Beloit, Wis.
Children:
I. Harriet M., b. April 10, 1850; d. in infancy.
II. Lewis A., b. Sept. 24, 1852.

III. George, b. Aug. 4, 1855.
IV. James C., b. Oct. 4, 1857; d. in childhood.
V. Parvin W., b. Sept. 28, 1859; d. in childhood.

Section 259

Lewis Henry Cary, son of John, Sec. 139, b. Morrow Co., O., Mar. 27, 1813; m. Martha Chamberlain, Jan. 8, 1839; removed to Toledo, Ia. Children:
I. A son; d. in infancy.
II. William P., b. Jan. 17, 1841; d. in childhood.
III. John Lewis, b. Feb. 24, 1843.
IV. Mary E., b. Feb. 28, 1845.
V. Lou, b. April 29, 1848; d. in infancy.
VI. Martha M., b. Sept. 9, 1849.
VII. Lucretia, b. Nov. 18, 1852.

Section 260

William Snook Cary, son of John, Sec. 139, b. Morrow Co., O., May 16, 1818; m. Mary A. Gordon, Feb. 21, 1843, and removed to Alvarado, Ind.
Children:
I. Mary Ann, b. Jan. 18, 1844; m. William H. Keyes, Jan. 18, 1865.
II. Laurana, b. Jan. 29, 1847; d. 1853.
III. Margaret J., b. Oct. 20, 1849; d. 1833.
IV. Levinna E., b. Nov. 11, 1851; d. 1853.
V. William G., b. Oct. 9, 1854.
VI. John L., b. Mar. 28, 1858.
VII. Nelson E., b. Nov. 29, 1861.

Section 261

John R. Cary, son of John, Sec. 139, b. Morrow Co., O., Aug. 7, 1826; m. Eliza S. Lewis, July 1, 1845; was a Minister of the Methodist Episcopal Church, and lived at Garden Grove, Ia.
Children:
I. Edward G., b. July 5, 1846.
II. Leonard B., b. June 26, 1848.
III. Emma, b. Jan. 25, 1851.
IV. John Lewis, b. May 18, 1854.
V. Alice B., b. Mar. 4, 1857.
VI. Clara B., b. April 3, 1859.

Section 262

George C. Cary, son of John, Sec. 139, b. Morrow Co., O., Mar. 20, 1823; m. Cordelia Purvis, Dec. 31, 1849; removed to Alvarado, Ind., and d. 1900.
Children:
I. Willard P., b. Oct. 10, 1850; d. in infancy.
II. Lewis W., b. Sept. 14, 1852, Rome City, Ind.; d. at Metz, Ind., Feb. 27, 1896; m. Anne Barber, April 12, 1876, and had
  1. Emmet B., b. Feb. 19, 1880; a Pharmacist.
  2. Emerson, b. Dec. 14, 1882; d. 1904.
  3. Edna Eugenia, b. Feb. 15, 1885; a Teacher, and both reside with the Mother in Cleveland, O.
III. Eugenia A., b. Mar. 15, 1855; m. Nathan Metz.
IV. George M., b. Aug. 29, 1857; d. 1881.
V. Hibbard E., b. June 20. 1861; d. in childhood.
VI. Lizzie O., b. May 11, 1864; m. Elmer Tees.
VII. Luta P.. b. Oct. 12, 1866; m. George Scott.
These reside in Edson, O.

Section 263

William Sayre Cary, son of Daniel, Sec. 140. b. Drakesville, N. J., Mar. 28, 1822; m. 1st, Phebe Northrup, Newton, N. J., who bore him three children, and d. Jan. 17, 1865; m. 2d, Sarah R. Cramer, May, 1868; he was a Surveyor and Farmer, and discovered Fire Sand on his farm; was prominent in the community, and d. June 28, 1902.
Children:
I. Ann Eliza, b. Feb. 4, 1853; m. Nicholas W. Hoffman, Lebanon, N. J., and had
  1. Albert Cary, b. Oct. 7, 1885; m. Addie Stillwell, Trenton, N. J., June 8, 1909.
II. Lyman Northrup, b. May 5. 1856, Hoboken, N. J., lived on old farm at Flanders, and about 1880 removed to Mandan, N. D., where he is in the Real Estate business; m. Anne Alison Clark, Washington, Pa., Dec. 12, 1894, and had
  1. Ethelind, b. Feb. 25, 1897.
  2. William Sayre, b. Nov. 18, 1898.
  3. James Alison, b. Sept. 18, 1900.
  4. Colin Reed, b. Jan. 5, 1905.
III. Lewis Daniel, b. Nov. 30, 1858; m. Carrie H. Salmon, Budd's Lake, N. J., June 18, 1896; he is a Civil Engineer, to which he adds farming, and getting out Fire Sand and Kaolin; they had
  1. A daughter; d. in infancy.
  2. Phoebe Dorothy, b. April 10, 1909; d. in infancy.

Section 264

John Cary, son of Zenas, Sec. 142, b. Colrain, Mass., July 24, 1810; m. 1st, Olive Watson, Feb. 27, 1835, who d. Oct. 2, 1852; m. 2d, Catherine Coolidge, Sept. 22, 1853, who d. Oct. 23, 1864; m. 3d, Lizzie J. White, Jan. 23, 1867, who d. June 23, 1909, Springfield, Mass. He d. Mar. 1, 1899, at North Adams, Mass.
Children:
I. Emerson J., b. May 3, 1837; d. Aug. 19, 1901, North Adams; m. Lydia D. Davenport, Aug. 29, 1858, and had
  1. Alice Lela, b. May 7, 1865; m. William H. Buck, Oct. 8, 1885, and had
  (1) Ray Cary, b. Aug. 20, 1886; m. Ethel Green, 1907, and had
    1. A daughter, b. Jan., 1909.
  (2) Gladys L., b. June 9, 1891.
  (3) Donald Le Roy, b. Mar. 12, 1893; d. 1900.
  2. Emerson J., b. May 12, 1872; m. Nellie G. Clark of Colrain, Jan. 7, 1892; m. 2d, Grace M. Harris, June 1, 1908, at Spokane, Wash.; Bureau of Animal Industry, Dept. of Agriculture.
II. Mary S., b. Jan. 12, 1840; d. 1851.
III. Fanny Olive, b. June 18, 1842; m. Horatio Nelson Buck, East Arlington, Vt., Jan. 1, 1892.
IV. Lydia A., b. Aug. 25, 1844; m. George O. Braman of North Adams, Mar. 19, 1873, and had
  1. Jason Cary, b. Aug. 1, 1874; m. Theressa C. Beck, April 21, 1909; a commercial traveler, North Adams.
  2. Arthur E., b. Aug. 23, 1876; m. Amey E. Tower of North Adams, June 16, 1897; commercial traveler, Springfield, Mass.
  3. John Watson, b. Aug. 4, 1883; bookkeeper B. & M., Springfield.
  4. Harold G., b. Sept. 27, 1885.
V. James P., b. May 18, 1848.
VI. Eva Elizabeth, b. Jan. 21, 1855; m. Emerson E. Watson, a R. R. engineer, who d. July 27, 1904.
VII. Ellen B., b. Aug. 25, 1858.

Section 265

George Cary, son of Zenas, Sec. 142, b. Colrain, Mass., July 4, 1812; m. 1st, Diana Shippee, Jan. 7, 1837, who d. Sept. 21, 1854; m. 2d, Dordana Shippee, Nov. 1. 1855, and lived in Colrain, where he d. July 10, 1871.
Children:
I. Clark Shepard, b. Oct. 3, 1838. Sec. 316.
II. Ella Diana, b. Oct. 5, 1856; d. 1859.

Section 266

William Whiting Cary, son of Zenas, Sec. 142, b. Colrain, Mass., Feb. 24, 1815; m. 1st, Britania Maxam, Colrain. Mass., July 5, 1838, who d. Aug. 9, 1842; m. 2d, Harriet M. Maxam, May 21, 1843, who d. Oct. 17, 1898. When 13 years of age one of his knees was injured, which crippled him for life; probably this turned his attention to Nature studies, and specially to the Honey Bee, which proved to be his life work, and he soon had the largest and most thriving Apiary in Western Massachusetts. In this he became an authority, and when the Italian bees were imported, he was selected as the best man to propagate them, and his specialty became the propagation of the Queen Bee, which he sent to all parts of the country. He was also engaged in the invention and manufacture of apiarian supplies. He was sympathetic and public spirited, and d. Dec. 9, 1884.

Children:

I. Sarah F., b. June 12, 1840; d. in childhood.
II. William H., b. July 19, 1842; d. in infancy.
III. William Henry, b. Dec. 18, 1846; d. in childhood.
IV. William Whiting, b. Nov. 6, 1848; m. Mary Frances Tripp, Feb. 22, 1871, and he well kept up the reputation of the family in his interest in propagating and distributing the Queen Bees, to which he has added manufacturing. They had

1. Lillian Emeline, b. Nov. 27, 1871.
2. Minnie Lulu, b. Nov. 14, 1874.
3. Herbert Francis, b. April 17, 1879; he in the third generation, keeps up the good repute of the family in Bee culture; m. Elizabeth Blagborough of Holyoke, Mass., Dec. 31, 1901, and had

(1) Harold Whiting, b. Oct. 4, 1903.
(2) Donald Edwin, b. Feb. 11, 1905.

4. Ethel Lena, b. June 19, 1883; m. Earl Willard Nichols of Colrain, July 18, 1906, and had

(1) Raymond E., b. June 17, 1909.

V. Sarah E., b. July 13, 1850; m. Charles W. Eastman of Bradford, Vt., Mar. 5, 1872, who d. Oct. 14, 1876; m. 2d, George E. Brown of Bradford, Vt., Aug. 29, 1883, who d. Mar. 9, 1901; m. 3d, Levi E. Call of Gardner, Mass., April 9, 1904.
VI. Viola Estella, b. Sept. 22, 1853; m. Frank Crozier of Readsboro, Vt., Jan. 17, 1887, and had 1. Ruth Cary, b. Jan. 31, 1892; d. in infancy.
VII. Charles F., b. May 16, 1857; d. in infancy.

Section 267

Levi Cary, son of Zenas, Sec. 142, b. Catamount Hill, Colrain, Mass., April 2, 1822; m. Fanny Jane Shippee, Nov. 27, 1845; they lived in Colrain and Con-

way, and several years at North Adams, Mass. He d. April 18, 1889, and his widow d. Oct. 24, 1899, at Turner's Falls, Mass.
Children:
I. Hoyt Francis, b. Oct. 11, 1847; m. and had six children, North Adams.
II. Arthur D., b. Mar. 1, 1853; d. in childhood.
III. Emma L., b. Oct. 1, 1855; d. in childhood.
IV. Nellie G., b. May 16, 1860; m. Mr. Williams, Turner's Falls, Mass.
V. Fred E., b. June 9, 1864, Orange, Mass.

Section 268

Josiah Cary, son of Zebulon, Sec. 143, b. Brookfield, Mass., Sept. 25, 1814; m. Anne Butler, 1843; he was a Carpenter, removed to Franklinville, N. Y., and d. Sept. 29, 1865.
Children:
I. Phebe Ann, b. Jan. 2, 1844.
II. William H., b. Jan 2, 1846.
III. Susan, b. May 7, 1849.

Section 269

Josiah Addison Cary, son of Josiah, Sec. 144, b. Brookfield, Mass., 1813; removed to Ohio, and was Supt. of the Asylum for the Deaf and Dumb at Columbus, where he d. Aug. 7, 1852. He m. Gertrude Jenkins, Oct. 23, 1844, who afterwards conducted a popular Young Ladies' Seminary at Philadelphia, Pa.
Children:
I. Mary Alice, b. May 5, 1846.
II. Norman White, b. Oct. 29, 1849.

Section 270

Nathan C. Cary, son of Avery, Sec. 145, b. North Brookfield, Mass., 1814; m. Frances T. Wilson, and lived in Roxbury, Boston, Mass.
Children:
I. Fanny Maria, b. 1846; m. Charles Albert Merrill, 1867, and had
1. Charles A., b. 1870; m. Clara Boutell, 1901, and had (1) Cary Merrill, b. 1902, and live at Los Angeles, Cal. II. William Avery, b. 1849; a Solicitor in Probate, Boston; m.
Mrs. Clara Pond Hutchins, 1901.
III. Mary E., b. 1854; d. in childhood.

Section 271

Samuel Avery Cary, son of Avery, Sec. 145, b. North Brookfield, Mass., 1823; m. Maria Cook, Boston, 1853, and settled at Elyria, O. Children:
I. Edward Avery, b. 1856.
II. Harriet, b. 1858; m. Walter G. Cleveland, Cleveland, O., and d. 1900.
III. Annie, b. 1861; m. George Martin.
IV. Mary, b. 1861; d. in infancy.
V. Samuel, b. 1866; m. and lives in Chicago.
VI. Fanny M.
VII. Kate; m. Walter G. Cleveland, 1902.
VIII. Nettie; m. and lives in St. Louis.

Section 272

Daniel Moulton Cary, son of Thomas H., Sec. 147, b. Springville, N. Y., June 25, 1831; m. Celestine Gates, Mar., 1856, and lived at Allen's Point, Wis.
Children:
I. Edward, b. 1857.
II. Benjamin, b. 1860.

Section 272-A

Susanna Cary, dau. of Barzillai, Sec. 149, b. Bridgewater, 1808; m. Luke Perkins, Auburn, Mass.
Children:
I. Rhoda Cary, m. Mr. Dinsmore.
II. Susan Elizabeth, m. Mr. Packard.
III. Vesta Snell, m. Isaiah A. Beals, and had
1. Arthur Loring.
2. Susanna Cary.
IV. Stillman Simeon, m. and had
1. Edward Lyman, who m. and had
(1) Dorothy Ellen.
(2) Mary Louisa.
V. George Albert.
VI. Martha Ellen.

Section 272-B

Rhoda Cary, dau. of Barzillai, Sec. 149, b. Bridgewater, 1821; m. Daniel S. Howard; she d. Dec. 4, 1868.
Children:

I. Warren Alcott, b. Dec. 20, 1839; m. Mary Agnes Stetson, Dec. 25, 1861, and had
  1. Mary Stetson, b. Nov. 19, 1862.
  2. Agnes Alcott, b. June 17, 1868; m. Edward T. Rock, Sept. 22, 1896, and had
    (1) Katherine. (2) Howard. (3) Warren. (4) Richard.
  3. Annie Cary, b. Nov. 22, 1870; d. 1872.
  4. Frank A., b. Dec. 17, 1872; m. Faith Rider, Sept. 22, 1902, and had
    (1) Allen R., b. Nov., 1903.
    (2) Warren, b. June 22, 1905.
    (3) Lucius A.
II. Lizzie Stone.

Section 272-C

Vesta Snell Cary, dau. of Barzillai, Sec. 149, b. Bridgewater, May 1, 1827; m. Henry K. Keith, Kingston, Mass. (b. Dec. 19, 1826; d. Aug. 9, 1909), July 18, 1847; she d. Feb. 5, 1903.

Children:

I. Lewis Henry, b. June 8, 1848, North Duxbury, Mass.; m. Laura L. Bailey, Kingston, and had
  1. Louise Cary, b. Dec. 9, 1872; d. Sept. 22, 1908; m. George H. Clark, and had
    (1) Kenneth Oldham.
  2. Anne Lewis, b. June 24, 1876; d. in infancy.
  3. Gertrude Willard, b. Nov. 16, 1879.
  4. Flelen Cynthia, b. Mar. 4, 1881; d. 1901.
  5. Clinton Thomas, b. Nov. 27, 1887.
II. Emma Cary, b. Feb. 25, 1850; d. Feb. 15, 1891; m. James L. Barker, Santa Barbara, Cal., and had 1. Henry L., b. Sept. 11, 1875, Kingston, Mass., a Correspondent of the Associated Press.

Section 273

Charles Cary, son of Caleb, Sec. 150 , b. East Machias, Me., 1835; m. Mary E., dau. of Luther Cary, 1857; lived in East Machias, and d. 1884.

Children:

I. William, b. 1858; d. 1865.
II. Lucy T., b. 1860; d. 1865.
III. Austin, b. July 31, 1865; educated at Bowdoin, taught for a year, and then engaged in University work; spent ten years in the U. S. Forestry Division, and in the work in the State of Maine; in forestry work for the Berlin Mills Co., Portland, Me.; holds degrees of B. A., M. A., and Phi Beta Kappa; explored in Labrador in 1892; Professor at Harvard.

IV. George Foster, b. 1867, and is a business man; grad. Bowdoin, 1888; Treas. Machias Savings Bank, 1897; Pres't Machias Banking Co., 1901; Overseer Bowdoin College; m. Lottie Colman, 1889, and had
   1. Charles Austin, b. 1900.
V. Edwin L., b. 1872; d. in childhood.

Section 274

Elisha Caleb Cary, son of Jonathan, Sec. 151, b. Cooper, Me., 1819; m. Vienna Bridgman, 1846, and lived in Cooper.
Children:
I. Laura E.
II. Veranus L.
III. Alvin S.
IV. Manly A.
V. Frank E.
VI. Elisha S.

Section 275

Henry S. Cary, son of Jonathan, Sec. 151, b. Cooper, Me., Aug. 4, 1822; m. Waity W. Palmeter, Cooper, Me., 1845, and lived in Cooper. Children:
   I. Elizabeth M., b. Mar. 3, 1848; m. George H. Foster, and had

REV. OTIS CARY, D. D.

   1. Charles Henry, b. Mar. 22, 1875.
   2. Laura E., b. April 29, 1877; d. in childhood.
   3. George E., b. May 9, 1883; d. in childhood.
   II. Emily, b. Sept. 5, 1850; m. Raymond A. Damon, Jan. 1, 1876, and had
   1. Alice Cary, b. Nov. 27, 1876; m. George Cary of Brockton, Mass., June 14, 1900, and had
   (1) George Arnold, b. May 18, 1905.
   2. Bertha E., b. Aug. 6, 1879; m. Alfred Miles, Hancock, Me.
   3. Arthur R., b. Feb. 22, 1884.
   III. Evelyn P., b. Jan. 10, 1859; d. about 1875.
   IV. Willard H., b. April 6, 1863; m. Hattie Stewart, Columbia, Me.; he d. Aug. 19, 1902.

Section 276

James Webber Cary, son of Luther, Sec. 152. b. East Machias, Me., Aug., 1819; m. Anna E. Allan, Oct., 1857; lived in Cooper, Me., and d. Feb., 1900.
Children:
I. Charlotte Amelia, b. Oct., 1858; in Moody Training School, Chicago.
II. John Allan, b. Mar., 1861; m. Frances McMullin, and had
1. James. 2. Alice Elizabeth.

Section 276-A

Martin L. Cary, son of Luther, Sec. 152, b. Cooper, Me., Sept., 1836; was a Sergeant in the 1st Rhode Island Cav., and in 1864 was severely wounded and discharged; he then became Foreman in the Corliss Steam Engine Works, Providence, and afterwards was engaged in caring for the interests of the heirs, so that in all he gave 42 years to the service of the family. He was a member of the North Congregational Church, and for many years a Deacon. In 1867, m. Mary M. Wattles, who d. April, 1904; he d. 1907.
Children:
I. Edwin Foster; m. Clara Louise Perry, and had
1. Eleanor.
2. Hope.
II. Walter W.; m. Margaret Forsyth, and had
1. Margaret.
2. Luther.
3. Ida.
4. Howard W.
5. Austin.
III. Alice; m. Arthur Dent, and had
1. Alston Cary.
2. Edwin Foster.
IV. Helen.

Section 277

Charles George Cary, son of Lewis, Sec. 155, b. Boston, Mass., 1824; m. Sarah O. Barnes, 1848, and was accidentally shot while hunting in 1853.
Children:
I. George Billings, b. 1849.
II. Francis Henry, b. 1851. %
III. Charles Warren, b. 1854.

Section 278

Thomas Webb Cary, son of Lewis, Sec. 155 , b. Boston, Mass., 1826; m. Caroline Parker, 1846.
Children:
I. Charles Parker, b. 1847.
II. Emma C., b. 1849.
III. Lewis Warren, b. 1851; d. in childhood.
IV. Adaline E., b. 1853.
V. Mary E., b. 1856.
VI. Calvin Chase, b. 1858.

Section 279

Alexander Claxton Cary, son of Isaac, Sec. 156, b. Boston, Mass., Feb., 1834; m. Mary Elizabeth Barker, Newton, Mass., 1857, who d. Aug. 7, 1907, New York City; he entered The New England Bank Note Co., of which his father was the Manager, and which was afterwards absorbed by The American Bank Note Co., and he removed to New York City and became the Manager. At the time of his death, which occurred Jan. 11, 1909, he had retired from active business.
Children:
I. Lillian; m. Arthur W. Stedman, Boston, 1878; d. 1881.
II. Alice.
III. Elizabeth; m. Arthur Blaney; m. 2d, Frank C. Farquhar, Boston, 1905; they had
 1. Lillian.
IV. Julia Willard.
V. Jane Solis.
VI. Mary Willard; d. about 1889.
VII. Alexander Claxton; m. Lillian Daly, New York, and had
 1. Alexander Claxton.
 2. Helen.
 3. Lillian.
 4. Willard Perkins, b. 1908.
VIII. Emma Cheney; m. Richard A. Monks. New York City.

Section 279-A

Mary Ann Cary, dau. of Hon. Otis, Sec. 157, b. Easton, Mass., Aug. 15, 1831; d. Feb. 20, 1901; grad. Mount Holyoke, 1851; m. Arza Benjamin Keith, a prominent Shoe Manufacturer of Campello (Brockton), Mass., April 25, 1854. She was a friend of sound learning, a church worker, and a helper in every good cause. Her brother's Poem, written for the Cary Reunion following her death, is a fitting tribute to her loving service.

> A self-forgetful life; and we
> Often forgot, like her, to see
> Whose hand it was that wrought the deed,
> Who spoke the word that met the need,
> Who labored on while none gave heed.
>
> But now we see what she saw not,
> And know the worth, which she forgot,
> Of her own self, as long she stood
> In sacrifice for others' good,
> A type of Christian womanhood.

Karuizawa, Japan, July 24, 1901.

Children:

I. Otis Franklin, b. July 27, 1855; d. in childhood.

II. Warren Burton, b. Oct. 6, 1857; grad, at Amherst, and is a Civil Engineer; m. Mrs. Luella Chapman Parke.

III. Marcia Ann, b. Sept. 10, 1859; grad, at Mt. Holyoke, and taught there 18 years; has studied at Worcester Polytechnic, Chicago, and Berlin.

IV. Herbert Cary, b. Dec. 24, 1861; is a Consulting Civil Engineer; m. Lillian Davenport; their eldest son has a Rhodes Scholarship, and the younger is at Yale.

V. Clara Louisa, b. Sept. 3, 1864; m. E. C. Bryant.

VI. Lucy Ella, b. Oct. 16, 1866; grad, of Chicago, and is Prof, of Bible Study, Western College, Oxford, O.

VII. Mary Helen, b. Nov. 9, 1868; grad. Mt. Holyoke and Columbia, and taught at Mt. Holyoke.

VIII. Sarah Emma, b. Nov. 11, 1870; grad. Mt. Holyoke and Tufft's, and an independent Investigator at Marine Biological Laboratory, Woods Holl, Mass.

IX. Cora Frances, b. June 16, 1873; m. Charles McLean Warren, Sept. 23, 1905, and they are Missionaries in Japan; they had

1. Dana Thurston, b. Oct. 8, 1906.
2. Mary Keith, b. Mar. 12, 1908.

X. Arza Henry, b. Mar. 11, 1875; m. Emma L. Thompson.

Section 279-B

Rev. Otis Cary, D. D., son of Hon. Otis, Sec. 157, b. April 20, 1851, Foxboro, Mass.; graduated from High School, 1868; from Amherst, 1872; from Andover, 1877, and was ordained to the Ministry the same year, and received his Doctor's degree 1904; m. Ellen Maria Emerson of Nashua, N. H., Dec. 18, 1877. In 1878 went to Japan as a Missionary of the American Board; engaged in evangelistic work in Okayama, Osaka, and Kyoto; in 1892 was Lecturer on Practical Sociology, and in 1900 became Professor of Practical Sociology and

Homiletics in the Doshisha Seminary. In the Japanese language he has been a fruitful author and translator, as well as preacher; his last work while on leave of absence in 1898-99, being a History of Christianity in Japan, in two large volumes. After thirty years in Japan, he went back, leaving his four children in school in America. He is also the author of the Later Cary Poems, the longer of which gives the story of the winning of the Cary Coat of Arms.

Children:

I. George Emerson, b. Jan. 27, 1884, Okayama, Japan; now in Andover Theological Seminary.

II. Walter, b. Jan. 8, 1886, Okayama, Japan; now in Medical School, Cleveland, Ohio.

III. Frank, b. July 18, 1888, Foxboro, Mass.; now at Amherst College.

IV. Alice Elizabeth, b. Nov. 2, 1900, Osaka, Japan; now at Northfield, Mass.

Section 280

Col. Samuel Cary, son of Abram, Sec. 159, b. in New Jersey, 1784; when a boy removed to the Northwest Territory with his parents; m. Sarah Goble, Oct. 25, 1803, at Cincinnati, O., and settled in Henry Co., Ind. He was a man of quiet and amiable temper, a nobleman by nature, and a great favorite of the Indians; was an early and prominent Mason, and came to his death by accident, Aug. 27, 1828. He had five sons in the Mexican War. His wife was a model woman, and d. at the age of 71 years.

Children:

I. Rhoda, b. Jan. 25, 1805; m. A. W. Reed of South Carolina, Oct. 2, 1823; d. at Grand Gulf, La., 1848, leaving four sons and two daughters.

II. Mary M., b. May, 1807; m. Dr. John Elliott, Oct. 25, 1826, and had one son and two daughters.

III. Drusilla, b. Feb. 3, 1809; m. J. B. Ferguson, Indianapolis, Ind., Dec. 18, 1823; d. 1853, leaving three sons and one daughter.

IV. Leonora, b. Nov. 12, 1810; d. 1814.

V. Martha, b. Oct. 6, 1812; m. Lorenzo D. Meeks, New Castle, Ind., Sept. 23, 1831, and had four sons and three daughters.

VI. Ebenezer, b. Oct. 6, 1812; m. Mary Elsrath; was a Captain in the Mexican War, and d. in the City of Mexico, 1848.

VII. Samuel Stephen Decatur, b. Mar. 29, 1815; m. Mary D. Owens, July 22, 1833, Newcastle, Ind., and had three sons and two daughters. He was in the Mexican War, and d. at Puebla, Mex., 1848. His widow went South, and his sons, Fielding G. and Martin, were in the Confederate service; the daughters d. childless.

VIII. Susanna, b. May 23, 1817; d. 1826.

IX. Oliver H. Perry, b. Feb. 26, 1819; was a Captain in the Mexican War, and Lieutenant-Colonel, 36th Ind., in the Civil War; m. Lois Hall, and had a daughter; lived at Marion, Ind.

X. Sarah A. M., b. Feb. 6, 1822; m. Bronson Swaim, Sept. 22, 1847, and had two sons and one daughter; lived at Knightstown, Ind.

XI. James Noble, b. June 18, 1823; was in the Mexican War, and d. soon after his return.

XII. John Test, b. 1825; was in the Mexican War; in 1850 went to California, and became distinguished as a Lawyer, and for years was Judge in Klamath County.

Section 281

Waitstill Munson Cary, son of Abram, Sec. 159, b. in New Jersey, 1785; removed with parents to Cincinnati, O., thence to Springfield, O., where he married Nancy Rock, July 9, 1805; removed with the first settlers to Knightstown, Ind., where he lived to an advanced age highly respected.

Children:

I. Abram, b. Nov. n, 1807; m. Elizabeth Sprause, and had
1. Nancy E., b. Sept. 1, 1849.
2. Waitstill M., b. Feb. 18, 1851.
3. Henrietta, b. Jan., 1853.
4. Joseph M., b. Oct., 1854.
5. Mary H., b. Nov., 1856.
6. Rosa E., b. Jan., 1862.

II. Martha, b. Jan. 20, 1809; m. 1st, Benjamin Stratton, Jan. 26, 1832; m. 2d, Jesse Hinshaw; had three sons and two daughters.

III. Mary, b. Nov. 7, 1810; m. Asa Heaton, Feb. 4, 1830, and had
1. Abram C.
2. Joseph W.
3. Waitstill M.

IV. Eleanor, b. Sept, n, 1812; m. J. M. Whitesill, Aug. 18, 1831, and had
1. James Lowry.
2. Charles Rock.

V. Phebe, b. April 4, 1814; m. Robert Huddleson, June 10, 1830, and had four sons and two daughters.

VI. Rosanna, b. Mar. 5, 1816; m. M. F. Edwards, May 5, 1836, and had two sons and three daughters.

VII. Caroline, b. 1818; m. D. Macy, 1834; d. 1836.

Section 281-A

Ebenezer Cary, son of Clement, Sec. 161, b. Suckasunna Plains, N. J., July 30, 1810; removed to Augusta, Ga., 1835; m. Martha Burr Stockton (a descendant of the New Jersey Stocktons, and connected with Aaron Burr), Feb. 22, 1843; she d. May 12, 1863, and he d. Mar. 4, 1884.

Children:

I. Martha, b. April 21, 1844; d. in infancy.

II. Silas Jennings, b. Dec. 23, 1845; d. Nov. 7, 1875; m. Annie L. Parker, Dec. 21, 1870, and had

1. Martha Eugenia, b. Oct. 31, 1869; d. in infancy.

2. Harry Francis, b. Nov. 28, 1874; m. Catherine Cornell, Macon, Ga., Nov. 8, 1900; he is General Passenger Agent of the Southern Railway, Washington, D. C.

III. Clement Cassius, b. Oct. 27, 1847; m Callia Benson, Jan. 26, 1871, is a member of the North Georgia Conference of the Methodist Episcopal Church, South, and lives at Atlanta, Ga.

IV. Joseph Burr, b. Oct. 8, 1849; d. in infancy.

V. Mary Elizabeth, b. Dec. 4, 1851; d. Jan. 15, 1879; m. Benjamin Toole, Dec. 21, 1870, and had

1. Madge Elizabeth, b. Nov. 26, 1871; d. in infancy.

2. Benjamin Franklin, b. Feb. 3, 1874; d. Sept. 28, 1900, Charleston, S. C.

3. Alice Lavinia, b. Jan. 2, 1876; m. Dr. De Leon Lewellen, June 25, 1902, and had

(1) Jesse De Leon, b. Aug. 18, 1903.

(2) Alice Cary, b. June 1, 1905.

(3) John Wyeth, b. July 24, 1908.

VI. Alice Matilda, b. Jan. 30, 1854; m. Benjamin F. Toole, Aug. 18, 1879, and had

1. Mamie Derry, b. June 6, 1881.

2. Irene Elizabeth, b. Nov. 7, 1882, Savannah, Ga.

3. Norman Cary, b. June 28, 1886, Wilmington, N. C.

VII. Ebenezer Francis, b. June 12, 1856; m. Mrs. Augusta Dodge Cooper, Sept. 1, 1883, who d. Nov., 1905, Macon, Ga.

VIII. Hattie Edith, b. May 17, 1863; d. in infancy.

Section 282

Henry Axtell Cary, son of Nathaniel, Sec. 162, b. in New Jersey, Nov. 4, 1816; was a Tanner, and m. Mary Bockover, 1839, and lived in Towanda, Pa.

Children:

I. Jefferson S., b. Oct., 1840, in U. S. Navy.

II. Frank B., b. April. 1842; killed in the battle of Chancellorsville, Va., 1863.

III. Ann Augusta, b. June, 1848.

Section 283

Lewis Cary, son of Nathaniel, Sec. 162, b. in New Jersey, June 13, 1820; m. Julia A. Ensign, Aug. 31, 1845; was an extensive Manufacturer of Coach Lamps at Newark. N. J.

Children:

I. Amelia, b. July 7, 1846.
II. William H., b. July 2, 1848.
III. John C, b. Jan. 19, 1851.
IV. Edward P., b. June 23, 1853; d. in infancy.
V. Alfred E., b. Oct. 23, 1855; d. in childhood.
VI. Emma M., b. Oct. 5, 1862.

Section 284

Dr. Isaac Cary, son of Nathaniel, Sec. 162, b. in New Jersey, Mar. 22, 1823; m. Harriet Rowe, Aug. 31, 1854; a Physician and lived at Norwich, N. J.
Child:
I. Frank R., b. 1856.

Section 285

William Henry Cary, son of William, Sec. 167, b. Graniteville, R. I., May 17, 1837, and was a Stonecutter; m. Claretta A. Davis, Jan. 13, 1861, at Pawtucket, R. I.
Children:
I. Frederick A., b. Dec. 29, 1865; d. in infancy.
II. Franklin E., b. Dec. 29, 1865; d. in infancy.
III. Henry, b. April 18, 1868; d. in infancy.
IV. Elma, b. April 18, 1868; d. in infancy.

Section 286

George W. Cary, son of George S., Sec. 168, b. Phenix Village, R. I., June 11, 1829, a Boot and Shoe dealer; m. Martha W. Hill, June 28, 1849, and lived in New Haven, Ct.
Children:
I. Edna Dora, b. Jan. 5, 1850; d. in childhood.
II. George S., b. May 6, 1852, and lived in New Haven.

Section 287

William H. Cary, son of George S., Sec. 168, b. Lippit, R. I., Aug. 31, 1831; m. Nellie N. Converse, May 19, 1862; a Farmer, and lived at Worcester, Mass.
Child:
I. William Pliny, b. Jan. 7, 1865.

Section 288

Edward M. Cary, son of George S., Sec. 168, b. Thompson, Ct., April 28, 1834; m. Esther J. Benham, Sept. 24, 1863; a Manufacturer, and lived at Detroit, Mich.
Child:
I. Edward Lincoln, b. Mar. 8, 1865.

Section 288-A

Olive Elizabeth Cary, dau. of Isaac, Sec. 172, b. Ontario, N. Y., Mar. 28, 1833; m John Franklin Harris (b. Sept. 29, 1831, Stowe, Vt.), Nov. 20, 1851, at Williamson, N. Y. Mr. Harris was educated at Stockbridge, Mass., and became Manager of various large Iron Works, and a large real estate owner, finally settling at Fort Edward, N. Y., where he was a leading citizen, respected by his townsmen, who named a Fire Company in his honor; he was prominent in the Church, in the public schools and in municipal life, and the President of the Village Corporation.
Children:
I. George De Forest, b. July 22, 1853, Ontario, N. Y.; m.
Marion B., dau. of Hon. Alexander Barclay of Argyle, N. Y.,
Feb. 3, 1876, and had
 1. Clarence C., b. Nov. 27, 1876, Fort Edward; m. Helen Elizabeth De Forest, Dec. 30, 1903, Fort Edward, and had
  (1) Marian De Forest, b. Dec. 28, 1905.
  (2) John Franklin, b. Oct. 25, 1907.
 2. A. Barkley, b. May 20, 1878.
These sons are in business with the father, who is a wholesale Coal Merchant in New York City, with branches in London, Albany, and Pittsburg.
 3. Mark De Forest, b. June 8, 1880; d. in childhood.
II. Della Medura, b. April 22, 1855, Hudson, N. Y.; m. George E. Rogers, Fort Edward, N. Y., Nov. 15, 1877, and had
 1. John Franklin, b. Oct. 16, 1878, Troy, N. Y.; m. Mabel Day, June 28, 1906, and had
  (1) William Emerson, b. Mar. 31, 1910.
 2. Emerson, b. June 19, 1880; d. in infancy.
 3. Marian Elizabeth, b. Oct. 17, 1881.
 4. William Arthur, b. May 29, 1886; grad. Rensselaer Polytechnic Inst.
III. Sarah Elizabeth, b. Feb. 19, 1857; d. in childhood.

Section 289

Calvin Cary, son of Richard M., Sec. 173, b. Boston, N. Y., Oct. 1, 1816; m. Orilla S. Drake, Nov. 30, 1837, who d. Aug. 21, 1868; removed to Johnstown, Wis., where he d. Nov. 26, 1858.

Children:
I. Rollin, b. Oct. 16, 1838; d. in infancy.
II. Aramitta, b. Aug. 25, 1843; d. in infancy.
III. Leland J., b. Sept. 27, 1846; d. 1863.

Section 290

Ephraim Cary, son of Richard M., Sec. 173, b. Boston, N. Y., Oct. 27, 1818; m. Emily Shumway, April 22, 1846, Johnstown, Wis., where he resided.
Children:
I. Orinda, b. Aug. 14, 1847; m. Mr. Roe.
II. Eugene L., b. Nov. 16, 1849.
III. Anne G., b. Nov. 13, 1851.
IV. Emma, b. May 28, 1856.

Section 291

Benjamin F. Cary, son of Richard M., Sec. 173, b. Boston, N. Y., Feb. 15, 1821; m. Sarah M. Skinner, Mar. 12, 1845, who d. June 17, 1873; m. 2d, Mary M. Magee, Nov. 26, 1874; he resided in Janesville, Wis., where he d. Feb. 9, 1885.
Children:
I. Levi F., b. July 16, 1846; d. in infancy.
II. Arthur W., b. Oct. 30, 1847; m. 1st, Laura M. Hull, Oct. 22, 1868, who d. Mar. 12, 1883; m. 2d, E. Belle Nickerson, Sept. 17, 1885, and had
   1. Ernest S., b. Jan. 2, 1870; d. in infancy.
   2. Harlin E., b. July 11, 1871; m. Clara Staples, June 27, 1900, and had
   (1) Ellsworth H., b. Nov. 17, 1902.
   (2) Olive M., b. Jan. 7, 1907.
   3. Edwin S., b. Aug. 27, 1878; m. Marne E. Clark, Oct. 29, 1902, and had
   (1) Donovan, b. Oct. 1, 1903.
   4. Orra Belle, b. Aug. 18, 1895; d. in infancy.
   5. Leta L., b. Mar. 1, 1897.
III. Emery, b. Sept. 7, 1849; d. in childhood.
IV. Eddie L., b. May 10, 1853, at Mannette, Wash.
V. Elmer E., b. Dec. 30, 1856; d. 1874.
VI. Lillian M., b. Jan. 30, 1858; m. Mr. Aldrich, Whitewater, Wis.

Section 292

Richard Cary, son of Richard M., Sec. 173, b. Boston, N. Y., April 8, 1830; m. Julia Osborn, Jan. 1, 1853, and lived at Johnstown, Wis.
Children:

I. A son, b. Aug. 31, 1856; d. in infancy.
II. Emery C., b. Mar. 12, 1860, Milton, Wis.

Section 293

Melvin Cary, son of Richard M., Sec. 173, b. Boston, N. Y., June 28, 1834; m. Helen Thayer, Oct. 4, 1851, and lived at Johnstown, Wis.
Children:
I. Delia L., b. April 18, 1860.
II. Edith M., b. Mar. 16, 1862.
III. Ida M., b. May 19, 1864.

Section 294

Sylvester L. Cary, son of Van Renssalaer, Sec. 178, b. Boston, Erie Co., N. Y., Feb. 22, 1827; was a public school Teacher at 14, a Sunday School Supt. at 18, and followed it 40 years; lived at Freeport, Ill., ten years; m. Clara J. Daniels, April 25, 1855, and observed their Golden Wedding, 1905; removed to Iowa in 1856, and to Jennings, La., 1883, when it had but 12 people. He was the first Station Agent on the Southern Pacific R. R., and also Emigration Agent. He is called the "Father" of Jennings by its 5,000 citizens; Father of the Rice industry, and President of the Iowa Colony; at 82 was personally raising 500 acres of Rice.
Children:
I. Alice S., b. April 16, 1856; m. N. S. Craig, M. D., Oct. 16, 1871.
II. Howard L., b. April 21, 1860; m. Armance Brillault, July 19, 1887, and had
1. Pearl Louise, b. July 18, 1889.
2. Howard B., b. July 15, 1891.
3. Eugene S., d. in infancy.
4. Clinton B., b. Oct. 19, 1898.
III. James V., b. Jan. 16, 1862; d. in infancy.
IV. Eddie S., b. June 28, 1864; d. 1884.
V. Curtis C., b. Sept. 28, 1867; m. Fanny Austin, Oct. 7, 1891, and had
1. Jennette P., b. Aug. 8, 1892.
2. Edward A., b. Mar. 25, 1893.

Section 295

John W. Cary, son of Van Renssalaer, Sec. 178, b. Boston, N. Y., Mar. 5, 1829; m. Harriet E. Midberry, July, 1849, and lived at Medoc, Ill.; member of the 74th Regt. Illinois, in the Civil War.
Children:

I. Sophronia, b. 1851.
II. Clara, b. 1856.
III. Inez, b. 1858.
IV. Emory, b. 1860.

Section 296

Alfred William Cary, son of Elijah, Sec. 184, b. Scotland, Ct., July 24, 1819; m. Sarah E. Cross, Mar. 24, 1844; a Mechanic and Farmer, and lived on the Homestead of his great-grandfather, John Cary, Sec. 49.
Children:
I. Sarah L., b. July 19, 1846.
II. Charles A., b. May 3, 1860.

Section 297

Henry Lorin Cary, son of Elijah, Sec. 184, b. Scotland, Ct., Nov. 21, 1824; m. 1st, Martha R. Griswold, Jan. 13, 1848; moved to Petersburg, Va., where his wife d. Nov. 17, 1855; m. 2d, Eliza Whittington, July 7, 1859, and moved to St. Paul, Minn.
Children:
I. Martha V., b. Nov. 12, 1855; d. in infancy.
II. George Henry, b. Mar. 23, 1860; d. in infancy.
III. William Henry, b. Jan. 19, 1861.
IV. Georgianna E., b. July 31, 1864.

Section 298

Theron Cary, son of William, Sec. 185, b. Scotland, Ct., Dec. 16, 1810; m. Hannah Bishop, July 8, 1844, and lived in Middletown, Ct., where he d. in 1885. He was a quiet man, but enjoyed the sparkle of wit; was a Deacon in the Baptist Church till his death.
Children:
I. Harriet B., b. Feb. 16, 1884; d. in childhood.
II. Edwin William, b. July 27, 1849; m. Harriet Ella Bacon, Nov. 26, 1873, a Manufacturer and lives at Lockport, N. Y., and had
　1. Howard Theron, b. Oct. 26, 1874; m. Maud Harris, May 28, 1903, who d. Oct. 12, 1904; is a traveling Salesman.
　2. Ernest Bacon, b. Aug. 1, 1877; grad, of Cornell, 1900, and is a Mechanical Engineer.
　3. Bessie Ella, b. April 30, 1884; grad, of Smith's College, 1908, a Phi Beta Kappa.
　4. Marjorie Gladys, b. June 20, 1894.

Section 299

Frederick William Cary, son of William, Sec. 185, b. Scotland, Ct., June 6, 1813; m. 1st, Henrietta R. Woodworth, Feb. 1, 1837, who d. July 9, 1852; m. 2d, Rachel Woodworth, Oct. 11, 1853, and lived in Greenville, Ct. He was a Deacon in the Congregational Church forty years, and Sunday school Supt., and was succeeded by his son, who held the office nearly twenty-five years. The old Cary Homestead was in Scotland, Ct., and when at one time the farm was divided between two heirs, the division line passed through the barn; so the building was divided where the line came, and each took what belonged to him, and rebuilt the portion which fell to the other.

Children:

I. Mary L., b. Nov. 28, 1838; m. Archibald Troland (b. May 21, 1831; d. July 2, 1907); she d. Feb. 8, 1908; both were earnest church workers.

II. Ellen M., b. Jan. 6, 1841; d. 1849.

III. Charles W., b. July 15, 1843; he was the great-great-grandson of Benjamin Holt, 1748-1809, Hampton, Ct., who was Ensign under Washington during the year 1777. He was mustered into Co. A, 18th Conn., July 24, 1862, and served in the Civil War till July 1, 1865; m. and had

1. Herbert Bishop.
2. Henrietta; m. Mr. Palmer.
3. Frederic William, b. Feb. 15, 1872, Norwich, Ct., and is a grad, of Williams, 1894, and was active in all College work; became City Editor of the Norwich Bulletin; in 1895 organized the Thomas Arms Co., and is interested in Church, Lodge, and Military affairs; m. Helen Darling, and had

(1) Mildred Jeannette, b. May 18, 1897.

IV. Andrew E., b. Dec. 11, 1845.

V. Frances W., b. Feb. 23, 1852; d. in infancy.

VI. Frederick, b. Dec. 9, 1854; d. in childhood.

VII. Walter L., b. May 15, 1857; d. in infancy.

Section 300

Horace Cary, son of William, Sec. 185, b. Scotland, Ct., Aug. 5, 1819; m. Cornelia E. Brown, of North Windham, Ct., June 14, 1847; removed to Bureau Co., Ill., 1853; in 1874 he removed to Joliet, where he d. Dec. 21, 1889.

Children:

I. William H., b. Windham, Ct., Nov. 2, 1848, and removed to Illinois with parents, 1853 5 m Mary E. Garten, and lived on a farm near Dover, where he d. Dec. 17, 1878; they had

1. Fannie E., b. Nov. 29, 1871; d. 1901.
2. William H., b. Jan. 26, 1873, and is a traveling Salesman, living in Chicago; m. Ella Kane, and had

(1) June Rose, b. Dec. 9, 1906.

3. Oren E., b. Jan. 1, 1876; was one of the Rough Riders; in Government service in the Philippines, and now stationed in California.

4. Elmer B., b. Feb. 4, 1878.

II. Herbert O., b. Windham, Ct., Mar. 6, 1850, and went West with parents; m. Anna E. Knight, and was for years Supt. American Steel & Wire Co., De Kalb, Ill.; also first Prest. Western Branch of the John Cary Descendants; now at Bangor, Mich.; they had

1. Charles M., b. Aug. 25, 1872; m. Isabelle D. Harkness; resides in Joliet, and had

(1) Eloise.

(2) Annabelle.

2. Herbert L., b. June 18, 1876; m. Bertha Kellogg; lives at Cleveland, O., and had

(1) Agnes B.

(2) Horace K.

3. A son; d. in infancy.

4. Ralph H., b. Aug. 11, 1882; m. Nellie M. Petersen, and had

(1) Henry O., b. Sept. 6, 1903.

5. George B., b. Oct. 4, 1884.

6. Mabel V., b. Aug. 10, 1887.

III. Edgar A., b. Mansfield, Ct., Dec. 29, 1851; came to Illinois in 1853, and is a prosperous Merchant in Joliet; m. Mary M. Lewis, Cresco, Mich., Oct. 30, 1875, and had

1. Jessie M., b. Aug. 22, 1876; m. Charles M. White; live in Joliet, and had

(1) Bessie Ruth, b. Feb. 4, 1900.

(2) Esther Cornelia; d. in infancy.

(3) Iona Margery, b. Dec. 24, 1902.

(4) Charles E.

(5) Mary Louise, b. Dec. 31, 1908.

2. Morris L., b. Oct. 20, 1878; enlisted in 3d Ill. Infty., Spanish War, and served in Porto Rico; m. Isabella McNabb, and live at Allegan, Mich.

3. Edgar A., b. June 30, 1880; was in 3d Ill. Infty., Spanish War, and served in Porto Rico, and then in the U. S. Navy; m. Clara Collins, and have one child.

4. Ruth L., b. Oct. 19, 1886; grad, of Olivet College, 1909, a High School Teacher.

5. Caroline E., b. Dec. 15, 1888.

6. Rex. L., b. April 3, 1891.

7. Anna L., b. Mar. 13, 1893.

8. Esther, b. April 26, 1894; d. in infancy.

IV. Frederick A., b. Windham, Ct., Mar. 28, 1853; m. 1st, Ella Showerinan, who d. Dec. 15, 1893; m. 2d, Mrs. Rose Hammond; he d. May 8, 1896, and the widow lives in Chicago; they had

1. Alice M., b. May 8, 1879; m. H. C. Nelson; live in Chicago, and had

(1) Dorothy A., b. Mar. 1, 1906.
2. Frederick A., b. June 8, 1881.
3. Luella, b. July 28, 1883; m. William Hasse, and had
(1) Wilbur D., July 24, 1904.
(2) Lester.
(3) William.
4. Horace, b. Oct. 8, 1890; d. in infancy.
5. Benjamin H., b. April 15, 1892.
V. Charles H., b. April 12, 1855; d. in childhood.
VI. Oscar E., b. Dec. 27, 1856; m. Kate D. Bush, live in Joliet, and had
1. Evelyn L., b. Feb. 8, 1882.
2. Frank B., b. July 9, 1883; m. Emma Evans, live Plainfield, Ill., and had
(1) Alta Loraine, b. Feb. 1, 1906.
(2) Bernice W., b. June 1, 1907.
3. Belle, b. Sept. 21, 1884.
4. Son; d. in infancy.
5. Irene, b. Dec. 29, 1887; d. in childhood.
6. Eugenia, b. Oct. 13, 1890.
7. Susan M., b. Oct. 4, 1893.
8. Joseph F., b. Mar. 13, 1896.
VII. Frank L., b. Dec. 10, 1859; m. Nellie Krater, live in Durand, Ill., and had
1. Bessie M., b. May 2, 1883; m. Charles Dunn.
2. Lola, b. Feb. 4, 1885.
VIII. Alice A., b. July 20, 1861; m. Alexander Storm, a Farmer; live at New Lenox, Ill., and had
1. Son; d. in infancy.
2. Florence L., b. May 13, 1893.
3. Donald Ross, b. Mar. 28, 1896.
IX. Dwight P., b. Aug. 21, 1863; m. Mary B. Bearse, who d. June, 1901; m. 2d, Jennie Gibson; he is Auditor of the N. W. Fuel Co., lives in St. Paul, Minn., and had
1. Roy D., b. Dec. 23, 1888.
2. Raiman B., b. Jan. 22, 1889.
3. Clarence, b. July 17, 1891.
4. Stella, b. Oct. 28, 1893.
5. Howard; d. in infancy.
6. John Winfield, b. Feb. 1, 1897.
X. Phebe J., b. July 16, 1866, Dover Ill.; a Teacher in the Chicago public schools.

Section 301

William L. Cary, son of Frederick, Sec. 186, b. Mt. Vernon, O., Sept. 25, 1822; was educated in the public schools and at Sloan's Academy; taught for some years, was a great reader, and took an interest in current affairs and politics, being an ardent Republican, and had the confidence of all who knew him; m. Eveline Graham, 1851; he d. Mar. 3, 1906.

Children:

I. Ralph Waldo, b. July 2, 1852; studied medicine and began to practice in 1879; moved to Monte Vista, Colo., 1883; m. Mae B. Bartlett, of Jerseyville, Ill., Mar. 6, 1890, and had
  1. Ralph Waldo, b. May 17, 1891.
  2. Julia Eveline, b. July 10, 1893; d. in childhood.
  3. Linna Mae, b. Mar. 29, 1897.
  4. Rachel Naomi, b. Feb. 15, 1903.
  5. Ruth Bartlett, b. Feb. 15, 1903; d. in infancy.

II. Henry Yale, b. Jan. 4, 1854; m. Clara Harvey, 1881, and lives on the homestead at Mt. Vernon; they have
  1. Ralph G., b. Sept. 3, 1882; m. Elizabeth Griggs, and live at Bowdle, S. D.
  2. Evelyn, b. Aug. 9, 1885; a successful teacher in Trinidad, Colo.
  3. Yale H., b. Oct. 25, 1888.
  4. Hubert H., b. April 9, 1891.

III. Samuel F., b. Oct. 11, 1856; educated at Ohio State University; m. Linna Bartlett, Jerseyville, Ill., 1884, and have
  1. Alice, b. Sept. 28, 1885; m. Dr. A. C. Listor, of Bellows Falls, Vt.
  2. Will W., b. April 13, 1887; grad. Ohio Wesleyan University, 1910.
  3. Frederick, b. Sept. 3, 1889.
  4. Florence, b. Jan. 12, 1891.
  5. Marion, b. Nov. 9, 1898; d. in infancy.

IV. John W., b. Oct. 9, 1858; d. Aug. 6, 1886, at Elroy, Wis.

V. Evelyn E., b. Aug. 24, 1860, Mt. Vernon, O.

VI. William L., b. Nov. 30, 1862. Sec. 319.

VII. Grant, b. Oct. 26, 1868; d. 1877.

Section 302

Winthrop H. Cary, son of Ralph, Sec. 187, b. Hartford, Ct., 1818; m. Sarah Hills, 1840, and lived at Hartford.

Children:

I. Ellen A., b. 1842.

II. Emily L., b. 1844.

Section 303

James S. Cary, son of Ralph, Sec. 187, Hartford, Ct., 1820; m. Betsey Ann Alger, 1847.

Child:

I. Lucien B., b. 1848; removed to Mississippi.

Section 304

George H. Cary, son of Ralph, Sec. 187, b. Hartford, Ct., 1823; m. Annie A. Haven, and lived at Hartford.
Children:
I. George H., b. 1852.
II. Frank S., b. 1854.

Section 305

James Beneijah Cary, son of James, Sec. 188, b. Canterbury, Ct., Aug. 22, 1810; m. Mary B. Adams.
Children:
I. Asa Bacon, b. July 12, 1835. Sec. 317.
II. Fitch A., b. 1838; m. and had a daughter, and lives at Central Village, Ct.
III. Mary Elizabeth, b. 1840; m. Henry B. Geer, Scotland, Ct.; died.
IV. George L., b. 1842; was in Co. A., 1st Ct. Cav., in the Civil War; Norwich, Ct.
V. Dwight, b. 1846; was in Co. F., 8th Ct., and killed at Antietam, Md., Sept. 17, 1862.

Section 306

Henry Hudson Cary, son of Sanford, Sec. 189, b. Scotland, Ct., July 2, 1814, where he lived a Farmer; m. Persis Geer, 1840.
Children:
I. Caroline Tracy, b. 1845.
II. Eliza Jane, b. 1849.

Section 307

Dwight Cary, son of Sanford, Sec. 189, b. Scotland, Ct., Feb. 24, 1817; m. Susan Bass, 1843, and was a Farmer.
Children:
I. Sarah Rosetta, b. 1844.
II. Marthaette, b. 1846; d. 1848.
III. Maryette, b. 1846; d. 1848.
IV. Ann Bradford, b. 1848.
V. Frank Winslow, b. 1850.
VI. Sanford, b. 1853; d. 1858.
VII. Jane Lucretia, b. 1856.
VIII. George Sanford, b. 1860.

Section 308

Walcott Cary, son of Sanford, Sec. 189, b. Scotland, Ct., June 29, 1819; a Farmer in Hampton, Ct.; m. Lucy Jane Burnham, Windham, Ct., 1842.
Children:
I. Mary Josephine, b. 1843; m Henry E. Holt, 1861.
II. Julian, b. 1846.
III. George Clinton, b. 1848.
IV. William Burnham, b. 1856.

Section 309

Jonathan T. Cary, son of Josiah, Sec. 202, b. Haddam, Ct., Mar. 31, 1823; m. 1st, Rhuca Mead, Mar. 7, 1844, who d. April, 1845; m. 2d, Lucy C. Lear, Mar. 10, 1849, and lived at Schenectady, N. Y.
Children:
I. A son, b. April, 1845; d. in infancy.
II. Susan M.
III. George Newton.
IV. Rhuca.

Section 310

Clark W. Cary, son of Josiah, Sec. 202, b. Haddam, Ct., Jan. 28, 1825; was an extensive Leather Merchant in New York City, of the firm of Mulford & Cary; m. Mary E. Doyle, Feb. 18, 1852; he d. Mar. 7, 1871.
Children:
I. Josiah Willard, b. Jan. 22, 1853.
II. Clark Henry, b. Oct. 19, 1854.
III. Mary Ida, b. Dec. 2, 1856.
IV. Albert Ferris, b. Feb. 27, 1859.

Section 311

Jedediah T. Cary, son of Josiah, Sec. 202, b. Haddam, Ct., Feb. 13, 1833; m. Lucy Ann Bromley, April 12, 1857.
Children:
I. Charles.
II. Albert.
III. Sarah Jane.

Section 312

Benjamin H. Cary, son of Josiah, Sec. 202, b. Jan. 26, 1835, Haddam, Ct.; m. Phebe E. Komorinskey, May 13, 1858, and lived in New York City.
Children:
I. Alice Eliza, b. Feb. 24, 1859.
II. Edwin Augustus, b. July 27, 1863.

Section 313

William Augustus Cary, son of Augustus Celanus, Sec. 206, b. Amesbury, Mass., June 12, 1848. After going through the public schools and a Business College, he became an Engraver and carried on this business for some years in Boston; entered the Electric Lighting business, and in 1884 became a Manager of Lighting Plants. He has Musical tastes, and plays the Flute and Violoncello, and this taste is inherited by members of the family; m. Maria Augusta Pitman (b. in Boston, 1849), 1869, and lives in Malden, Mass.
Children:
I. William A., b. 1870; d. 1893; was a talented Musician and Artist.
II. Annie Lee, b. 1872; m. John R. Purdy, M. D., who d. of typhoid fever in London, two months after the marriage; they had Arthur C., b. 1901; she m. 2d. Herbert C. Shattuck, and had Herbert C., b. 1907.
III. Mary Gertrude, b. 1873; m. Frank N. Folsom, 1899; d. 1910.
IV. Edith Walker, b. 1874; m. Arthur S. Fisher, and their daughter, Marion Gertrude, has at the age of seven manifested remarkable talent in playing the piano.

Section 314

Rev. William Bracket Cary, son of Hon. Jeremiah Eaton, Sec. 210, b. Cherry Valley, N. Y., Aug. 8, 1841; m. Harriet Elizabeth Pate (b. London, Eng., Feb. 14, 1847, dau. of William and Harriet Wasted Pate, who was an Engraver and Publisher of fine engravings), Feb., 1871, at Brooklyn, N. Y. In Aug., 1861, he enlisted in the 5th New York Cav., and was promoted to Sergeant, 2d and 1st Lieutenants, and Captain; this Regiment served with distinction, and was engaged in nearly all the battles of the Army of the Potomac, besides raids, scouting, and skirmishes. After the War he resumed his studies and grad, at the Union Theological Seminary, 1871; went to Kansas as a Home Missionary for five years; was settled at Old Lyme, Ct., 1876-1883; at North Stonington, Ct., 1883-1899, then retired to the old Home place at Windsor, Ct. In 1899 was elected to the Legislature, and drafted the bill for the Indeterminate Sentence, which became a law in 1901; since then he has been in literary work.
Children:

I. Joseph Pate, b. Oct. 13, 1872; grad, at Lafayette College and Union Theo. Seminary, and went as Missionary to the State of Washington; m. Harriet Janet Gray, June 1, 1898.
II. William Eaton, b. Nov. 21, 1874; d. 1898.
III. Albert Ely, b. Mar. 26, 1876.
IV. Alice Louise, b. Jan. 31, 1878; d. in childhood.
V. Ella Elizabeth, b. Nov. 29, 1879.
VI. Anna De Lacy, b. May 14, 1882.
VII. Helen, b. Jan. 12, 1885.
VIII. Allen, b. Jan. 12, 1885.
IX. Jennie Wheeler, b. July 21, 1891.

Section 315

William Cary, son of Daniel Morris, Sec. 254, b. Feb. 2, 1833; m. Lucy Ellen Ohara, lived at Siloam Springs, Ark., and d. 1907. Children:
I. F. P., b. July 29, 1859; a Banker at Jet, Okla.; m. Susan E. ___ and had
1. Ethel Powell.
II. Dr. Charles Allen, b. Nov. 27, 1861; m. Emma Heck, Nov. 27, 1890; a grad, of Iowa State College, 1885 and 1887, and studied in Germany; was Asst. State Veterinarian of Iowa and So. Dak.; now Veterinarian of Alabama; they had
1. Elwyn Allen, b. April 11, 1892.
2. Alice Phebe, b. Sept. 3, 1893.
3. Alice, b. June 16, 1894.
III. Walter E., b. Dec. 25, 1872.
IV. Wilford P., a Merchant at Jennings, La.

Section 316

Clark Shepard Cary, son of George, Sec. 265, b. Colrain, Mass., Oct. 3, 1838; m. Mina L. Goodell, of Readsboro, Vt., April 10, 1867. He was a man of genuine integrity, native affability, and all enjoyed the cordial reception and generous entertainment at the "Mountain Home Farm" on Catamount Hill; he was a large man, weighing 350 pounds, and one of his sons stands "six feet four" in his stockings. He d. Jan. 8, 1894, honored and beloved.
Children:
I. Charles Wilbur, b. Sept. 24, 1872; has been engaged in Educational work, and now Manager of the Cary Teachers' Agency, Hartford, Ct.; m. Grace M. Cleveland, Mar. 24, 1897.
II. George Walter, b. Sept. 24, 1872; m. Edith M. Clark, of Sunderland, Mass.; m. 2d, Sarah E. Avery, Jan. 6, 1910, and lives at Greenfield, Mass.; they had
1. Ruth Clark, b. Mar. 31, 1898.

Section 317

Brig. Gen. Asa Bacon Cary, son of James Beneijah, Sec. 305, b. Canterbury, Ct., July 12, 1835; grad, from the U. S. Military Academy, West Point, 1858; served continuously on active duty until July 12, 1899, when he was retired by operation of law as Paymaster General of the United States Army. He m. Laura M., dau. of Hon. Stodard B. Colby, Montpelier, Vt., July 29, 1867. His home is Vineyard Haven, Mass.
Children:
I. Edward Colby, b. Santa Fe, N. M., April 20, 1871; grad, from U. S. Military Academy, West Point, 1893; served in the Spanish War, and while 2d Lieut. was made an Adjutant-General of Vols., and afterward Major of the 42d U. S. Vols. He served five years in the Philippines, and is now Captain U. S. A., and stationed at Boston, Mass. He m. Ruth, dau. of Maj. George H. Palmer, Aug. 1, 1895, and had 1. Laura, b. Jan. 15, 1897, Fort Spokane, Wash.
II. Edith, b. Nov. 4, 1878, Washington, D. C.; m. Maj. Merriwether Lewis Walker, Corps of Engineers, U. S. A., Sept. 30, 1904.

Section 318

Knibloe Bouton Cary, son of Rev. Seth C., Sec. 206-B., b. Mar. 26, 1882, Beverly, Mass.; grad. Gardner High School, 1898; Boston Latin School, 1899; Boston University, 1903. Entered the employ of the John A. Dunn Company, Gardner, Mass., 1903.

Section 319

William L. Cary, son of William L., Sec. 301, b. Mt. Vernon, O;, June 30, 1862; grad, at Cincinnati College and in Law, in 1888; is General Counsel and Secretary of the U. S. Telephone Co., Columbus, O.; m. Ella K. Taugher, of Mt. Vernon, 1897.
Children:
I. Helen, b. June 4, 1900.
II. Josephine, b. Jan. 22, 1905.
III. William L., b. Nov. 27, 1910.

www.ingramcontent.com/pod-product-compliance
Lightning Source LLC
Chambersburg PA
CBHW032108090426
42743CB00007B/278